Explorations in Interdisciplinary Reading

Explorations in Interdisciplinary Reading

Theological, Exegetical, and Reception-Historical Perspectives

EDITED BY

Robbie F. Castleman,

Darian R. Lockett,

AND

Stephen O. Presley

PICKWICK *Publications* · Eugene, Oregon

EXPLORATIONS IN INTERDISCIPLINARY READING
Theological, Exegetical, and Reception-Historical Perspectives

Pickwick Publications
An Imprint of Wipf and Stock Publishers
199 W. 8th Ave., Suite 3
Eugene, OR 97401

www.wipfandstock.com

PAPERBACK ISBN: 978-1-4982-2966-1
HARDCOVER ISBN: 978-1-4982-2968-5
EBOOK ISBN: 978-1-4982-2967-8

Cataloguing-in-Publication data:

Names: Castleman, Robbie F., editor. | Lockett, Darian R., editor. | Presley, Stephen O., editor.

Title: Explorations in interdisciplinary reading : theological, exegetical, reception-historical perspectives / edited by Robbie Castleman, Darian R. Lockett, and Stephen O. Presley.

Description: Eugene, OR: Pickwick Publications, 2017 | Includes bibliographical references.

Identifiers: ISBN 978-1-4982-2966-1 (paperback) | ISBN 978-1-4982-2968-5 (hardcover) | ISBN 978-1-4982-2967-8 (ebook)

Subjects: LCSH: Bible—Hermeneutics. | Bible—Theology. | Bible—Criticism, interpretation, etc.

Classification: LCC BS543 E9 2017 (print) | LCC BS543 (ebook)

Manufactured in the U.S.A. 05/15/17

Contents

Abbreviations

ABD	*The Anchor Bible Dictionary*. 6 vols. Edited by David Noel Freedman. New York: Doubleday, 1992.
CBR	*Currents in Biblical Research*
BBR	*Bulletin for Biblical Research*
BDAG	Walter Bauer, Frederick W. Danker, W. F. Arndt, and F. W. Gingrich. *Greek-English Lexicon of the New Testament and Other Early Christian Literature*. 3rd ed. Chicago: University of Chicago Press, 2000.
DTIB	*Dictionary for Theological Interpretation of the Bible*
THNTC	The Two Horizons New Testament Commentary
IOTS	Brevard S. Childs. *Introduction to the Old Testament as Scripture*. Philadelphia, PA: Fortress, 1979.
JBL	*Journal for Biblical Literature*
JETS	*Journal of the Evangelical Theological Society*
JSNT	*Journal for the Study of the New Testament*
JSNTSup	Journal for the Study of the New Testament Supplement Series
JTS	*Journal of Theological Studies*
NDBT	*The New Dictionary of Biblical Theology*
NICNT	New International Commentary on the New Testament

NIGTC	New International Greek Testament Commentary
ANF	*Ante-Nicene Fathers*
NPNF1	*Nicene and Post-Nicene Fathers*, Series 1
NPNF2	*Nicene and Post-Nicene Fathers*, Series 2
LXX	The Septuagint
NTS	*New Testament Studies*
OG	Old Greek
PNTC	Pillar New Testament Commentary
SBL	Society for Biblical Literature
SBLGNT	*Society for Biblical Literature Greek New Testament*
SNTSMS	Society for New Testament Studies Monograph Series
TDNT	*Theological Dictionary of the New Testament* 10 vols. Edited by Gerhard Kittel and Gerhard Friedrich. Translated by Geoffrey W. Bromiley. Grand Rapids: Eerdmans, 1964–76.
TDOT	*Theological Dictionary of the Old Testament* 14 vols. Edited by G. Johannes Botterweck and Helmer Ringgren. Translated by Geoffrey W. Bromiley et al. Grand Rapids: Eerdmans, 1974–2004.
ZNW	*Zeitschrift für die Neutestamentliche Wissenschaft*

Contributors

D. Jeffery Bingham, Dean and Professor of Theology, School of Theology, Southwestern Baptist Theological Seminary, Fort Worth, TX.

Craig Blaising, Jesse Hendley Chair of Biblical Theology, Southwestern Baptist Theological Seminary, Fort Worth, TX.

Susan I. Bubbers, Dean, The Center for Anglican Theology, Liturgy, and Spiritual Formation, Inc, Orlando, FL.

Robbie F. Castleman, Professor of New Testament and Theology, John Brown University, Siloam Spring, AR.

Darian R. Lockett, Associate Professor of Biblical and Theological Studies, Talbot School of Theology, Biola University, La Mirada, CA.

Gregory S. MaGee, Associate Professor of Biblical Studies, Taylor University, Upland, IN.

J. Richard Middleton, Professor of Biblical Worldview and Exegesis, Northeastern Seminary at Roberts Wesleyan College, Rochester, NY.

Stephen O. Presley, Associate Professor of Church History, Southwestern Baptist Theological Seminary, Fort Worth, TX.

Andrew J. Schmutzer, Professor of Biblical Studies, Moody Bible Institute, Chicago, IL.

J. David Stark, Associate Professor and Director, Faulkner University Online, Montgomery, AL.

Lissa M. Wray Beal, Professor of Old Testament, Providence Theological Seminary, Otterburne, Manitoba, CA.

Introduction

Darian R. Lockett &
Stephen O. Presley

The tension between reading Scripture as primarily a historically situated text on one hand and binding canon addressed to a community of faith on the other constitutes a crucial issue for biblical interpretation. This tension, moreover, is felt in different ways in the various academic disciplines. Scholars who work in Biblical Studies, Biblical Theology, Patristics, and Systematic Theology all approach scripture with different assumptions and methods. Considering the ways each of these disciplines approach Scripture and biblical interpretation, the "Biblical Theology, Hermeneutics, and Theological Disciplines" study group within the Institute of Biblical Research established a four-year project aimed at clarifying the relationships between these diverse lines of inquiry into scriptural interpretation found in each of these disciplines. The goal of this project was to foster a sustained discussion in the context of an academic community (IBR) where exploratory papers might be proposed, composed, and rewritten for a final publication.

Unique to this project was the process through which each paper was developed. First, early in the Spring a call for papers when out and two or three ideas were selected based upon their diversity and quality. Second, each paper was written by these individual authors and then shared initially with the entire group. Third, during the summer months leading up to the fall conference of IBR, readers from the research group commented on the papers and interacted with each author. Fourth, each author then redrafted the paper with these comments in mind. Finally, each rewritten paper was then presented at our annual fall meeting where further comments were offered. Therefore, the final draft of each paper represents the work of these individual authors, yet at the same time, embodies the collaborative process of the study group itself. This was truly an exercise in interdisciplinary thinking and writing about biblical interpretation. Thus, a unique aspect of this volume is both its exploration of the integration of Biblical Studies and Theology as well as the exploratory collaborative process through which these papers were composed. The volume embodies the very integrative approach it seeks to analyze and promote.

This research project, and the present volume resulting from it, offers valuable insights into the integration of Biblical Studies and Theology as sub-disciplines within the academy. The essays collected here fall naturally into the following sections: Exegetical Explorations, Reception-Historical Explorations, and Theological-Practical Explorations. While each of these sections reflects approaches to biblical interpretation framed within separate disciplines, they also exhibit a healthy inter-collegiate dialogue over these critical issues.

The volume opens with the section labeled "Exegetical Explorations" that considers the intersection of biblical studies and theology in Old Testament (Schmutzer and Middleton) and New Testament (Stark and Lockett) exegesis. Schmutzer's essay, "The Suffering of God: Love in Willing Vulnerability," explores the role of narrative in the Old Testament's dramatic portrayal of the suffering of God and this founded upon the biblical drama itself rather than abstract metaphysical properties. Schmutzer argues that God has always related to his creation in willing vulnerability. This entails inevitable emotional pain that is experienced in the life of God resulting from his committed relationship with his rebellious creatures. As such, a theology of the suffering of God is evident throughout the testimony of Scripture, not just the passion of the crucified Lord. Through such biblical texts as Genesis 6:5–6; Numbers 14:1–45; Hosea 11:8–9, and Revelation 5:6, Schmutzer illustrates how: (1) the history of interpretation has overwhelmingly been afraid of the emotional and verbal particularity of God in Scripture, and so interpreters have resorted to a philosophical theism; (2) and that a theology of divine pathos draws human affliction into the orbit of profound relationship, not just membership.

In J. Richard Middleton's essay, "A Psalm against David? A Canonical Reading of Psalm 51 as a Critique of David's Inadequate Repentance in 2 Samuel 12," he explores the relationship between reading these two texts together. He begins arguing that out of 150 Psalms in the Masoretic Text, seventy-three are connected to David in some way through their superscriptions. The most famous of these is Psalm 51, which references the liaison with Bathsheba and the subsequent confrontation with the prophet Nathan (2 Samuel 11–12), suggesting that the psalm is David's prayer of confession on that occasion. Although there are, indeed, a few phrases in the body of Psalm 51 that might suggest this particular incident, there are others that actually problematize such a connection. The major point of disjunction between the psalm and the Samuel narrative is that the psalm focuses on forgiveness followed by restoration of the broken sinner, whereas David in the narrative simply confesses and is summarily forgiven by Nathan (who had previously misrepresented God's will in 2 Sam 7:3); the result is that David's life and family continue in shambles, without moral reformation. Here Middleton explores the possibility of an intertextual reading of Psalm 51 and 2 Samuel 11–12, where the psalm's more robust conception of repentance (beyond mere confession) calls into question aspects of David's inadequate response recounted in the prose narrative of 2 Samuel. In this intertextual reading, he draws on wider biblical perspectives (in both Testaments) concerning the normative shape of the moral life and the need for disciplined restoration after sin.

Turning to the New Testament, J. David Stark focuses on Paul and the law in his essay: "Paul, Apostle of Torah Obedience: Retheologizing Torah Obedience in the Letter to the Romans." He notes, that commonly, Paul of Tarsus is portrayed as an "apostle of grace" who preached a "Torah-free" gospel and, consequently, opposed making Torah obedience a requirement for Gentile Christians. So far as it goes, this sketch contains important truths. For Paul, "the works of the Torah" should never be an identity locus for the Christian community. What often fails to be appreciated—with serious consequences for understanding Pauline thought—however, is the degree to which Paul himself rewrites and retheologizes what counts as proper Torah obedience. Concentrating particularly on Romans 2:1–16 and tracing corollaries into the balance of the letter, Stark shows how Paul's rereading of Torah obedience allows him holistically to commend this obedience even to Gentiles as such. He then connects this retheologizing movement to subsequent testimony within the Christian tradition (e.g., Augustine) and draws out the significance for similarly theological readings of Christian scripture by contemporary interpreters.

Rounding out the "Exegetical Explorations" section, Darian Lockett investigates a more methodological question regarding the role of history in the interpretation of James as Christian Scripture ("Necessary but Not Sufficient": The Role of History in the Interpretation of James as Christian Scripture"). Asking the question: "How important is history to interpreting the general letters?" Lockett specifically addresses the hermeneutical question of the role and importance of history (especially social-historical reconstruction) in the interpretation of the Epistle of James. After assessing the genre of James, which itself narrows the historical aperture of access into the letter's context, Lockett argues that while history is in particular ways necessary, it is not sufficient of itself (especially as it is defined under the auspices of historical-criticism) to interpret James as Christian Scripture.

Moving beyond the Old and New Testament, the second section of the volume considers "Reception-Historical Explorations" and focuses on how the early church (in this case Irenaeus and Origen) received and read Holy Scripture. These essays show how the earliest Christian communities at the fountainhead of the tradition began to develop their understanding of the relationship between Scripture and theology. Just as the essays in the previous section entertain the particular aspects of reading the Old and New Testaments, these essays consider both the strengths and challenges of reading the whole Bible as Christian Scripture.

D. Jeffery Bingham's essay, "Against Historicism: The Rule of Faith, Scripture, and Baptismal Historiography in Second-Century Lyons," is a study of competing historiographies. Bingham contrasts the historiography of historicism and its hermeneutic with that of an ancient Irenaean approach. The former, Bingham argues, is an approach to history, Scripture, and early Christianity that is wholly secular and severed from ecclesiology, which ultimately leads away from the reliability of the biblical texts. The latter, on the other hand, is a thoroughgoing ecclesiological model of historiography and hermeneutics where a community of faith indwelt with the Spirit serves as a unique, privileged group of biblical exegetes. Irenaeus exhorts the Christian community to read the Scriptural material in coherence with the church's Rule of Faith received at baptism, which supersedes any authority in non-ecclesiastical sources.

Staying with the Bishop of Lyons, Stephen O. Presley narrows his focus upon a particular work of Irenaeus (*Epideixis*) and reflects upon what this somewhat neglected work shows modern readers about Irenaeus' hermeneutic ("From Catechesis to Exegesis: The Hermeneutical Shaping of Catechetical Formation in Irenaeus of Lyons"). While the seedbed of catechetical instruction is evident within the New Testament, Presley notes that the practice of catechumenate began to take shape in the post-apostolic age. As the church expanded rapidly throughout the ancient world, the need arose for a formal instruction in the faith. Thus, in the waning years of the second century Irenaeus of Lyons composed his own catechetical work entitled the *Epideixis* or Demonstration of Apostolic Preaching. Presley argues that Irenaeus' general purpose in the *Epideixis* is actually hermeneutical. This work instructs a young catechist on the proper manner of reading scripture and encourages him to follow his example of scriptural interpretation. Second, the prevailing assumption governing Irenaeus' scriptural hermeneutic is a theological perspective described in *Epideixis* 5: the Spirit-inspired prophets announce the coming of the Son, and coming of the Son interprets the prophets. This implies that Irenaeus' hermeneutic is carried out in the very words of scripture. Throughout Irenaeus' work, scripture does not merely provide support for his arguments, but instead the language of scripture is integrated within his arguments. This suggests that catechesis, for Irenaeus, is Scripture catechesis. Presley shows that under the administration of his scripture hermeneutic, Irenaeus applies a variety of particular intertextual methods of linking and connecting texts. Some of these interpretive strategies include: narratival arrangements, prophecy-fulfillment, prosopological interpretation, and intentional connections between the words of a prophet and apostle. The Bishop of Lyons is not beholden to any standardized method of interpretation, but under the guidance of the rule of faith and the inspiration of scriptures, he carefully crafts together the textual tiles of the scriptural mosaic. All together, these aspects clarify the distinctive hermeneutical nature of Irenaeus' catechetical instruction in the *Epideixis*.

Finally, in her essay, "Land Entry and Possession in Origen's *Homilies on Joshua*: Deep Reading for the Christian Life," Lissa Wray Beal considers the way Origen interpreted of the book of Joshua in light of contemporary discussion of the theological interpretation of Scripture. She explains how Origen's hermeneutical method addressed potential difficulties in the book and notes how different his approach was from modern historical critical approaches. Wray Beal analyzes Origen's interpretative work through the lenses of Christology, Soteriology, and Christian praxis and gives special attention to Origen's treatment of problematic texts regarding warfare and the ban. She closes her essay with a reflection on the possibility of reclaiming Origen's readings for today. However, Origen's christological hermeneutic, according to Wray Beal, is helpful but ultimately inadequate to engage the text's own discrete witness. Instead, she proposes a more developed trinitarian hermeneutic as a better reading of Joshua as Christian Scripture.

The concluding section of this volume moves the conversation to the topics of Systematic Theology, Biblical Theology, and Practical Theology. Each of these essays considers ways that Scripture and theology interact, especially in conversation with the disciplines of Biblical Studies. Several of these essays are preliminary and exploratory as they set a framework for a conversation that must be developed further. This is especially true of the first essay, "Integrating Systematic and Biblical Theology: Creation as a Test Case," by Craig Blaising. His brief essay epitomizes the exploratory nature of this volume as he casts a vision for some possibilities of fruitful interaction between Biblical and Systematic Theology, particular in terms of the doctrine of creation. His essay is no mere discussion of methodology or prolegomena, but instead uses the topic of creation as a lens though which he facilitates a conversation between these disciplines. Blaising's essay begins with a brief survey of the place of creation in various systematic theologies including discussions of creation *ex nihilo*, anthropology, and teleology. He then compares these uses with the narrative and redemptive focus of creation prevalent in biblical theologies. Finally, in the closing pages he briefly surveys a few key points that could be fruitful talking points between these disciplines as a way to consider how they might interact.

Next, Susan Bubbers's essay, "A Guiding Principle and a Question-based Strategy for Integrating Biblical, Systematic, and Practical Disciplines," considers one's posture and disposition while engaging Scripture. Her essay takes a more methodological turn as she considers the issues necessary for integrating the biblical and theological disciplines. Taking Blaising as her starting point, Bubbers raises a host of hermeneutical questions—constituting a "question-based strategy for interpretation"—relevant to the synthesis of Biblical Studies, Systematic Theology, Practical Theology, and Liturgy. Bubbers' central observation is that the nature of God must serve as the guiding principle for theological interpretation.

Finally, in his essay "Biblical Theology in the Service of Ecumenism: Eschatology as a Case Study," Gregory MaGee not only pulls together the various strands running through these essays, but naturally provides a fitting bookend for this volume. Specifically, MaGee's essay reflects upon the intersection of Biblical and Systematic Theology as they shed hermeneutical light upon the interpretation of Scripture such that the outcome is identifying an ecumenical common ground. MaGee argues that the ecumenical benefits of a biblical-theological approach can be observed especially when applied to the eschatologically rich depiction of a new heavens and earth in Isaiah 65:17–25. Here Biblical Theology helps broker systematic-theological disputes between competing eschatologies. MaGee concludes that with the perspectives and discoveries of both Biblical and Systematic Theology scholars can engage in constructive conversations about differences while still recognizing the common core beliefs that continue to unite them. As these conversations have occurred in the area of eschatology, MaGee insists, some theological differences, while not being eliminated altogether, have been diminished, leaving less of a gulf between opposing positions. Suggestive of further study, MaGee observes that other topics for which Biblical Theology could act (and has undoubtedly already acted) as a catalyst for theological unity include the nature and authority of Scripture, atonement, election in salvation, cosmology, and ethics. He argues that reinforcing consensus in the center and flexibility on the margins for these various debated topics, Biblical Theology is well suited to move the discussion forward in the direction of greater agreement and understanding, without extinguishing the passion for further discovery in these areas. Finally, MaGee concludes, biblical theologians have made significant contributions towards eschatological consensus that is firmly rooted in the authority of God's revelation but is broad enough to be considered truly ecumenical in scope. Perhaps Biblical Theology can be mobilized in similar ways to build consensus in other theological areas as well.

Together this collection of essays is a good starting point for an important hermeneutical conversation that must continue. Those who work in the classical disciplines of Theology and Biblical Studies must come to the table and share the best of what we have to offer in order to foster an even richer and deeper understanding of the Church's Scriptures. We hope you will enjoy these explorations and may they inspire you to consider some hermeneutical explorations of your own.

1

The Suffering of God

Love in Willing Vulnerability

ANDREW J. SCHMUTZER

Introduction

NOTHING ILLUSTRATES OR HONORS suffering like a story. And, when we are trying to understand our pain and our trials, we look for a story that will be revealing.[1] Learning, communicating, and remembering actually reflect a mode of living, a worldview. Whether some define life, God, and suffering through empirical information, an "act of God," or others relate through cultural stories and myths, we need to understand how Scripture presents its redemptive drama.

In truth, whenever we allow the Scripture to become fragmented, it is in danger of being diluted and absorbed into our individual narratives.[2] To be sure, suffering always "writes" a powerful personal story—which we need to hear in far more testimonies!—but our stories are not what redeem people's lives. They show how lives are redeemed. This really concerns our hermeneutic. Understanding the Bible's story of the suffering of God is all about how God presents himself in Scripture, and this is a theo-drama far more riveting than most know! To get here, though, we need to do some digging.

1. Moore, *Care of the Soul*, 56–65.

2. Bartholomew and Goheen, *Drama of Scripture*, 12.

Exploring Story and Defining Terms

Two Illustrative Accounts

In the Greek play, *The Frogs,* Aristophanes writes about Dionysus and Xanthias. They embark on a trip into the underworld to resurrect a skilled poet. As they are passing through Hades, they both claim to be gods. So they construct a decisive test: both of them will be flogged, and they conclude, "Whichever of us squeals first or even bats an eyelid isn't a god at all."[3] In other words, true deity is defined by freedom from pain and suffering.[4] Emerging from this stoic philosophy, The Unmoved Mover may reflect Aristotle's metaphysics, but these same commitments also shaped the core trajectory of the theology of God in the early church.[5] But is God really this unresponsive and sealed off from pain? Is the life of God really detached from the pain of his own creation? Is this really the God of the Christian Scriptures? Assuredly not!

As one of the leaders in the anti-apartheid struggle in South Africa, Allan Aubrey Boesak discusses another kind of illustrative story. In his book, *Dare We Speak of Hope?* he writes about the Khoi people of the Eastern Cape. He notes three distinctives of their faith: (1) a supreme being, named Tusi-Goab, is the Giver, Protector, and Sustainer of all creation; (2) the people's dependence on and resonance with nature; (3) and awareness that their "human-being-ness depended on the life-giving interrelationships with other human beings."[6] Tusi-Goab fights on behalf of his creation and helpless people, not just for himself. In Tusi-Goab's fight against evil, Boesak explains:

> [T]hough God was victorious, they say in that ancient and ongoing battle God was wounded in the knee. That is why the supreme being is called Tusi-Goab, which literally means "wounded knee" . . . Tusi-Goab was in the first place not a

3. Aristophanes, *Frogs*, 179.

4. Placher, *Vulnerable God,* 4.

5. While Lister is convinced the "Hellenization hypothesis" has distorted the theology of the early church fathers, I find his claim overblown, due, in large part, to his lack of primary sources (cf. Seneca's *Moral Essays*, "On Providence"); see Lister, *God Is Impassible and Impassioned.* I agree with D. A. Carson's assessment that "conservatives themselves have sometimes been too unaware of how far they have 'sold out' to Greek philosophical traditions" (*How Long, O Lord?,* 166). More convincing is the Greco-Roman impact as outlined by Bauckham, "Only The Suffering God Can Help," 6–12; also Hankinson, *Cause and Explanation in Ancient Greek Thought*, esp. 116–20, with much translation of original material.

6. Boesak, *Dare We Speak of Hope?,* 34.

> God of power and might, but of woundedness and empathetic solidarity, a God who fought on behalf of God's creation and children, and who was willing to be wounded for their sake. . . . Because Tusi-Goab is wounded, the ancients go on to say, God understands the woundedness and woundability of God's creation, of God's children. . . . It may well be that this is the answer to the oft-debated question why the Khoi in South Africa so easily opened their hearts to the Christian gospel. . . . The lure of the Christian faith could only have been in the fact that they discovered in the crucified Jesus, with the wounds in his hands, feet, and side, so much of the image of Tusi-Goab, the God whose name is "Wounded Knee."[7]

Boesak poignantly argues that we can speak of hope "only if we speak of woundednes."[8] Because of the profound evil, systemic suffering and social injustice that Boesak lived through under Apartheid, he concludes, "hope is fragile, for it is the hope of the vulnerable, of those at the bottom of the well."[9]

Seriously . . . A Suffering God?

Though hardly the theological scandal it was once, the theology of a suffering God still runs up against several "roadblocks." On the one hand, these two illustrative accounts need not be multiplied in order to show how intellectually post-modern and un-omnipotent a suffering God can seem to some. On the other hand, it is stunning that some ancient non-Western religious traditions can be so richly oriented around a "wounded deity."[10] Simon Chan explores a context-specific theology, noting how European reflection moved sharply toward a theology of a suffering God after WWII, as a counter-measure to the unprecedented mechanized evil of the twentieth century. By contrast, key strands of Asian theology moved decidedly in the opposite direction, cordoning God off from human pain and brutal regimes, in order to oppose the fear of ancestral spirits and demonic oppression more common in Asian cultures. The transcendence and immanence of God find different emphases, depending on the cultural codes of a group and the meaning they attach to their suffering. Western theology has

7. Ibid., 37–38.

8. Ibid., 24–42.

9. Ibid., 42; quoting the phrase by Bell, *Faces at the Bottom of the Well*, 1992.

10. See Chan, *Spiritual Theology*, 15–39; also Kitamori, *Theology of the Pain of God*.

prioritized objective certainty, and this has led to a dogmatism ill equipped for the dialogic categories of a relational theology.

Much of the problem has been the tendency of Western Christian theology to view God in categories of rational abstraction and political triumphalism; categories that cannot accept the affectability of God or the Khoi and their God with a "wounded knee."[11] But, as Walter Brueggemann rightly observes, the God of biblical orthodoxy functions at neither end of the spectrum: New Age vagueness nor classic austereness.[12] The way laity long to relate to their approachable God has, at times, felt muted before a "bar-of-justice" theology. Where is the tender "shepherd of the sheep" (Heb 13:20) who "gathers the lambs and gently holds them close to his heart" (Isa 40:11, NIV)? This same paradigm is charged to Church leaders, "being examples to the flock" (1 Pet 5:3). This is the same God of both testaments, and he still comes to the aid of frail sheep.

It is our contention that God relates to his creation in willing vulnerability and the inevitable emotional pain that is experienced in the life of God that results from his committed relationship with his rebellious creatures. Further, we claim that a theology of the suffering of God is evident throughout the testimony of Scripture, not just the passion of the crucified Lord.[13] Our study will explore numerous biblical passages, rather than pursue abstract philosophical or metaphysical arguments for divine perfection, simplicity, ultimate power, or perfect freedom—arguments that take on a logic of their own, usually detached from the real drama of biblical texts.[14] Observing the suffering of God in Scripture is not a simple enterprise. Considering the relational life of God—within the inner-Trinitarian relationship and among God's standard human agents—requires a hermeneutic of discernment, not deduction; a relational theology, not objectivist epistemology.[15] Lutheran theologian, Robert W. Jenson, is surely correct when he argues that the suffering of God is best defined by the biblical drama itself, not metaphysical properties.[16]

11. See the excellent study of Kessler, *Old Testament Theology*, 381–445.

12. Brueggemann, *Unsettling God*, 1.

13. Some classic biblical texts that disclose the suffering of God include: Gen 6:5–6; Hos 9:15; 11:8–9; Isa 49:15; 63:9, 15; 66:13; Jer 18:7–10; 31:20; Pss 78:40–41, 58–59; 103:13. Two of the best volumes addressing the Suffering of God are Fretheim, *The Suffering of God*; and Mouw and Sweeney, *The Suffering and Victorious Christ*.

14. For celebration of reformed metaphysical austerity, see Dolezal, *God Without Parts*. A classic philosophical theism is Weinandy, *Does God Suffer?*

15. Vanhoozer, *Is There a Meaning in This Text?*, 426.

16. Jenson, *Systematic Theology: Volume 1*, esp. 100–102, 125–45.

Metaphors have raised another problem. The claim that metaphors are simply accommodative language to speak of God is linguistically and hermeneutically naïve. As G. B. Caird points out, "We have no other language besides metaphor with which to speak about God."[17] Terence E. Fretheim helpfully explains, "Metaphors do reveal an essential continuity with the reality which is God." The real danger, however, "is either interpreting metaphors literally in every respect or (more commonly today) denying any essential relationship between the metaphor and God."[18] The interpreter must determine where the point of comparison lies. "But to conclude that such language reveals nothing of God's essential personhood makes all such language pointless."[19] When God is given human characteristics, it reveals a God who is living and personal—One who is committed to interaction with people. As Terence E. Fretheim states:

> Christians should have no difficulty using such language for God, for in Jesus Christ God has acted in a remarkably anthropomorphic way. A direct line connects this kind of language for God and God's becoming flesh in Jesus Christ, "the image of the invisible God" (Colossians 1:15). In this human being God reveals to us most supremely who God is, how God relates to us and the world, and the depths to which God will go for our salvation.[20]

Unfortunately, classic epistemology is embarrassed by the anthropomorphic aspects of God—in both testaments. In fact, such language has been transposed or explained away in generic notions of God.[21] But this dismissal of emotional aspects in the language for God runs into the fallacy of circular logic, as Kevin J. Vanhoozer explains. This hermeneutic assumes that the interpreter already knows either what God is like, or what the author of the biblical text knew God to be like, and can thus differentiate between the language which is intended to correspond to God's true nature and actions, and that which is not.[22] So any biblical text that speaks of divine

17. Caird, *Language and Imagery of the Bible*, 174. "Thus anthropomorphism is something more than the imposing of man's preconceived and limited images on the divine. There is something that answers back in perpetual dialogue" (ibid., 182).

18. Fretheim, "Repentance of God," 51; emphasis added.

19. Mathews, *Genesis 1–11:26*, 344.

20. Fretheim, *About the Bible*, 58–59; emphasis added.

21. Brueggemann, *Unsettling God*, 2.

22. Vanhoozer, *Remythologizing Theology*, 60; see especially "Impassible Passion? Suffering, Emotions and the Crucified God" (387–432), and "Impassible Compassion? From Divine *Pathos* to Divine Patience" (434–67).

passibility is simply dismissed. But no biblical text or passage argues divine impassibility.[23] Broadly speaking, classical theism is itself, a hermeneutic "on guard."

Sadly, some "frozen categories" of biblical orthodoxy have stressed the legal work and transcendent life of God, to the exclusion of his immanent presence with and relational pain over rebellious humankind, whom he sent his son to save.[24] The profile of God, popularized within every generation of theologians and pastors, is often a God who is stubbornly "other"—above the fray of human ills, ablaze in glory and power, completely apart and unaffected.[25] In effect, God has been marooned on an island of unapproachable sovereignty by his own image bearers, stripped of his emotions, addressed by abstract titles, hailed in monikers of "victory," and defined by terms that are offensively negative to seeker and saint, alike: immutable, impassible, impeccable, ineffable, and so on. So much definition—*via negativa*—shuns the vulnerable love and emotional spectrum of God's own person. This is not the portrait of God in Scripture.

We must pause and ask some vital questions. How does God relate to human pain, injury, violence, and involuntary suffering? Can a God who does not or cannot experience suffering in some sense really be said to "know" the tides of pain that sweep through his own world? How are humans to enter a genuinely personal relationship with a secluded God? Can a God who is unable to sympathize—at cost to himself—really be said to love? Because humans are made in the image of God, can our unique connection with God be limited to emotion or reason, or does God relate more holistically with us?

I submit that Scripture reveals great breadth and depth in the life of God. From Creator to Savior, God has always chosen to be vulnerable. In the freedom of his love toward all creation, especially humankind, this results in a spectrum of his own suffering.

23. That said, some appeal to *theological syllogism*, regarding divine ontology to defend impassibility. Paul Helm, for example, argues: (1) God is timelessly eternal, (2) whatever is timelessly eternal is unchangeable, (3) and whatever is unchangeable is impassible. (4) Therefore, God is impassible. See Helm, "The Impossibility of Divine Passibility," 119. In counterpoint to Helm, see the excellent essay by Bauckham, "In Defense of the Crucified God," 93–118.

24. Even some of the greatest creeds of contemporary faith obscure these biblical truths. The Westminster Confession of Faith states that God is "infinite in being and perfection, a most pure spirit, invisible, without body, parts, or passions; immutable, immense." This is a proud statement of *apatheia*.

25. See the insightful cultural critique of Brueggemann, *Unsettling God*, 1–17.

Some Terms and Tenets

While most of these topics of our study could be expanded further, our purposes require us at least to consider some of the primary terms and tenets in this relational theology of God. First, several important terms must be defined.

1. *Impassible*—used in classical theology to claim that God cannot suffer, since he cannot be affected by anything external to himself.
2. *Passibility*—refers to God being affected by and responsive to the external world.
3. *Pathos*—both suffering (= pain) and passion (= emotion), capable of "disturbing" pure reason.
4. *Apatheia*—divine impassibility; divine constancy, expressed as immutability (= static).

Most significant is the term impassibility, meaning God does not experience emotion or suffering. As William C. Placher explains it:

> Divine impassibility served two functions. It ruled out vulgar passions: no more rapes, no more private vengeance. At the same time, it preserved divine power. Part of what power seemed to mean, after all, is that one can affect others for good or ill but yet remain unthreatened by them, invulnerable. It is the most powerful ruler who is safe and secure from external threat . . . For God, then, impassibility guarantees omnipotence.[26]

In other words, God feels neither pain nor pleasure from the actions of other beings. But the testimony of Scripture, as we shall see, actually shows otherwise. In the end, terms such impassible are not helpful, as the profile of God is far more complex, interactive, and dialogical than such negative terms allow. God's love makes him willingly involved in the lives of people—God is not stoic and unaffected. Again, however, there was a rich cultural backdrop that fueled this stoic worldview.[27] More accurate to the biblical testimony is the claim of Thomas J. Oord, when he writes, "God acts intentionally and sympathetically" toward his creation.[28]

26. Placher, *Vulnerable God*, 5.

27. Bauckham explains the Greek philosophical thought that shaped classic theology's aversion to a suffering God in "Only the Suffering God Can Help," 7.

28. Oord, *Nature of Love*, 17.

Christians of all theological stripes are now rethinking the impassibility of God, for several reasons, and now argue that God is the "deeply moved 'First Mover.'"[29] Roger Olson states:

> Some evangelical theologians believe that the God of classical theism is not much better than the God of panentheism; if the latter is too dependent and weak, the former is too impersonal and despotic. How can the God of classical theism be the compassionate God of the biblical narrative, they ask?[30]

John S. Feinberg expresses similar dissatisfaction. For him, the claims of both classic theism and process theism are inadequate. On the one hand, the self-sufficient, immutable sovereign God of classical theism, he claims, is "too domineering, too austere, and too remote to be at all religiously adequate."[31] On the other hand, the adapting, power-sharing God of process theology, Feinberg claims, is not strong enough to sustain and revitalize hope that all things will be well. He proposes a third model: the King who cares.[32]

The roots of contemporary impassiveness reach back into philosophical commitments of impassibility in an earlier era. This discussion illustrates how these terms have been used, most often, to isolate God from any "outside" suffering.[33] While we have briefly touched on some "strands" comprising a theology of the suffering of God, we can also list some core tenets of a suffering God; One who is actively engaged in vulnerable relationship with people. A theology of the suffering of God draws on some core realities of God's emotional life and activity, as portrayed in Scripture.

- God maintains his compassionate-love toward people (Exod 34:6b–7; James 5:11).
- God is in constant relatedness with his creation. God's life with his creation is always incarnational. From the highly relational metaphors (Isa 42:14; 66:13) to his theophany in human form (Genesis 18–19), God is constantly interacting, drawing himself into potential pain (Hos 11:8).

29. Callen, *Discerning the Divine*, 23.

30. Olson, *Westminster Handbook*, 190.

31. Feinberg, *No One Like Him*, 31.

32. D. A. Carson also registers his methodological disagreement with impassibility (Carson, *How Long, O Lord?*, 165).

33. See Wolterstorff, "Suffering Love," 209–10.

- God is willingly vulnerable toward people (Gen 6:5–6). Jesus Christ is the fullest expression of God, and he suffered greatly (John 14:9; Phil 2:7–8). Far from divine child abuse, Jesus Christ gave up his own life (1 John 3:16).
- God is affectable, evident in his emotional life. God freely loves, and in that love is willing to risk great anguish and suffering (Ps 78:40–41; Jer 18:7–10).
- God is personally consistent, amid great pain (Pss 90:2; 95:9–10; Heb 13:8).

God's availability to his creation results in a rich vulnerability matched by new initiatives of discipline and restoration. God's dialogic commitment causes him to be impinged upon—brought to areas of agony, grief, and joy.[34] However, the emotional life of God does not diminish the unchanging character of his promissory purposes.[35]

Key Biblical Passages Involving God's Suffering

Genesis 6:5–6

> The LORD saw that the wickedness of man was great in the earth, and that every intention of the thoughts of his heart was only evil continually. And the LORD was sorry that he had made man on the earth, and it grieved him to his heart.

From creation on, God is affected by the events in his world. The LORD's "seeing" counters the "sons of God" who "saw" (v. 2). God is no robot or some static principle. Rather, God engages intimately with his creation, to further his transcendent purposes.[36] "Sorry" describes the emotional anguish of God (cf. Exod 13:17; Jer 31:19), which is further explained by the final clause: "and it grieved him to his heart" (v. 6b). God's "pained-heart" (*wayyiṯ ʾaṣ ṣēḇ ʾel-libbô*, v. 6) responds to humankind's "wicked-heart" (*libbô . . . ra ʿ* v. 5), and recalls the first judgment involving the woman's "pain" (*ʿiṣ ṣᵉḇōnēk,ʾeṣeḇ*, 3:16) next to the man's "pain" (*ʿiṣ ṣāḇôn*, 3:17).

The relational ecosystem includes the pain of the broken-hearted Creator toward humans who were intended to act differently. "God's judgment is not a detached decision . . . the judgment is a very personal decision, with

34. Brueggemann, *Unsettling God*, 5.

35. Fretheim, *Suffering of God*, 5–8; 109–13.

36. Mathews, *Genesis*, 344.

all the mixed sorrow and anger that go into the making of decisions that affect people who one loves. Grief is always what the Godward side of judgment looks like."[37] While pre-flood humanity has a scheming heart, God responds with a wounded heart, filled with pain.[38] As Walter Brueggemann observed, God has altered his course:

> It has effected an irreversible change in God . . . . It is now clear that such a commitment on God's part is costly. The God-world relation is not simply that of strong God and needy world. Now it is a tortured relation between a grieved God and a resistant world. And of the two, the real changes are in God.[39]

Exodus 3:7–10

> I have surely seen the affliction of my people . . . and have heard their cry . . . I know their sufferings, and I have come down to deliver them . . . the cry of the people of Israel has come to me . . . Come, I will send you to Pharaoh that you may bring my people . . .

God addresses Moses as his chosen agent, the means of Israel's deliverance. But Moses will force God into a compromise in his divine plan (4:14). Alongside this portrait of resistance from Moses, there emerges a profound revelation of God's intimate attention.[40] In verse 7, three key verbs highlight God's full engagement on their behalf: "seen . . . heard . . . know." What the narrator notes about God in 2:24–25 is now stated from God's own mouth. This is God's first speech since he gave Jacob permission to descend to Egypt (Gen 46:1–4). They are not merely "sons of Israel," instead, their "affliction . . . cry . . . and sufferings" have arisen to God as "my people"—noted twice! (3:7, 10; cf. Gen 18:21).

There is a new level of knowing for God (cf. 3:7; cf. 33:12–17) that changes his relationship with his people and incites a dynamic act of redemption: "Come, I will send you" (v. 10).[41] With this spectrum of God's senses activated (v. 7) he is now physically mobilized into the very midst of their trouble.[42] The severity of Israel's oppression provokes a radical

37. Fretheim, *Suffering of God*, 112.

38. Mathews, *Genesis*, 341.

39. Brueggemann, *Genesis*, 73, 81.

40. Childs, *Book of Exodus*, 73.

41. Fretheim, *Suffering of God*, 83–84.

42. Brueggemann, "Exodus," 712.

intervention from God.[43] This is a God who "comes down to deliver" (v. 8), incarnated in the mouth of Moses (4:11) and, even with "the staff of God in his hand" (4:20)!

Numbers 14:1–45

> And all the Israelites grumbled against Moses and Aaron, and the whole assembly said to them, "If only we had died in Egypt! . . . We should choose a leader and go back to Egypt." . . . Then Moses and Aaron fell facedown . . . "Only do not rebel against the LORD." But the whole congregation talked about stoning them . . . The LORD said to Moses, "How long will these people treat me with contempt? How long will they refuse to believe in me? . . . I will strike them down with a plague and destroy them . . . " Moses said to the LORD, "In accordance with your great love, forgive the sin of these people, just as you have pardoned them from the time they left Egypt until now." The LORD replied, "I have forgiven them, as you asked."

The grief and fear that Moses and Aaron show, by falling facedown (v. 5), sets the stage for the sudden manifestation of God's glory in his wrath (v. 10; cf. Exod 16:7). God's glory is his royal grandeur, and in the context of his anger, can appear in a storm-like theophany (1 Sam 7:10; Ps 29:3, 7). While God desires fellowship from his people, he does not force their obedience. So, for good reason, Joshua and Caleb passionately try to avert God's anger (v. 6). God's anger appears over five hundred times in Scripture, precisely because people use their freedom to act in rebellion and defiance against God's tender love and instruction (cf. Exod 34:6–7; Ps 95:8–11).

What God does next is stunning—he laments! Horst D. Preuss is correct, "When even YHWH himself laments, then this demonstrates something about the God who suffers with his people."[44] "How long . . . contempt"; "How long . . . refuse" (v. 11); "How long . . . grumble against me?" (v. 27). "Lament is always an integral part of the wrath of God."[45] God uses the very language of his servants who cry out to him (Pss 6:3; 13:1–2). This is not a quest for information, but combines divine (1) complaint with (2) anguish (cf. Exod. 16:3, 7–9).[46] In fact, God's memory of past actions

43. Mann, *Book of the Torah*, 101.

44. Preuss, *Old Testament Theology*, 2:248. Preuss also includes these texts: Jer 2:10–13, 31; 3:20; 8:7; 12:7–13; 15:5–9, and 18:13–15a.

45. Fretheim, *Suffering of God*, 110.

46. Ibid., 121.

only intensifies the painfulness of the present. God is not a dispassionate accountant. On several occasions he genuinely struggles over what shape the people's future will take: "Why should I forgive you? Your children have forsaken me . . . Should I not punish them for this?" (Jer 5:7–9, NIV; cf. 2 Sam 24:11–13; Joel 2:12–13).

How the people respond to God's efforts to repair the relationship determines the shape of the future that God and his people will have together.[47] To see God's anguish and change of decision, it is helpful to observe the switch between parties in Numbers 14.

A The Congregation Rebels and God's Glory Appears (vv. 1–10)

B Moses Intervenes and Asks God to Forgive (*selaḥ*, vv. 11–19)

B' God Forgives in Response to Moses' Request (*selaḥ*, vv. 20–25)[48]

A' The Congregation Receives a Mitigated Punishment (vv. 26–38)

It is entirely God's prerogative to activate their punishment through the standard cause-consequence sequence; that is, moving from announcement of judgment to execution of judgment.

But Moses intervenes at this key juncture with a three-part plea:

1. God's reputation as a powerful deliverer is at stake (vv. 13–14),
2. Mass destruction lets the wicked determine the fate of the righteous (vv. 15–16),
3. God's revealed nature requires that God be motivated by grace as much as the need for justice (vv. 17–19).[49]

This three-part argument forms the foundation for Moses' dire request that God "forgive the sin of these people" (v. 19).[50] Observe that Moses' request is not based on any repentance from the people, just the magnanimous character of their covenant-keeping God (cf. Exod 34:6–9; Neh 9:17–19).[51]

47. Ibid., 123.

48. In the Old Testament, *selaḥ* is only used with God as the subject (46x). In other words, it is the only word used exclusively for God's forgiveness.

49. Balentine, *Prayer in the Hebrew Bible*, 132–33.

50. If pre-flood humanity had had a mediator like Moses, like Israel experienced in the wilderness period, maybe the suffering would have been modified. Regardless, after the flood we see God in *self-limitation* (Gen 8:21). A flood is no longer an option for God.

51. Balentine, *Prayer in the Hebrew Bible*, 134.

God's response to Moses is immediate and positive: "I have forgiven them as you asked" (v. 20). Unlike humans, God's pain and emotion do not incapacitate him. Nevertheless, forgiveness does not preclude punishment.[52] But death will only come to those who maintained disbelief in the face of God's mighty acts of deliverance (cf. Ps 95:9). God will not wipe them out "all at one time" (v. 15). Moses succeeded in changing God's course of action, and no priest or ritual sacrifice was involved. Though still angered by their collective rebellion, this text illustrates how God "invites participation in the accomplishing of divine will."[53]

God's judgment is viewed in terms of a breakdown in personal relationship, and all the accompanying effects of anger and pain. At stake is a relationship, not a contract. "To bear the suffering, while making continuing efforts to heal the relationship, means at least that God chooses to suffer for the sake of the future of that relationship."[54]

Psalm 78:40–41

> How often they rebelled against him in the wilderness
> and grieved him in the desert!
> They tested God again and again
> and provoked the Holy One of Israel.

Psalm 78 extols God's faithfulness in Israel's history—at great cost to God. This is the unique contribution of the historical psalms (e.g., Pss 78, 105, 106), which recount the story of God's relationship with his people. As the second longest poem, Psalm 78 recounts how deeply God's relationship with Israel finds him vulnerable, not mechanical. The purpose is not to convey facts, but to show that the responses God was drawn into while guiding a wayward nation had an ongoing impact in the life of God and Israel's theological tradition.[55]

Psalm 78 moves through two broad panels.[56] Following the introduction (vv. 1–11), the first historical recital recounts key events in the wilderness (vv. 12–32), and the second recital recounts their march from Egypt to Canaan (vv. 40–64). Each recital briefly notes an occasion of national rebellion (vv. 17–20; 56–58) which is then followed by an extensive account

52. Hausmann, "*sālaḥ*," 262.

53. Balentine, *Prayer in the Hebrew Bible*, 143.

54. Fretheim, *Suffering of God*, 124–25.

55. Jacobson, "'Faithfulness of the Lord,'" 121.

56. The helpful rhetorical outline of Clifford, *Psalms 73–150*, 43.

of the spurning of God, his anger, and Israel's subsequent discipline (vv. 21–31; 59–64). Each panel closes with God's readiness to forgive and begin anew (vv. 32–39; 65–72). Sadly, "Their heart was not steadfast toward him" (v. 37a), so God acknowledges "that they were but flesh" (v. 39a).

The nation's constant rebellion is matched by God's ongoing grief. Just as Israel's rebellion continually reoccurred, so God's personal grieving was not a one-time experience (cf. Num 14:22).[57] The word for "grief" (*'aṣab*) here refers to pain and hurt (e.g., Gen. 6:6; Pss 16:4; 127:2; 147:3). God's grief is as current as people's disobedience.[58] In fact, the entire period of wilderness wandering was "loathsome" or "disgusting" (HCSB) to God (Ps 95:10). But God remains committed to a relationship that deeply grieves him. The "Holy One"—the unique and transcendent God—is still moved to act "When they are diminished and brought low through oppression, evil, and sorrow" (Ps 107:39; cf. 106:44–45).

Divine anger is highlighted in Psalm 78, for good reason. This psalm mentions God's anger seven times, more than any other psalm. It is important to understand that God's anger is relational, is not a reckless emotion (cf. 78:38).[59] Anger is not innate to God's nature, but appears because of his vulnerable relationship to sinners. God is provoked because of his relational commitment. Further, God's anger is not the opposite of his faithfulness. God's anger flares up because of his relational commitment. Though they grieved God's heart, "he was merciful and forgave their sins and didn't destroy them all. Many a time he held back his anger" (v. 38, NLT). By his own admission, God is "slow to anger" (Exod 34:6), not devoid of it. As William P. Brown states, "Divine indignation is no blind rage. God, rather, has the moral resolve and emotive wherewithal required to execute justice continually and without compromise."[60]

Hosea 11:8–9

> How can I give you up, O Ephraim? How can I hand you over, O Israel?
>
> How can I make you like Admah? How can I treat you like Zeboiim?
>
> My heart recoils within me;

57. Fretheim, *Suffering of God*, 111.
58. Ibid.
59. Jacobson, "Faithfulness of the Lord," 123.
60. Brown, *Seeing the Psalms*, 182.

my compassion grows warm and tender.

I will not execute my burning anger; I will not again destroy Ephraim;

for I am God and not a man, the Holy One in your midst,

and I will not come in wrath.

There is no greater display of God's pathos as a loving parent than Hosea 11. Not surprisingly, this is a suffering love. God's love has been obstinately shunned—past and present (vv. 1–2a). So Israel's judgment is now inevitable. Of all ironies, Israel will "return" (*šuḇ*) to Egypt, because they refuse to "return" (*šuḇ*) to God! (v. 5; cf. 2:6–7). Their rebellion has forced God to activate their means of destruction through Assyria (vv. 5–6). God's pain is acute: "My people are determined to turn from me. Even though they call me God Most High, I will by no means exalt them" (v. 7).

In verse 8, God begins intense self-questioning. These words are soaked with wrenching emotion. Four rhetorical questions occur in one verse, highlighting a rich paradox—he is the sovereign-broken, God! This is turmoil, not timidity. God reconsiders the extent of destruction. Whereas Admah and Zeboiim were destroyed with the cities of Sodom and Gomorrah (Gen 19:21, 25; Deut 29:23), God's parenting-love will curb the degree of Israel's judgment. The reference to these ancient cities highlights both precedence and manner. While the wickedness of these cities caused them to be "overthrown" (*hāp̱aḵ*, Gen 19:21, 25), now it is God's caring heart that is "overthrown" (*hāp̱aḵ*, Hos 11:8b)! The daring use of this verb (*hāp̱aḵ*) describes the sudden agitation and "shake-up" of God's heart.[61]

While God begins by "pouring out his heartfelt agony" (v. 8a), he concludes by describing the sharp emotional effect Israel's pending judgment has on him—the heart of God "recoils" or "is torn" (NLT).[62] The sharp justice of the Judge is overwhelmed by the tender compassion of the Parent (cf. 1 Kgs 3:26). God maintains his mysterious freedom that willingly stoops to the messiness of his wayward child. The rebellious son will not be stoned (cf. Deut 21:18–21). The declaration that "I loved him" (11:1a) is also mingled with persistent sorrow and, together, will prevent the final ruin of his loved ones.[63] God does not suffer as mortals do. He does not lash out to destroy the deserter, venting frustration. God's anger is restorative, not revengeful.

61. Seybold, "*hāphakh*," 426–27.

62. Patterson, "Hosea," 68.

63. Fretheim, *Suffering of God*, 120.

So the boundaries represented in his "I will not" statements (3x) distinguish the balanced emotional life of the "Holy One" from humankind.[64]

Again, God's pained memory shows through (11:1–8), and causes profound suffering for God (v. 8–9).[65] In God's love, the destruction is drawn down, though they have not even repented!

Jeremiah 9:1[Heb. 8:23]; 9:10[Heb. 9:9]; 13:17; 14:17–18

> O that my head were waters, and my eyes a fountain of tears, that I might weep day and night for the slain of the daughter of my people! (9:1)

Weeping is a social behavior, utilizing tears that are meant to be seen.[66] Tears are standard fare in laments (cf. Pss 6:9; 39:13; 102:10), and this pain is evident in the book's beginning (3:21; 4:19; 6:26; 7:29). In the "weeping poems" of Jeremiah, the parent-child relationship illuminates God's behavior and deep emotion.[67] In his ministry, Jeremiah finds God to be patient, compassionate, merciful, and long-suffering (3:12; 13:14; 15:15). Yet because God is the agent of destruction as well as lover of the nation, love and anger mingle in God's tears (cf. Jer 31:20; Isa 63:15).

While it can be difficult to determine who the speaker is in these biblical texts, if God speaks in any of them, then God weeps.[68] J. J. M. Roberts argues persuasively that God's weeping is couched in the form of "city laments" common to Mesopotamia. These laments depict deities weeping over their precious cities.[69] The parallel to Jesus weeping outside Jerusalem should not be missed (Matt 23:37–38). In the case of Jeremiah, I believe the prophet is expressing God's suffering. Terence E. Fretheim's comment is a helpful guide:

> The suffering prophet and God are so interconnected that it is difficult to sort out who is speaking in many texts. Nor should one try to make too sharp a distinction. As if with one voice, prophet and God express their anguish over the suffering of the people. . . . These texts should be interpreted in terms of the prophet's embodiment of God's mourning. . . . At least, Jeremiah's mourning is an embodiment of the anguish of God,

64. Chisholm Jr., *Handbook on the Prophets*, 362.
65. Fretheim, *Suffering of God*, 143.
66. Bosworth, "Tears of God," 25.
67. Ibid.
68. Ibid., 27.
69. Roberts, "Motif of the Weeping God," 132–42.

showing the people the genuine pain God feels over the hurt that his people are experiencing.[70]

The movement of 8:18—9:1 has one speaker, arguably YHWH. There are not multiple voices here (contra 12:1–6; 15:10–21), though the persona of both prophet and God may be present. Emotive phrases like "O that" (*mı-yittēn*) connect the close of chapter 8 with the opening of chapter 9. "Day and night" underscores the depth and duration of grief. The speaker wishes to continue weeping, uninterrupted (cf. Ps 42:4; Lam 2:18).[71]

The God who "exalts" and "sings" over restored Israel (Zeph 3:17) also weeps over Israel's pending destruction. The tears are a plea for the people to turn around.

> I will take up weeping and wailing for the mountains, and a lamentation for the pastures of the wilderness. (9:10)

Again, there is no change of speaker surrounding verse 10. The people's fear of abandonment (8:19; 9:2) is actually what God is about to do (12:7–8)! But rather than leaving Jerusalem and fleeing to the wilderness (9:2), God makes a wilderness out of Jerusalem (cf. Luke 19:41–44).[72] The people "are so deeply enmeshed in evil that they lack the will to repent."[73] God is weeping and lamenting over the loss of a treasured relationship.

> But if you [pl.] will not listen, my soul will weep in secret for your pride;
>
> my eyes will weep bitterly and run down with tears,
>
> because the LORD's flock has been taken captive. (13:17)

Here the weeping, though "in secret," is noted for the entire community. Reference to "life/soul" (*nep̱eš*) adds to the sincerity of "secret" tears that affect the innermost parts. "They arise from an interior emotion rather than an insincere display."[74] Again, the goal is to prompt the people toward restoration of the relationship. Even as Jeremiah's tears embody God's, the Old Testament prophet is often an extension of the divine theophany.

> You shall say to them this word:
>
> "Let my eyes run down with tears night and day,
>
> and let them not cease . . .
>
> If I go out into the field . . . and if I enter the city . . . " (14:17–18a)

70. Fretheim, *Suffering of God*, 160–161.
71. Bosworth, "Tears of God," 33.
72. Craigie, et al., *Jeremiah 1–25*, 145.
73. Ibid.
74. Bosworth, "Tears of God," 38.

In 14:17–18 God commands Jeremiah to quote a message to his people: "say to them this word" (17a). This means that the following first person pronouns ("my, I", vv. 17–18) refer to God and his lament. God's tour of his royal city and its adjacent territories prompts God's weeping mourning in a communal lament. Like Jer 9:10, the text of 14:17–18 single out the weeping of God. But as J. J. M. Roberts observes, "the anthropomorphisms involved in such a portrait of God are simply too striking for most commentators to entertain seriously."[75] God's sorrow is intensified because of the false optimism of prophets' message. The response of the people is too little, too late.[76] This is the portrait of a God in deep sorrow for the "blows" of punishment that he must bring, and the devastation that follows. As David A. Bosworth notes:

> Tears signify deep distress, especially when an important relationship is threatened or terminated . . . Weeping is a powerful non-verbal expression of distress and need, and the weeping of YHWH is revealed to the people . . . They should respond with empathy for a suffering God and seek to sooth YHWH's pain by their own repentance . . . The revelation that YHWH's experience of the punishment is sorrow rather than satisfaction serves an important function.[77]

Yet God's impassibility is also found outside the Gospels. One of the most poignant examples can be found in Revelation.

Revelation 5:6

> And between the throne and the four living creatures and among the elders I saw a Lamb standing, as though it had been slain . . .

While it is common for Christians to comfort each other with the words: "He's still on the throne," that is only where John begins (4:2). A passive appeal to God's sovereignty may sound good (e.g., "Turn it over to God"), but these words offer no care to the rape victim, no reprieve for the depressed, no solace to those betrayed by their spouse, and bring no timely intervention for the martyr's family.[78] A "bigger" picture is needed for our profound stories of suffering.

75. Roberts, "Motif of the Weeping God," 135.

76. Bosworth, "Tears of God," 40.

77. Ibid., 44–45.

78. Stevenson, *Slaughtered Lamb*, 129–30.

Afraid that the scroll might be permanently sealed, with no mediator able to open it, John starts "weeping loudly" (v. 5) in the heavenly throne room (cf. Isa 6:8). Then he is informed that the "Lion of the tribe of Judah" and the "Root of David" is qualified to open the scroll (cf. Gen 49:9; Isa 11:1–5). Both titles identified the Messiah as the conqueror of the nations, one ready to destroy the enemies of God's people. These were standard texts and titles for Jewish messianic hope in the first century (cf. 1QSb 5:24, 29).[79] At one level, this is imagery of a new David who secures a military victory over Israel's enemies. But John never sees this lion. This scene is actually not about the slaying of the wicked (cf. Isa 11:4).

John *hears* about the conquering Lion, but when he turns to look, he *sees* a slaughtered "Lamb" (v. 6; cf. Isa 53:7)![80] For John, the auditory is often redefined by the visual (cf. 1:10–12; 7:4, 9; 9:16–17).[81] John makes this identification by the ritual marks of slaughter. Neither the Lion nor the title will appear again in the book. The Lamb, however, will appear over twenty-eight times to designate the exalted Christ. Resurrected, the lamb now stands. This highlights his sacrificial role. The scene climaxes with the Passover Lamb (1 Cor 5:7) ready to lead a new Exodus (Rev 5:9–10; cf. 17:14). Taken together, the mix of titles for the Lion and Lamb forms a new symbol—conquest by sacrificial death![82] This composite now explains how the ancient Scriptures are fulfilled.[83] Jewish expectations have been changed. Evil has been defeated by a sacrificial death, not military conflict.[84] And those delivered are from all nations (5:9–10).

This is a stunning picture of power redefined in weakness![85] "The Lamb is the embodiment of the Lion, not its replacement."[86] This is Revelation's most lingering image. On the historical horizon, this is a scene of impressive might, especially for those who have "little power" (3:8)—like

79. Bauckham, *Climax of Prophecy*, 214.

80. "Looking as if/though it had been slain" (ESV, NIV, CEB) is not clear enough to be helpful. "As advertised" means *actually* advertised, not just in words. See Beale, *Book of Revelation*, 352. The Greek *esphagmenon* (perf. ptcp., "having been slain") expresses an ongoing condition resulting from a past act. The struggle among translations to reflect this dynamic is obvious: "seemed to have been slain" (JB), "a lamb that appeared to have been killed" (NET), "looked as if it had been slaughtered" (NLT), are interpretively unclear, with "like a slain lamb" (HCSB) or "a lamb with the marks of slaughter upon him" (NEB), being preferable.

81. Stevenson, *Slaughtered Lamb* 133.

82. Bauckham, *Climax of Prophecy*, 215.

83. Ibid.

84 Bateman IV, et al., *Jesus the Messiah*, esp. "Messiah Confessed," 336–39.

85. Stevenson, *Slaughtered Lamb*, 133.

86. Ibid., 143.

the Philadelphian believers (3:7–13). To the eyes of faith, the cross is not victimization or "divine child abuse," but the willing choice of the "Lamb of God" (John 1:29), who reigned from the cross (John 19:19). Christ joined humanity, in his suffering. This has always been the divine relational commitment. "God saves the world by taking its suffering into the very heart of the divine life, bearing it there, and then wearing it in the form of a cross."[87] Suffering, not force, was the key to his victory.

The death of the Passover Lamb was so significant, that this sacrificial image was permanently taken up into heaven. The flesh of the Word "is taken into the inner triune life of the Godhead as a permanent, now eternal feature, scars, history, glory and all, as a permanent sacrament."[88] This is what Peter Hicks calls "the eternal scarring of God."[89] I agree with Hicks when he states: "Somehow, evil in all its forms—sin and suffering and death—has been taken eternally into the Godhead; the marks of slaughter on the Lamb are eternal; there is blood on the throne of heaven."[90] John's vision of the wounded Lamb goes well beyond the notion of Christ's death as an event in history; he transforms the crucifixion into a principle of cosmic proportion which, in turn, serves as a starting point for understanding what it means to live faithfully in a world characterized by profound suffering (cf. 6:9–11).[91]

Conclusion

At present, I believe biblical studies are making the freshest contributions in the study of the suffering of God.[92] That said, several theological and practical points should be made.

First, so much interpretation has been nervous of the verbal and emotional particularity of God in Scripture, and so interpreters resorted to a philosophical theism. I agree with Timothy Wiarda when he observes, "Apologetic and theoretically oriented interests drive much of the modern discussion of divine passibility."[93] These approaches tacitly deny that their interpretation is hermeneutically socialized at all. Yet there are clearly certain rationalistic abstractions and triumphalist commitments that prioritize

87. Fretheim, *Creation Untamed*, 119.

88. Hughes III, "Catching the Divine Breath," 538.

89. Hicks, *Message of Evil & Suffering*, 75–76.

90. Ibid., 81–82.

91. Stuckenbruck, "Revelation," 1546.

92. Also the opinion of Castelo, "Continued Grappling," 364–72; see also Wiarda, "Divine Passibility," 159–73.

93. Wiarda, "Divine Passibility," 171.

power and autonomous sovereignty, particularly in the Western tradition. Jürgen Moltmann observes that the Church Fathers mistakenly saw only two alternatives: (1) essential incapacity for suffering, and (2) fateful subjection to suffering. Fortunately, fresh nuances are now defining this conversation. I propose that God's willing vulnerability—expressed in passionate love—more accurately reflects the redemptive drama.[94] The biblical metanarrative needs to reassert itself amid a flood of conceptual studies. In this case the story of suffering in the life of God is actually the meaning of doctrine, and following his suffering will press us closer to God's theo-drama.[95]

Second, for the contemporary reader, the suffering of God also dips deeply into a distasteful paradox: "the weakness of God is stronger than men . . . though he was rich, yet for your sake he became poor" (1 Cor 1:25b; 2 Cor 8:9). Defining salvation as liberation and power as perfection, we have sidestepped the majesty of God who "stoops" into humankind in frail flesh, living in scandalous weakness. Or, as Michael S. Horton puts it, "Christ's will to weakness is stronger than modern humanity's will to power, and that which the supermen of our age regard as opium for the masses."[96] God's love precedes power, rightly argues William C. Placher. "A God defined in terms of power is precisely not a reliable rescuer, because power provides no guarantee of concern . . . it is his silent suffering that paradoxically confirms his identity as the true Messiah."[97] This is a harsh truth for a religious culture more interested in validation than restoration.

Third, we noted at the outset that we would have to dig, and that includes staring into the darkness of our own hearts. We are petrified of weakness! Manipulation and violence are actually false alternatives to real power, where we turn when we are too weak to risk vulnerability.[98]

> Human beings seek power because they are afraid of weakness, afraid of what might happen should they be vulnerable, and so the drive for power that looks like the purest expression of freedom proves in significant degree inspired by an enslaving fear that dares not risk vulnerability . . . Probe violence and the quest for domination far enough, and one always finds the fear of weakness.[99]

94. Cf. Moltmann, *Trinity and the Kingdom of God*, 23.

95. Placher, *Vulnerable God*, 15, quoting Frei, *Types of Christian Theology*, 126.

96. Horton, *Place for Weakness*, 89.

97. Placher, *Vulnerable God*, 14, 18.

98. Ibid., 20.

99. Ibid., 18, 21; emphasis added.

We have projected an "isolating" power onto God that he never claims for himself. Instead, he routinely prefers the company of orphans, widows, and the poor (Ps 113:5–9)—the weaklings of the world. Only a God who is weak in power but strong in love is really strong enough to take on the pain of the world.[100]

Fourth, understanding the suffering of God helps mend the shattered lives of believers who have known painful and alienating suffering. For broken, betrayed, and persecuted believers, a suffering Savior makes following our Lord credible, not just possible (cf. Heb 2:17–18; 4:15–16). In a world steeped in terrorism, this reality also matters. Being a disciple of the "First Wounded" creates a new reality through a fresh view that many suffering believers need. The wounded redeemed can follow this kind of Shepherd. Being a disciple of one who does not hide his sorrow or wounds is beyond comforting, it calms the deep-down places that have no words, only groans (cf. Rom 8:26–27; Heb 7:25). This relationship of the scarred Lamb to his suffering sheep helps us say "No" to surrogate attachments that promise relief, but only enslave. This "man of sorrows" (Isa 53:3) does not ask us to go where he has never been—this is a precious discipleship, indeed. He not only died for us, he is also willing to suffer with us.

Fifth, embracing a suffering and scarred God draws human affliction into the context of profound relationship not membership. This provides a nurturing point of departure for the hurting—beyond "divine knowledge." This relationship draws from a shared place of suffering that is capable of calling the believer out of their commodified lifestyle and their addiction to technology.[101] But connectivity is not intimacy. So, it is not surprising that mechanical solutions to suffering have seduced the contemporary church away from the rawness of pain, away from the gift of communal grief-sharing and our basic need for human community. The suffering of God can stimulate a practice of bearing others' pain that we might rather deny as unspiritual or unproductive. But this is no pill or "like" button. It is all about following the wounds of our risen Lord in a time when affliction is increasingly something of an embarrassment to "refined faith."

Nicholas Wolterstorff writes, "It is said of God that no one can behold his face and live." "I always thought this meant that no one could see his splendor and live. A friend said perhaps it means that no one could see his sorrow and live. Or perhaps his sorrow is his splendor."[102]

100. Ibid., 21.

101. Brueggemann, *Reverberations of Faith*, 203–4.

102. Sittser, *Grace Disguised*, 148 (quoting Wolterstorff, *Lament for a Son*, 81).

Bibliography

Aristophanes. *The Frogs*. Translated by D. Barrett. London: Penguin, 1964.

Balentine, Samuel E. *Prayer in the Hebrew Bible: The Drama of Divine–Human Dialogue*. Overtures to Biblical Theology. Minneapolis: Fortress, 1993.

Bartholomew, Craig G., and Michael W. Goheen. *The Drama of Scripture: Finding Our Place in the Biblical Story*. Grand Rapids: Baker Academic, 2004.

Bateman IV, Herbert W., et al. *Jesus the Messiah: Tracing the Promises, Expectations, and Coming of Israel's King*. Grand Rapids: Kregel Academic, 2012.

Bauckham, Richard. *The Climax of Prophecy: Studies on the Book of Revelation*. Edinburgh: T. & T. Clark, 1993.

———. "In Defense of the Crucified God." In *The Power and Weakness of God*, edited by N. M. de S. Cameron, 93–118. Edinburgh: Rutherford, 1990.

———. "'Only The Suffering God Can Help': Divine Passibility in Modern Theology." *Themelios* 9 (1984) 6–12.

Beale, Gregg K. *The Book of Revelation*. Grand Rapids: Eerdmans, 1999.

Bell, Derrick. *Faces at the Bottom of the Well: The Permanence of Racism*. New York: Basic, 1992.

Boesak, Allan Aubrey. *Dare We Speak of Hope? Searching for a Language of Life in Faith and Politics*. Grand Rapids: Eerdmans, 2014.

Bosworth, David A. "The Tears of God in the Book of Jeremiah." *Biblica* 94 (2013) 24–46.

Brown, William P. *Seeing the Psalms: A Theology of Metaphor*. Louisville, KY: Westminster John Knox, 2002.

Brueggemann, Walter. "Exodus." In *The New Interpreter's Bible* 1. Nashville, TN: Abingdon 1994.

———. *Genesis*. Interpretation. Atlanta, GA: John Knox, 1982.

———. *Reverberations of Faith: A Theological Handbook of Old Testament Themes*. Louisville, KY: Westminster John Knox, 2002.

———. *An Unsettling God: The Heart of the Hebrew Bible*. Minneapolis, MN: Fortress, 2009.

Caird, G. B. *The Language and Imagery of the Bible*. Philadelphia, PA: Westminster, 1980.

Callen, Barry L. *Discerning the Divine: God in Christian Theology*. Louisville, KY: Westminster John Knox, 2014.

Carson, D. A. *How Long, O Lord? Reflections on Suffering and Evil*. Second Edition. Grand Rapids: Baker, 2006.

Castelo, Daniel. "Continued Grappling: The Divine Impassibility Debates Today." *International Journal of Systematic Theology* 12 (2010) 364–72.

Chan, Simon. *Spiritual Theology: A Systematic Study of the Christian Life*. Downers Grove, IL: InterVarsity, 1998.

Childs, Brevard S. *The Book of Exodus: A Critical, Theological Commentary*. Old Testament Library. Louisville, KY: Westminster, 1974.

Chisholm Jr., Robert B. *Handbook on the Prophets*. Grand Rapids: Baker Academic, 2002.

Clifford, Richard J. *Psalms 73–150*. Abingdon Old Testament Commentaries. Nashville: Abingdon, 2003.

Craigie, Peter C., et al. *Jeremiah 1–25*. Word Biblical Commentary 26. Dallas, TX: Word Books, 1991.

Dolezal, James. *God Without Parts: Divine Simplicity and the Metaphysics of God's Absoluteness*. Eugene, OR: Pickwick, 2011.

Feinberg, John S. *No One Like Him: The King Who Cares*. Foundations of Evangelical Theology. Wheaton, IL: Crossway, 2001.

Frei, Hans. *Types of Christian Theology*. New Haven, CT: Yale University Press, 1992.

Fretheim, Terence E. *About the Bible: Short Answers to Big Questions*. Revised and Expanded. Minneapolis, MN: Augsburg, 2009.

———. *Creation Untamed: The Bible, God and Natural Disasters*. Grand Rapids: Baker, 2010.

———. "The Repentance of God: A Key to Evaluating Old Testament God-Talk." *Horizons in Biblical Theology* 10 (1988).

———. *The Suffering of God: An Old Testament Perspective*. Philadelphia: Fortress, 1984.

Hankinson, R. J. *Cause and Explanation in Ancient Greek Thought*. Oxford: Oxford University Press, 2001.

Hausmann, J. "סָלַח sālaḥ." In *Theological Dictionary of the Old Testament* 10:258–65. Grand Rapids: Eerdmans, 1999.

Helm, Paul. "The Impossibility of Divine Passibility." In *The Power and Weakness of God: Impassibility and Orthodoxy*, edited by Nigel M. de S. Cameron, 119–40. Edinburgh: Rutherford, 1990.

Hicks, Peter. *The Message of Evil & Suffering*. The Bible Speaks Today. Downers Grove, IL: InterVarsity, 2006.

Horton, Michael S. *A Place for Weakness: Preparing Yourself for Suffering*. Grand Rapids: Zondervan, 2006.

Hughes III, Robert D. "Catching the Divine Breath in the Paschal Mystery: An Essay on the (Im)passibility of God, in Honor of Elizabeth Johnson." *Anglican Theological Review* 93 (2011) 527–39.

Jacobson, Rolf A. "'The Faithfulness of the Lord Endures Forever': The Theological Witness of the Psalter." In *Soundings in The Theology of Psalms: Perspectives and Methods in Contemporary Scholarship*, edited by Rolf A. Jacobson, 111–38. Minneapolis: Fortress, 2011.

Jenson, Robert W. *Systematic Theology: Volume 1, The Triune God*. New York: Oxford University Press, 1997.

Kessler, John. *Old Testament Theology: Divine Call and Human Response*. Waco, TX: Baylor University Press, 2013.

Kitamori, Kazo. *Theology of the Pain of God*. Eugene, OR: Wipf & Stock, 1958.

Lister, Rob. *God Is Impassible and Impassioned: Toward a Theology of Divine Emotion*. Wheaton, IL: Crossway, 2013.

Mathews, Kenneth A. *Genesis 1–11:26*. New American Commentary 1A. Nashville, TN: Broadman & Holman, 1996.

Mann, Thomas W. *The Book of the Torah*. Second Edition. Eugene, OR: Cascade, 2013.

Moltmann, Jürgen. *The Trinity and the Kingdom of God: The Doctrine of God*. Translated by Margaret Kohl. London: SCM, 1981.

Moore, Thomas. *Care of the Soul: A Guide for Cultivating Depth and Sacredness in Everyday Life*. New York, NY: HarperPerennial, 1994.

Mouw, Richard J., and Douglas A. Sweeney. *The Suffering and Victorious Christ: Toward a More Compassionate Christology*. Grand Rapids: Baker, 2013.

Olson, Roger. *The Westminster Handbook to Evangelical Theology*. Westminster Handbooks to Christian Theology. Louisville, KY: Westminster John Knox, 2004.

Oord, Thomas J. *The Nature of Love: A Theology*. St. Louis: Chalice, 2010.

Patterson, Richard D. "Hosea." In *Minor Prophets: Hosea–Malachi*. Cornerstone Biblical Commentary. Carol Stream, IL: Tyndale, 2008.

Placher, William C. *Narratives of a Vulnerable God: Christ, Theology, and Scripture*. Louisville, KY: Westminster John Knox, 1994.

Preuss, Horst D. *Old Testament Theology. Volume* 2. Old Testament Library. Louisville, KY: Westminster John Knox, 1996.

Roberts, J. J. M. "The Motif of the Weeping God in Jeremiah and Its Background in the Lament Tradition of the Ancient Near East." In *The Bible and the Ancient Near East*, edited by Cyrus H. Gordon, et al., 361–74. Winona Lake, IN: Eisenbrauns, 2002.

Seybold, K. "הָפַךְ hāphakh." In *Theological Dictionary of the Old Testament*, 3:423–27. Grand Rapids: Eerdmans, 1999.

Sittser, Jerry. *A Grace Disguised: How the Soul Grows Through Loss*. Grand Rapids: Zondervan, 2004.

Stevenson, Gregory. *A Slaughtered Lamb: Revelation and the Apocalyptic Response to Evil and Suffering*. Abilene, TX: Abilene Christian University Press, 2013.

Stuckenbruck, Loren T. "Revelation." In *Eerdmans Commentary on the Bible*, edited by James D. G. Dunn, 1.535–76. Grand Rapids: Eerdmans, 2003.

Vanhoozer, Kevin J. *First Theology: God, Scripture, and Hermeneutics*. Downers Grove, IL: InterVarsity, 2002.

———. *Is There a Meaning in This Text?* Grand Rapids: Zondervan, 2002.

———. *Remythologizing Theology: Divine Action, Passion, and Authorship*. Cambridge Studies in Christian Doctrine 18. New York: Cambridge University Press, 2010.

Weinandy, *Thomas G. Does God Suffer*. Notre Dame, IN: University of Notre Dame Press, 2000.

Wiarda, Timothy. "Divine Passibility in Light of Two Pictures of Intercession." *Scottish Journal of Theology* 66 (2013) 159–73.

Wolterstorff, Nicholas. *Lament for a Son*. Grand Rapids: Eerdmans, 1987.

———. "Suffering Love." In *Philosophy and the Christian Faith*, edited by T. V. Morris, 196–237. Notre Dame, IN: Universitiy of Notre Dame Press, 1990.

2

A Psalm against David?

A Canonical Reading of Psalm 51 as a Critique of David's Inadequate Repentance in 2 Samuel 12[1]

J. Richard Middleton

Out of 150 psalms in the Masoretic Text (MT), seventy-three are connected to David in some way through their superscriptions. Although in the majority of these cases the connection is limited to the cryptic expression לְדָוִד ("of David") or מִזְמוֹר לְדָוִד ("a psalm of David"),[2] thirteen of these seventy-three psalms make an explicit link to some event in David's life by the use of a long heading or narrative ascription. The most famous is Psalm 51, which references the liaison with Bathsheba and the subsequent confrontation with the prophet Nathan (found in 2 Samuel 11–12). A surface reading of the superscription suggests that the psalm is David's prayer of confession when confronted with his sin.

This paper intends to explore the connection between Psalm 51 and the incident narrated in 2 Samuel 11–12. As a preliminary, I will explore the possible meanings of לְדָוִד, as well as the textual connection of psalms

1. I owe a debt of gratitude to Chris Williams for his helpful feedback on an early draft of this paper. Special thanks are also due to Robbie Castleman, Darian Lockett, Greg MaGee, Susan Bubbers, and Stephen Presley (participants in the Biblical Theology, Hermeneutics, and the Theological Disciplines research group of the Institute for Biblical Research), for their encouragement and insightful suggestions on the latest draft.

2. This accounts for sixty-two of the cases (thirty-four and twenty-eight, respectively). The remaining eleven superscriptions have some other noun before לְדָוִד, such as מִכְתָּם, תְּפִלָּה, מַשְׂכִּיל, or שִׁגָּיוֹן.

superscriptions to the body of the psalms, taking into account the divergent testimony of the MT, the Septuagint (LXX), and the Dead Sea Scrolls (DSS). Next, I will examine specific language in the body of Psalm 51 that alludes to or resonates with the narrative of 2 Samuel 11–12, and which plausibly leads the reader to envision some sort of connection between the two texts. Yet, in counterpoint to such an expectation, I will highlight language in the psalm that problematizes the connection with the Bathsheba/Uriah incident by generating dissonance with aspects of the story. Taking as my cue the complex relationships with the David narrative evoked by the language of the psalm, I want to explore the possibility of an intertextual reading of Psalm 51 and 2 Samuel 11–12, where the psalm might function to call into question aspects of David's response recounted in the prose narrative.

The Ambiguity of the Davidic Psalms Superscriptions

Let me start with the issue of "Davidic" psalm superscriptions. There is at best an ambiguous connection between these superscriptions and either the historical David or the David of the biblical narratives. First of all, the preposition לְ in לְדָוִד is not the standard way to designate authorship in Hebrew;[3] on the contrary, its most common meanings are *to*, *for* or *belonging to*.[4] Given the semantic range of the preposition לְ, the following interpretive possibilities have been proposed for לְדָוִד: 1) addressed to or offered to David; 2) belonging to David; 3) for the use of David; 4) on behalf of David; 5) about David; or, possibly, 6) authored by David (the so-called *lamed auctoris*).[5]

One of the problems in deciding which sense of the preposition ought to be favored in any particular instance is that the psalms superscriptions tend to be in the form of brief notes and thus we have very little semantic context to go by. The ambiguity of the preposition לְ is well illustrated in the superscription to Psalm 88, where it is used in what are probably three

3. The LXX translates almost every case of לְדָוִד in the psalms superscriptions by the dative τῷ Δαυιδ and only rarely by the genitive. Outside the psalm superscriptions, the only probable use of the so-called *lamed auctoris* in the MT is in Hab 3:1.

4. Bill Arnold and John Choi (*A Guide to Biblical Hebrew Syntax*, 110–14) give no less than fourteen possible uses of the preposition לְ. However, not all these possibilities are relevant to the meaning of לְדָוִד.

5. For these proposals, see Craigie, *Psalms 1–50*, 33–34; and Goldingay, *Psalms*, vol. 1, 27. Mark S. Smith (*The Priestly Vision of Genesis 1*, 146) translates the Akkadian cognate to לְ similarly in the superscription to the Baal cycle of myths: "about (literally 'to') Baal," or perhaps more technically speaking, "belonging to (the series of tablets called) Baal (*lbʿl*, in *KTU* 1.6 I 1)."

different senses: 1) a psalm לְ the sons of Korah; 2) לְ the leader [or chief musician]; 3) a *Maskil* לְ Heman the Ezrahite. In Psalm 51, likewise, we have: 1) לְ the leader; 2) a psalm לְ David. But which specific sense goes with which phrase in either superscription? To further complicate matters, while "David" in לְדָוִד can designate the second king of Israel, the name can also stand for any king in the Davidic line or even, in its messianic use, for a hoped for ruler like David.[6]

But the ambiguity of how psalm superscriptions are connected to David is evident not just from the possible meanings of the preposition לְ. We must also take into account the textual variations found between the MT, the LXX, and the DSS as to *which* psalms are Davidic (whatever "Davidic" signifies).[7]

The following chart ("'Davidic' Psalms in the MT Compared with the LXX and DSS") is a schematic guide to these variations.[8]

6. In the body of the psalms, "David" is used in connection primarily with the Davidic covenant and the Davidic line (Pss 18, 78, 89, 122, 132, 144).

7. These variants will be enough to show the complexity of the issue, but the picture becomes even more complex when other versions (such as the Syriac) are canvassed.

8. The numbering of most of the psalms is different in the MT and LXX, since Ps 10 is attached to Ps 9 in the LXX, which results in MT Ps 11 becoming Ps 10 in the LXX. The numbering harmonizes again by Ps 146 since MT Ps 147 is split into two psalms in the LXX.

"Davidic" Psalms in the MT Compared with the LXX and DSS*

MT	LXX	MT	LXX	MT	LXX
Book I		Book II		Book V	
3	3	*(43)*	42	108	107
4	4	51	50	109	108
5	5	52	51	110	109
6	6	53	52	-------------	
7	7	54	53	122	121
8	8	55	54	*(123)*	*(122)*
9	9 [MT 9-10]	56	55	124	123
(10)		57	56	-------------	
11	10	58	57	131	130
12	11	59	58	-------------	
13	12	60	59	133	132
14	13	61	60	-------------	
15	14	62	61	*(137)*	136
16	15	63	62	138	137
17	16	64	63	139	138
18	17	65	64	140	139
19	18	-------------		141	140
20	19	68	67	142	141
21	20	69	68	143	142
22	21	70	69	144	143
23	22	*(71)*	70	145	144
24	23	-------------			
25	24	Book III			
26	25	86	85		
27	26	-------------			
28	27	Book IV			
29	28	*(91)*	90		
30	29	-------------			
31	30	*(93)*	92		
32	31	*(94)*	93		
(33)	32	*(95)*	94		
34	33	*(96)*	95		
35	34	*(97)*	96		
36	35	*(98)*	97		
37	36	*(99)*	98		
38	37	-------------			
39	38	101	100		
40	39	-------------			
41	40	103	102		
-------------		*(104)*	103		

* Psalms with superscriptions connecting them to David in either the MT or LXX are highlighted in **bold** in the relevant column. Psalms in **bold with grayscale highlighting** have long superscriptions connecting them to an event in David's life. Psalms in *(italics with parentheses)* are missing superscriptions connecting them to David in the relevant column (MT or LXX). The two psalms in the MT column in *(italics with parentheses)* that also have grayscale highlighting have long superscriptions connecting them to David in the DSS, but not in the MT. Psalms without Davidic superscriptions in the MT, LXX, and DSS are not listed in the chart.

Whereas the MT connects seventy-three psalms to David (in both long and short superscriptions), the DSS connect two more psalms from the Masoretic Psalter to David.[9] The LXX, however, links no less than eighty-five psalms found in the Masoretic Psalter with David.[10] It also adds Psalm

9. We should note that twenty-four psalms from the MT are not represented in the DSS; although these psalms were likely included, they are now missing due to manuscript deterioration. Of these twenty-four, fourteen have "Davidic" superscriptions in the MT (one with a long heading).

10. Note that the numbers given here (and below, concerning long headings) are based on Albert Pietersma's judgments in his translation of LXX Psalms (*A New English*

151 (which seems to be related to two separate psalms in the DSS), linking it to David with a long heading.[11] But the DSS take the cake (specifically, the great Psalms scroll from Cave 11) in claiming that David authored 3,600 psalms, plus other songs, totaling 4,050 (some of which seem to be tragically missing from our collections)!

What of the textual evidence for the long headings that link various psalms to events in David's life? Here we also find variations between the MT, LXX, and DSS. Whereas thirteen psalm superscriptions in the MT make an explicit connection to events in the David story, the DSS connect two extra psalms from the Masoretic Psalter, while the LXX adds three others (and these are different from the two in the DSS).

This admittedly brief survey of "Davidic" superscriptions in the MT, LXX, and DSS suggests that psalms superscriptions were still in a state of flux even into the early first century of the Common Era (when the Qumran Psalms scroll from Cave 11 is dated). This would indicate that the superscriptions are later than the psalms themselves, and cannot be taken as definitive historical evidence for Davidic authorship (or for any original connection to David, even beyond the question of authorship).[12] This is so despite the fact that both MT and LXX superscriptions participate in the verse-numbering scheme of the psalms, since verse numbering only entered the manuscript tradition at a later stage.

How then are we to interpret the long headings, especially those that link particular psalms (like Psalm 51) to events in David life? Although they are likely later scribal additions, these superscriptions are now part of the canonical text and may be read as clues as to how some later biblical interpreters understood these psalms. John Goldingay proposes that we view the long superscriptions like contemporary lectionary suggestions. The linking of two or more lectionary texts does not necessarily indicate any original

Translation of the Septuagint), which diverges in some cases from the older edition of Alfred Ralfs (this reflects different scholarly opinions about which phrases in psalms superscriptions are original to the LXX).

11. Contrary to prevailing opinion that LXX Ps 151 is derived from the two DSS psalms (11Q5 Ps 151A & B), Tyler Williams ("Psalm 151") makes a persuasive case for the original integrity of LXX Ps 151, the entirety of which is based on 1 Samuel 16–17 (David as shepherd and harpist, followed by his subsequent victory over Goliath), while 11Q5 Ps 151A & B is expansionistic, adding details not found in 1 Samuel 16–17.

12. This does not mean that a superscription couldn't preserve a genuine historical connection to David (on this possibility, see Craigie, *Psalms 1–50*, 35). My point is simply that the presence of a superscription cannot, by itself, be taken as definitive evidence of this.

relationship between them; rather, what we have are scribal or editorial suggestions that it might be fruitful to read particular texts together.[13]

So, let us take up the challenge of a responsible intertextual, canonical reading and see what sort of fruit is borne in the case of Psalm 51 and 2 Samuel 11–12.[14]

Resonances of Psalm 51 with the Narrative of 2 Samuel 11–12

The first thing to say is that the scribes or editors who linked Psalm 51 with 2 Samuel 11–12 were not engaging in wild flights of fantasy.[15] There are, indeed, at least six sets of verbal and thematic links between the two texts.

1. The Acknowledgment of Sin

The most obvious, and most important, is found in verse 4 (MT verse 6).[16] The first couplet of this verse reads: "Against you, you alone, have I sinned, / and what is evil in your eyes I have done." The first line of this couplet ("Against you, you alone, have I sinned") vividly evokes David's confession

13. Goldingay, *Psalms*, vol. 1, 29. Along the same lines, James Luther Mays (*Psalms*, 53) describes the psalms superscriptions as "inner-biblical exegesis." For a fuller discussion of the issue, see Childs, "Psalm Titles and Midrashic Exegesis."

14. There are many types of intertexual readings, not all attentive to context. Indeed, the origins of the term "intertexuality" (Kristeva, *Desire in Language*) suggest that the meaning of a text is a production of the reader with little by way of external controls. Although I acknowledge the legitimacy of exploring such wild intertextuality in certain contexts (see Middleton, "From the Clenched Fist to the Open Hand"), this essay intends to work with a much more limited notion of intertexutality, comparing and contrasting Ps 51 with the narrative of 2 Sam 12. For another example of intertextual reading (in this case between two psalms), see Middleton, "Role of Human Beings."

15. One commentator who attempts to link Ps 51 with an originally Davidic context is Michael Goulder (see *The Prayers of David*, 51–69). Although Goulder's hypothesis is a fascinating critical proposal, and is intended to make sense of parts of the psalm he thinks are often misunderstood by others, just about every point in his interpretation could be challenged. This shows the difficulty of reconstructing a plausible original connection of the psalm to David (indeed, of any psalm to an original historical context). In deference to this difficulty, I hold in abeyance the historical question of whether some author or editor *intended* Ps 51 as a critique of David. Instead, I will focus on textual *effects* of the psalm, when read as part of the biblical canon.

16. All verse references to Ps 51 in this essay will use the English numbering, which is two lower than the MT numbering scheme. The difference is because the superscription, which is counted as verses 1–2 in the MT, is unnumbered in English translations.

in 2 Sam 12:13, "I have sinned against YHWH." Both texts, the psalm and the narrative, utilize the verb חטא with the preposition לְ.

2. The Phrase "Evil in [Someone's] Eyes"

This evocation is intensified by the next line of the couplet ("and what is evil in your eyes I have done"), which echoes the three-fold use of the phrase "evil in [someone's] eyes," found in both chapters 11 and 12 of 2 Samuel. Whereas in 2 Sam 11:25 David tells Joab (through a messenger) that he should not let Uriah's death "seem evil in your eyes," two verses later the narrator tells us "it was evil in YHWH's eyes" (2 Sam 11:27), thus putting into sharp contrast the moral perspectives of God and the king of Israel. Then, in the following chapter, Nathan explicitly accuses David of despising YHWH "by doing what is evil in his eyes" (2 Sam 12:9).

So the first couplet in Ps 51:4 has clear and powerful resonances with important language in 2 Samuel 11–12, giving the impression that this is, indeed, David's confession after Nathan's accusation.

3. God's Righteous Judgment

The second couplet in verse 4 cements the impression that this is David's confession by calling our attention to God's just verdict of guilt (though in the narrative this *preceded* the confession). When the psalmist *follows* his confession of sin in verse 4 by immediately telling YHWH that he is therefore "righteous in [his] speaking / and blameless in [his] judgment," this evokes the guilty verdict and sentence that Nathan delivered from YHWH in 2 Sam 12:7–12 (and perhaps 12:14).[17]

4. The Plea for God's to Be Gracious

But there are other resonances too. The psalmist's opening plea, "Be gracious to me, O God" (51:1), calls to mind David's explanation in 2 Sam 12:22 for why he fasted prior to his son's death: "for I said, 'Who knows, YHWH may be gracious to me and the child will live'" Both texts use the same verb חנן for being gracious.

17. These lines from the psalm also echo the language of Deut 17:9, which uses the phrase "the word of judgment" for the verdict given by priests.

5. The Emphasis on Interiority

Then there is the emphasis in Ps 51:6 on God's desire for אֱמֶת (truth or faithfulness) and חָכְמָה (wisdom) in the inner or secret parts, a motif continued in the psalmist's petition in verse 10 for a clean heart and a steadfast or firm spirit.[18] This emphasis on positive interiority is the flip side of Nathan's assertion in 2 Sam 12:12 that David had committed his sin in secret (in contrast to the judgment, which would be public).[19] Although the words for interiority are not the same in the psalm and the narrative, this thematic link between them suggests that in the psalm David has come to a realization of the need for core personal integrity, a consistent inner disposition toward what is right.[20]

6. Deliverance from Bloodshed (דָמִים)

One more line in the psalm might suggest a further link with the Samuel narrative. In verse 14 the psalmist pleads, "Deliver me from bloodshed, O God," which could be taken as an allusion to the murder of Uriah (in 2 Samuel 11). Although the murder is not mentioned in the superscription to the psalm (only the adultery with Bathsheba), David is explicitly described in 2 Sam 16:8 as "a man of bloodshed," using the same word (דָמִים) found in our psalm.[21]

However, "Deliver me from דָמִים" is not likely a request for forgiveness, since דָמִים (despite the translation "bloodguilt" in the NIV; "bloodguiltiness" in the KJV and ESV) does not typically refer to the *guilt* that accrues

18. The emphasis on interiority is also suggested by verse 3, where the psalmist says he is constantly aware of his sin.

19. Indeed, whereas David's judgment will be "before all Israel and before the sun" (2 Sam 12:12), the psalmist confesses (in Ps 51:3): "my sin is continually before me" (using the same word נֶגֶד for "before").

20. There are other elements of the psalm that might suggest it is Davidic, though these do not necessarily connect to the episode in 2 Samuel 11–12. Included among these would be the psalmist's appeal for God's holy Spirit not to be taken from him (51:11), since this would fit with 2 Sam 16:13, where the Spirit of YHWH came on David at this anointing. Also relevant is the psalmist's plea for a "willing," "generous" or "noble" (נְדִיבָה) spirit (51:12). While this translation is derived from the use of the adjective נָדִיב in places like Exod 35:5 and 22 (where it is used to describe the people's generous *heart*), as well as 1 Chr 28:21, 2 Chr 29:31 and Isa 32:5, the noun נָדִיב can also mean "prince" or "noble," as in Job 2:28, Prov 25:7, and Song 7:2, thus suggesting the possibility of a literal meaning of "princely" or "royal" for the adjective in our psalm (see Goulder, *Prayers of David*, 60).

21. In 1 Chr 22:8 David is said to have shed "much blood," using both the singular and the plural.

from the act of killing or shedding blood, but rather to the act itself or to death as the consequence of the guilt (that is, punishment for the act). So the psalmist's plea in verse 14 would be for deliverance not from guilt taken on its own and certainly not from the subjective feeling of guilt. Nor could he be pleading for deliverance from committing the crime—that has already happened. Rather, the psalmist is most likely asking for deliverance from his own death (that is, the punishment that comes with guilt, the consequence for having shed blood). This certainly fits with 2 Sam 12:13, where David's death is mentioned as the punishment for his sin.

Dissonance between Psalm 51 and the Bathsheba/Uriah Incident

But not everything in the psalm fits the narrative. Having examined ways in which Psalm 51 resonates with the narrative of 2 Samuel 11–12, it is now time to note some divergences, beginning with some that suggest the psalm was not written with the narrative in mind. Although I will begin with four preliminary elements of dissonance between the psalm and the narrative, my focus will be on the most significant disjunction (which arises from the psalm's emphasis on the need for moral reformation after sin). Not only might this disjunction between Psalm 51 and the narrative of 2 Samuel cause us to question the adequacy of David's repentance, it raises important considerations about the nature of repentance in the moral life of the church today.

1. David's Death Is Averted yet the Psalmist Pleads for Deliverance from Death

If the psalmist is, indeed, pleading for deliverance from death in verse 16 (as the word דָמִים suggests), this introduces an element of dissonance between the psalm and the narrative of 2 Samuel, since Nathan tells David that his death has been averted through God's forgiveness (he has, in other words, already *been* delivered from דָמִים). Why then would David (in the psalm) plead for deliverance from his own impending death? Wouldn't this imply his lack of trust in the prophetic announcement that God had spared his life?

2. David Is Immediately Forgiven yet the Psalmist Pleads Continually for Forgiveness

Another area of dissonance arises from the psalmist's pleas for forgiveness. Whereas the psalmist pleads with God at some length for forgiveness, via the metaphor of cleansing (in verses 1–2, 7 and 9), David is immediately granted forgiveness in 2 Sam 12:13 after his two-word confession of sin: חָטָאתִי (I-have-sinned) לַיהוה (against-YHWH). So unless the psalm is viewed as an expansion of David's two-word confession, the lengthy pleading for forgiveness in the psalm would suggest that he did not entirely believe Nathan's pronouncement of God's forgiveness (or at least found it difficult to accept). Like the plea for deliverance from death, the extended plea for forgiveness, if attributed to David, might show a certain lack of trust on his part.[22]

Rescuing David—Ritual Cleansing and Not Forgiveness?

One way to perhaps rescue David from this charge would be to view the psalmist as pleading not for forgiveness per se, but for some sort of ritual cleansing that accompanies, or follows upon, forgiveness;[23] the *hyssop* of verse 7 might be meant literally.[24] But even if the hyssop is metaphorical, the idea might be that, having already received forgiveness, the psalmist is now seeking to be publicly restored to the community (by having the stain of sin liturgically removed).

In support of this emphasis on ritual it might be noted that the three words for sin (פֶּשַׁע; עָוֹן; חַטָּאה) mentioned in Ps 51:1–2 are also found in the Day of Atonement ritual (Lev 16:21). While I do not believe we need to conclude that the psalm was explicitly composed for this ritual,[25] the singular and plural forms of the varied nouns for sin scattered throughout the psalm seem to indicate a broader situation than David's predicament in 2 Samuel

22. It might be suggested that this extended plea for forgiveness might represent the depth of David's awareness of his sin. Yet besides being quite different in tone from the his two-word confession in the narrative, an extended plea of this sort *after forgiveness has been offered* suggests a wallowing in guilt that is not healthy in the process of repentance and healing.

23. The idea that the psalmist might be appealing for ritual cleansing and *not* forgiveness is an extrapolation from the view of some commentators that the psalmist is seeking ritual cleansing either *along with* or as a *means to* forgiveness (inner cleansing); for the emphasis on ritual cleansing, see Goldingay, *Psalms*, vol. 2, 122–40; Goulder, *Prayers of David*, 51–69.

24. Goulder suggests that the hyssop refers to a purgative drink David was to take as part of the ritual of atonement for his sin (Goulder, *Prayers of David*, 56–57).

25. Contra Mays, *Psalms*, 199.

11–12. Yet the psalm is certainly amenable to ritual or liturgical use, since its expansive language for sin would be applicable to all supplicants (no matter what their particular wrongdoing).[26]

But what are we to make of the proposal of some sort of ritual cleansing? Could this help overcome the divergence between the psalmist's insistent pleas for cleansing and the forgiveness immediately offered to David?

If the cleansing in the psalm were, indeed, a reference to a public or communal ritual, we could raise the question of whether David is ever portrayed as engaging in any such ritual; he is not. We could also ask whether he seems to be restored to the community after 2 Samuel 12; he seems in some significant ways alienated in the chapters that follow (more on that later).

The Psalm's Focus on Interiority Suggests Forgiveness Is the Issue

Alternatively, we could challenge the idea that the psalmist is seeking ritual cleansing. Given the strong focus on interiority in the psalm (including the interiorization of sacrifice in verse 17), it is more likely that language of cleansing is being used figuratively—to designate forgiveness, the removal of a stain on the conscience.

Another indication, beyond the thematic focus on interiority, that forgiveness is the issue in the psalm, rather than ritual cleansing, is language in verses 1–2 that echoes Exod 34:6–7, the revelation of God's character to Moses in connection with the forgiveness of Israel's sin of idolatry (the golden calf). The same three words for wrongdoing (חַטָאה; עָוֹן; פֶּשַׁע) that first appear in verses 1–2 of the psalm, and recur throughout (in both nominal and verbal forms), are found also in Exod 34:7, where they describe the sort of evil that God forgives (without any mention of ritual). But whereas these three words for sin occur in both Exodus 34 and the Day of Atonement ritual, the Exodus text has further resonances with the psalm.

It is significant that Ps 51:1 alludes to the description of YHWH's core character in Exod 34:6. Thus the opening plea for God to "be gracious to me" (חָנֵּנִי) "according to your love" (כְּחַסְדֶּךָ) and to blot out sins according to the excess of "your compassions" (רַחֲמֶיךָ) echoes God's self-revelation to Moses as "gracious" (חַנּוּן), "compassionate" (רַחוּם) and abounding in "love" (חֶסֶד).

These allusions to Exodus 34 make it plausible that the psalmist's pledge in verse 13 to teach transgressors "your ways" is also an allusion to

26. Indeed, we might say that the psalm's expansive terminology covers (or, better, uncovers/exposes) a multitude of sins.

the golden calf narrative. The psalmist's pledge may hearken back to Moses' request to God in Exod 33:13 to "show me your ways" (which, in context, are ways of mercy) or it may possibly echo Exod 32:8, where YHWH tells Moses that in constructing the calf the people "have turned aside from the way which I commanded them" (referring to the moral path they should have taken).[27]

When these multiple allusions to the golden calf episode are taken together, they cumulatively suggest that the psalmist is appealing to this paradigmatic example of YHWH's forgiveness in the past as the basis for being forgiven in the present. He is asking God to act in accordance with the divine character as revealed to Moses and forgive an individual's sin as he did the sin of the community.

And if forgiveness is, indeed, the issue in the psalm, and we read it as David's prayer, then David is portrayed as pleading for forgiveness despite the fact that forgiveness was immediately announced as soon as he confessed his sin in the Samuel narrative. The psalm could thus serve to question David's trust in God's word.

3. David's Only Petition is for the Life of His Son

A related area of dissonance between the psalm and the narrative is that while the psalm is dominated by petition (first for forgiveness or cleansing in verses 1–2, 7, and 9, and then for restoration in verses 6b, 8, 10–12 and 18), David's sole petition in the narrative is that his son's life be spared (2 Sam 12:16, echoed in verse 22).[28] Indeed, David engages in a public ritual of mourning over his son's impending death, in connection with his petition, but there is no comparable mourning concerning his own sin or its consequences for Bathsheba or Uriah (and certainly no ritual for restoration to the community).

27. Beyond the specific linguistic resonances between Ps 51 and the golden calf episode, there is the significant similarity in content between both, where the focus is on the forgiveness of serious sin (idolatry in the Exodus text, unspecified sin in Ps 51), for which there is no sacrifice possible. And the death of David's son, which occurs despite the forgiveness of his sin (2 Sam 12:18), might reflect Exod 34:7, which combines forgiveness with "visiting the iniquity of the parents upon the children."

28. The prominence of petitions (twenty-one in all) in Ps 51 is evident when we analyze the psalm for the typical elements of an individual lament: Petition (1–2, 6b–12, 14a, 15a, 18); Complaint (3–5); Confession of Trust (6a, 16–17); Vow of Praise (13–15). Thus Mays comments: "Petitions are in control of the structure throughout; the prayer begins, continues, and concludes in the asking mode" (Mays, *Psalms*, 198).

4. Was David's Sin against YHWH Alone?

This leads to what is perhaps the most egregious line in the psalm, when read against the background of 2 Samuel 11–12. In verse 4 the psalmist claims that his sin was solely against God: לְךָ (against you), לְבַדְּךָ (you alone), חָטָאתִי (I have sinned); whereas David's sin was patently also against Bathsheba and Uriah.

In defense of David (if he were the author of the psalm), it is understandable that he would concentrate on his sin against God, since no less than three times in 2 Samuel 12 he is told (in no uncertain terms) that he has despised or scorned YHWH or YHWH's word (verses 9, 10, and 14); and David himself confesses that he sinned against YHWH (verse 13).[29]

But while this theological focus is understandable, the narrowing down of the scope of the sin in Psalm 51 to exclude the sociological would nevertheless be inappropriate if this were David's prayer.[30] Indeed, we could imagine that if David had said in 2 Samuel 12, "Against YHWH, YHWH alone, have I sinned," this might well have been followed by Nathan's rebuke for his moral shortsightedness![31]

How Psalm 51 Might Call into Question the Adequacy of David's Response to God

But of all the areas of dissonance between the psalm and the Samuel narrative, the most instructive is generated by the psalmist's request in verse 10

29. One way to explain the exclusive theological focus of this statement would be to take it in the same vein as the psalmist's claim in verse 5 that his sinning began before birth, even at conception. The psalmist is so overwhelmed by his sense of guilt before God that this generates hyperbolic assertions. This leads the NET Bible to moderate the psalmist's extreme statement in verse 4 by translating "you alone" as "you above all."

30. In one sense this narrowing down might well fit the David of 2 Sam 12, since he becomes more and more inwardly focused as the narrative progresses, the climax of this interiority being verses 17–23. Here we see David isolated in his prayers. His refusal to "rise from the ground" at the urging of the elders may certainly communicate the burden of his grief, but it also creates a disconnection between those around him that still care about the hurting king. This isolation is evident in the servants' unwillingness to share with David the news of the child's death, to the point where David has to learn the news through eavesdropping. Finally, the accumulation of first-person singular verbs and pronouns in verses 22–23 emphasizes the individualized focus that David has (we only hear a hint of Bathsheba's grief in verse 24). Yet while this excluding of the social/interpersonal aspect of sin in Ps 51 might fit the David of the narrative, it would not be *ethically* appropriate, if it was, indeed, David's prayer. (A special thanks to Chris Williams for bringing this point to my attention.)

31. A point made also by Goldingay, *Psalms*, vol. 2, 128.

for a pure heart (לֵב טָהוֹר) and a steadfast spirit (רוּחַ נָכוֹן) and in verse 12 for a willing spirit (רוּחַ נְדִיבָה)—a request that is related to God's desire for faithfulness in the inner person (which was articulated in verse 6).

The Need for Moral Reformation after Confession of Sin

Not only is this request never voiced by the David of the Samuel narrative, it is (more importantly) never fulfilled in David's life. While the David of the narrative certainly has the broken spirit (רוּחַ נִשְׁבָּרָה) and broken and crushed[32] heart (רוּחַ נִשְׁבָּר וְנִדְכֶּה) that the psalmist says is a true, godly sacrifice in verse 17, he does not get beyond this to the moral reformation of character presupposed in the psalm.

As Mark Boda suggests in his comprehensive study of repentance in the Old Testament, biblical repentance typically involves more than "oral declarations expressing penitential desire whether in prayer or speech, including admission of sin and culpability"; such oral confession of sin certainly characterizes the David of the 2 Samuel narrative. But this is not enough. Full biblical repentance involves also *affective* change ("full engagement of internal orientation, all one's heart") and *behavioral* manifestations ("actual change in lifestyle and patterns of living").[33]

Boda cites a number of psalms to show that "the admission of sin is considered a prelude to a fundamental change in affection and behavior."[34] Among his parade examples are Pss 143:8, 10; 119 (*passim*); 40:6–8 [MT 7–9]; 86:11; 25:14; 32:8–9; 51:10, 13 [MT 12, 15].[35] His climactic example is none other than Psalm 51, noting "there is a clear shift in the psalm beginning with verse 10 as the psalmist cries out for a fundamental transformation in his inner character with the creation of a clean heart, the renewal of a steadfast spirit and the sustenance of a willing spirit."[36] But there is no evidence that the David of the Samuel narrative experienced any significant moral transformation after his confession (and immediate absolution by Nathan).[37]

32. Although the traditional translation of "crushed" in verse 17 is "contrite," the same verbal root for "crushed" (דכה) is used for the bones the psalmist says God has "broken" (דִּכִּיתָ) in verse 8.

33. Boda, *"Return to Me,"* 31.

34. Ibid., 117.

35. Ibid., 117–8.

36. Ibid., 118.

37. It might be objected that this is an argument from silence. However, we need to realize that the narrator's characterization of David in 2 Sam 12 is a highly nuanced (and intentional) portrayal; so we are warranted in attending to both what is *said* and what

David's Post-Confession Diminution/Passivity

Indeed, David is a much diminished person after 2 Samuel 12, as if the confrontation with his own sin took all the wind (רוּחַ) out of him. This diminution is evident in his passivity towards the rape of his daughter Tamar by her half-brother Amnon. Although David is angry (2 Sam 13:21), he does nothing either to comfort his daughter or to confront the rapist. Indeed, his passivity allows Absalom to stew in the juices of revenge and then serve it up cold to Amnon two years later (2 Sam 13:23–37).

But even after Absalom's murder of Amnon, David does nothing for three years, even though the text reports his strong emotions concerning both sons (2 Sam 13:38–39). Even with Absalom living in Jerusalem (through Joab's initiative) and yearning to see his father, which finally does happen after two years (2 Sam 14:28–33), David's inaction leads to such alienation from his son that this generates Absalom's revolt and takeover attempt on the kingdom (2 Sam 15:1–13).

And during the civil war with Absalom, David is a pathetic, maudlin figure (2 Sam 15:30, 18:3–5); indeed, after Absalom's death Joab has to reprimand David to pull himself together, to prevent the desertion of the troops (2 Sam 19:1–7). And there are other examples of the diminution of David's character that could be given from 2 Samuel.[38] But suffice it to say that David never recovers morally in the narrative.[39]

The contrast is significant: while the psalmist is broken and crushed in spirit *prior* to receiving forgiveness, and so pleads desperately for cleansing and restoration, the David of 2 Samuel is broken and crushed in spirit *after* receiving forgiveness and remains an ambivalent character for the rest of the Samuel narrative.

---

is *not said*. We have no access behind the biblical text to some pre-narrative "David."

38. Two examples would be David's initial passivity in concluding the war with the Ammonites right after Nathan's reprimand (2 Sam 12:26–28) and his fatalistic response to Shimei's cursing when he and his entourage are fleeing Jerusalem to escape Abasalom's army (2 Sam 16:5–13).

39. David M. Gunn discerns a strange invigorating of David's character during his flight from Absalom despite his ensuing passivity; see Gunn, *The Story of King David*, 101–2. However, this is not the same as moral recovery. The lack of moral reformation on David's part is evident in his change of mind regarding his oath to Shimei that he would not be killed (2 Sam 19:18–23). On his deathbed David instructs his son Solomon to kill Shimei, self-servingly construing his earlier oath to mean only that he himself would not personally do the killing (1 Kgs 2:8–9). This invigoration on David's part (if we may so name it) could be viewed as an (unethical) overreaction to his prior passivity. It is certainly not the same as moral recovery.

A Virtue Ethics Understanding of Sin and Moral Reformation

It is certainly commendable that David immediately confessed his sin (2 Sam 12:13) once convicted by Nathan's parable (2 Sam 12:1–4), in conjunction with the prophetic word (2 Sam 12:7b–12). Indeed, this parable, which was not technically part of the prophetic word ("Thus says YHWH" only begins in 7b), was an insightful strategy on the prophet's part to get the king to realize the enormity of his sin. Nathan was probably wise to begin with this self-involving parable, given the fact that David had only rarely ever been corrected by anyone during his rise to power and his consolidation of the kingdom.[40] This was not a man used to having his will be opposed.

With this in mind, the narrative of Samuel does not portray the transgression of boundaries depicted in the Bathsheba/Uriah incident as an isolated episode that comes out of the blue, with no warning. Rather, the preceding narrative portrays David as a rising leader who does not let anyone get in his way; and while he may not do outright evil during his rise to power, he seems to be a full-steam-ahead sort of person, who figures out what he wants and goes for it. And he gets away with everything he does.

In the narrative of David's rise to power, he conquers Goliath, single-handedly slays a hundred Philistines, marries Saul's daughter, receives an oath of fealty from Saul's son (and heir), escapes from Saul on multiple occasions, and receives the benefit of Joab's elimination of potential opposition (so that his hands are technically clean; yet he doesn't dismiss Joab from being his general).

A possible analogy for David's rise is that of a very fast (and skilled) race car driver, who just barely survives going off the road time and again as he takes hair-raising curves and overtakes other drivers. He gets used to surviving by the skin of his teeth. But one day he goes too far and spins out of control. The Bathsheba/Uriah incident is David's major crash.

A Christian understanding of virtue ethics suggests that good and evil actions are not isolated events in a person's life. Rather, character (whether good or evil) is built up bit by bit as we engage in habitual actions over time,

40. Among the few times when David is brought up short by external agency are the following (all in 2 Samuel 6–7). First, there is his initial failed attempt to bring the ark to Jerusalem, where the death of one of those carrying the ark leads David to postpone trying again for three months (2 Sam 6:1–11). Second, there is Michal's critique of his half-naked dancing in the presence of serving girls when he finally brings the ark to Jerusalem (2 Sam 6:20), and it is more likely that her consequent barrenness (2 Sam 6:23) was the result of her denying David the marriage bed than the typical (patriarchal) assumption either that David denied her or that God punished her. Third, we have YHWH's clear refusal of David's plan to build a temple in Jerusalem as YHWH's domicile (2 Sam 7:5–7), after Nathan had given him the go-ahead (2 Sam 7:1–3).

and this character is likewise evidenced in the actions or behavior that we engage in. So David's pattern of behavior (and thus his character) has been building up to the crash in 2 Samuel 11–12.

Virtue ethics applies not just to David's pre-crash actions, but also to what is needed post-crash. As he staggers away from the wreck, immediate blanket absolution (which Nathan gives) is a quick fix, like putting a Band-Aid on a serious wound. But this is clearly not enough. David needs to reform his driving habits (read: moral character).[41]

Questioning the Adequacy of Nathan's Bare Offer of Forgiveness

This leads me to wonder about the adequacy of Nathan's immediate absolution, without setting in place any process for moral reformation and renewal, especially since the major point of disjunction between Psalm 51 and the Samuel narrative is that the psalm focuses on forgiveness followed by restoration of the broken sinner, whereas David in the narrative simply confesses and is summarily forgiven by Nathan.[42]

Here it is perhaps not irrelevant to remember that Nathan had previously misrepresented God's will in 2 Samuel 7. Having immediately affirmed David's desire to build a temple for YHWH (2 Sam 7:3), he had to be corrected that same night by YHWH that this was *not* in fact the divine will (2 Sam 7:4–16).[43] So Nathan may have the instincts of a pleaser or a yes-man, as far as David is concerned.[44] At any rate, the result of Nathan's immediate offer of forgiveness (with no follow-up) in 2 Samuel 12 is that David's life and family continue in shambles, without recovery in the rest of 2 Samuel.[45]

41. This goes beyond the fact that David is brought up short and loses his sense of bravado. What he now needs is not a simple restoration of self-confidence, but a re-building of moral fiber, which is a more difficult process.

42. For further insightful analysis of the integral place of moral reformation in genuine repentance in both the Old Testament and Jewish tradition, see Wilson, *Exploring Our Hebraic Heritage*, 206–27 (chap. 11: "Entering His Gates: On Repentance and Prayer"). Wilson's account is similar to Boda's emphasis on what we might call the relationship of *faith* (turning to God) and *good works* (the moral change attendant upon faith).

43. Without putting too fine a point on it, we may say that Nathan here functions as a false prophet.

44. Special thanks to my student Bryan Picciotto for emphasizing the inadequacy of Nathan's offer of forgiveness in a paper entitled "Nathan's Parabolic and Prophetic Rhetoric."

45. The fact that so many interpreters have read the narrative of 2 Sam 12 without raising suspicions about the "cheap grace" that Nathan offers is testimony to the dominance of a truncated Protestant/pietist understanding of repentance. Yet even Billy

Communal/External Dimensions of Repentance in Psalm 51

While an emphasis on the interior transformation of the individual has already been made clear from the psalm (culminating in verse 17), it is significant that the psalm moves beyond the individual and the interior in two ways, neither of which finds a parallel in the David of 2 Samuel.

First, we have the vow in verses 13–15, consisting in the psalmist's promise to praise God and teach sinners God's ways. The vow is a typical element of individual laments (of which Psalm 51 is an example), where the psalmist pledges an appropriate response to God's anticipated answer to his prayer.[46] Yet nowhere in the Samuel narrative after God's forgiveness does David proclaim God's praise or teach transgressors God's ways (either God's moral standards or God's gracious forgiveness—drawing on the two meanings of God's *ways* in the golden calf episode).[47]

The second way in which the psalm moves beyond an interior focus is its concluding prayer for the building (or rebuilding) of Jerusalem and the public offering of righteous sacrifices once again (verses 18–19). These verses are sometimes taken as a post-exilic addition to an earlier psalm, supplementing the original's single-minded emphasis on inner sacrifice with a "correction" regarding the validity of public, communal sacrifices; this is entirely plausible as a historical guess.

However, it is also possible that the entire psalm is pre-exilic and verses 18–19 refer to the need to complete the building of the city walls that David started in 2 Sam 5:10 (the walls were, indeed, completed by Solomon; 1 Kgs 9:15 and 11:27). The completion of the walls would then be a sign of God's restorative grace to the forgiven king.

Or the entire psalm could be exilic or post-exilic, with the psalm's emphasis on interiority and grace reflecting a similar emphasis found in exilic texts like Jer 31:31–34, 32:38–40; and Ezek 36:26–27. In that case, the final

---

Graham evangelistic crusades were not content with a "decision" for Christ, but required new converts to engage in some minimal "follow-up," which included personal faith sharing and a process of integration into a community of believers.

46. Claus Westermann has suggested that psalms of individual lament may contain any combination of three types of laments or complaints: Thou-laments (which address God as the source of the problem), they-laments (which cite human enemies), and I-laments (where the psalmist acknowledges his own guilt); the complaints in Ps 51 consist entirely of I-laments. See Westermann, *Praise and Lament in the Psalms*, 66–67.

47. Indeed, the David of the Samuel narrative is not typically portrayed as a pious YHWH worshiper (with the exception of his dancing before the ark in 2 Samuel 6, a text that mixes political and religious motives); and he is certainly not portrayed as following the injunctions of Deut 17:18–20 concerning regular reading of the Torah that he might diligently observe God's laws.

verses of the psalm might suggest that after the broken/crushing experience of exile, Jerusalem would once more be restored (as Jer 31:38 anticipates), just as the psalmist anticipates he will be.

Whether these verses are integral to the original psalm or a post-exilic addition, the concluding emphasis on communal, visible, external (re) building hints at the very sort of restoration David needed to undergo.[48]

A Canonical Reading of Psalm 51 as a Critique of David's "Repentance"

The contrast between the psalmist's desire for a pure heart and a steadfast and willing spirit (in verses 10 and 12) and the *lack* of such steadfastness in the case of David after 2 Samuel 12 is suggestive of a canonical reading that highlights the need to go beyond confession and forgiveness of sin to moral reformation, the disciplined reshaping of character after sin. Confession and forgiveness, while necessary for repentance, are not enough. Since it is the cumulative deformation of character over time that leads to egregious sins like adultery and murder, the requisite moral reformation would involve both an *inner* steadfastness (of heart/spirit) and visible, *outer* actions to match—neither of which David attained to after his forgiveness in 2 Samuel 12. Such is the result of taking the superscription of Psalm 51 seriously as a guide to reading intertextually.[49]

It is not the purpose of this paper to claim that Psalm 51 was written explicitly as a critique of David. However, taking my cue from the content of the psalm when read in connection with the David narrative, and also from the use of the preposition לְ in the body of psalm (לְךָ; "*against* you" in verse 4) and in 2 Sam 12:13 (לַיהוה; "*against* YHWH"), might we be justified in taking מִזְמוֹר לְדָוִד in the superscription to Psalm 51 as a psalm *against* David?

Bibliography

Arnold, Bill T., and John H. Choi. *A Guide to Biblical Hebrew Syntax*. Cambridge: Cambridge University Press, 2003.

48. The fact that these are all guesses (we simply do not know the historical origins of the psalm) does not prevent us from mining the text for its possible connection to the David of the Samuel narrative.

49. It is an open question whether reading other "Davidic" psalms together with relevant narratives in 1 or 2 Samuel would bear significant interpretive fruit. That would be an interesting topic for further research.

Boda, Mark J. *"Return to Me": A Biblical Theology of Repentance*. New Studies in Biblical Theology. Downers Grove, IL: IVP Academic, 2015.

Childs, Brevard S. "Psalm Titles and Midrashic Exegesis." *Journal of Semitic Studies* 16 (1971) 137–50.

Craigie, Peter C. *Psalms 1–50*. Word Biblical Commentary 19. Waco, TX: Word Books, 1983.

Goldingay, John. *Psalms*, vol. 1: *Psalms 1–41*. Baker Commentary on the Old Testament Wisdom and Psalms. Grand Rapids: Baker, 2006.

———. *Psalms*, vol. 2: *Psalms 42–89*. Baker Commentary on the Old Testament Wisdom and Psalms. Grand Rapids: Baker, 2007.

Goulder, Michael. *The Prayers of David (Psalms 51–72): Studies in the Psalter, II*. London: T. & T. Clark International, 2004.

Gunn, David M. *The Story of King David: Genre and Interpretation*. JSOTSup 6. Sheffield, UK: JSOT Press, 1978.

Kristeva, Julia. *Desire in Language: A Semiotic Approach to Literature and Art*. New York: Columbia University Press, 1980.

Mays, James Luther. *Psalms*. Interpretation. Louisville, KY: John Knox, 1994.

Middleton, J. Richard. "From the Clenched Fist to the Open Hand: A Postmodern Reading of the Twenty-Third Psalm." In *The Strategic Smorgasbord of Postmodernity: Literature and the Christian Critic*, edited by Deborah C. Bowen, 307–25. Newcastle, UK: Cambridge Scholars, 2007.

———. "The Role of Human Beings in the Cosmic Temple: The Intersection of Worldviews in Psalms 8 and 104." *Canadian Theological Review* 2.1 (2013) 44–58.

Picciotto, Bryan. "Nathan's Parabolic and Prophetic Rhetoric: Examining the Communication in 2 Sam 12:1–15a." Unpublished paper presented at the Canadian Evangelical Theological Association annual meeting, Kitchener-Waterloo, ON, May 27, 2012.

Pietersma, Albert, and Benjamin G. Wright, eds. *A New English Translation of the Septuagint*. Oxford and New York: Oxford University Press, 2007.

Smith, Mark S. *The Priestly Vision of Genesis 1*. Minneapolis: Fortress, 2010.

Westermann, Claus. *Praise and Lament in the Psalms*. Translated by Richard N. Soulen. Atlanta: John Knox, 1981.

Williams, Tyler F. "Psalm 151: An Orphan in the Greek Psalter." Unpublished paper presented at the Canadian Society of Biblical Studies annual meeting, Carleton University, Ottawa, ON, May 26, 2009.

Wilson, Marvin R. *Exploring Our Hebraic Heritage: A Christian Theology of Roots and Renewal*. Grand Rapids: Eerdmans, 2014.

3

Rewriting Torah Obedience in Romans for the Church

J. David Stark

Commonly, Paul of Tarsus is portrayed as an "apostle of grace" who preached a "Torah-free" gospel and, consequently, opposed requiring Torah obedience for Gentile Christians. So far as it goes, this sketch contains important truths. For Paul, "the works of the Torah" should never be an identity locus for the Christian community.[1] What often fails to be appreciated however—with serious consequences for understanding the rest of Pauline thought—is the degree to which Paul himself rewrites and retheologizes what counts as proper Torah obedience.

In this connection, the concept of the "trace" may be a helpful rubric for this discussion. It has been said that "the (pure) trace is differance"—namely, "the differance which opens appearance. . .and signification"—and thus, "the trace is . . . the absolute origin of sense in general."[2] Prototypically, the trace combines both the past's moving away, the future's moving forward, and what remains from them as influencing and informing the

1. E.g., Rom 3:1—4:25; 9:30—10:13.

2. Derrida, *Grammatology*, 62, 65. There is no intention here either to engage or to underwrite Derrida's entire hermeneutical program. As the following discussion should show, however, there seem to be several points of contact among phenomena relevant to thinking about Paul's retheologizing Torah obedience and how Derrida develops the (non-)concept of the "trace." Of course, where this interaction fails to help, readers are invited kindly to look past it. Cf. Lewis, *Mere Christianity*, 166.

present.[3] "Trace," therefore, includes the idea of "remainder," but it does so specifically in connection to the "non-remainder."[4] That is, neither what passes away nor what the present suggests for the future is itself already present, but precisely in its being absent, it exerts force upon and shapes what remains.[5]

Strictly speaking, the "arche-trace"—that is, the foundation for subsequent traces—is always found absent if one seeks it phenomenologically. Even so, it is a found absence.[6] This absence's force, to some extent, still makes itself known. In communication, "real meaning" is both genuinely transferred—"understanding" is a thing that happens—and never fully present, hence the need for interpretation, the possibility of *mis*understanding, and the fact that communication itself is never outmoded in favor of "direct meaning transfer."[7]

This framework seems helpful for contextualizing this discussion in at least two respects. First, Paul's perspective on Torah obedience is part of the string of traces feeding into later reception history. This trace's force is felt, but it is also not fully present. The later tradition draws on Paul's argument, but the tradition also (helpfully or otherwise) leaves parts of that argument untraced and so under erasure in those later contexts. In his own context, Paul's staunchest opposition very arguably came not from pseudo-Pelagians or proto-Romanists but from other Second Temple Jews who were asking different questions while seeking to tell the story of Yahweh's faithfulness to Israel.[8]

Second, this context within Second Temple Judaism highlights how Paul's argument and those of his contemporaries are themselves "tracing" the traditions they have inherited. Each manner of constructing Yahweh's history with Israel traces certain elements, puts others under erasure, and constructs the total story in its own way.[9] Confessionally, the church

3. Derrida, *Grammatology*, 61, 67.

4. Ibid., 66.

5. Ibid., 67, 70–71; Derrida, *Writing and Difference*, 12.

6. Derrida, *Grammatology*, 61; Smith, *Jacques Derrida*, 76; Spivak, "Translator's Preface to *Of Grammatology*, by Jacques Derrida," xv–xx. I am grateful to John Burkett for the helpful reference to Smith's *Derrida*.

7. Smith, *Who's Afraid of Postmodernism?*, 31–58.

8. Wright, *Justification*; Wright, *Paul and the Faithfulness of God*.

9. Handling possible criticisms of a "grand narrative" approach to Second Temple Jewish thought need not detain this argument. E.g., Dunn, *Jesus Remembered*, 470–77. The relevant point is simply that "worldview" can reasonably be described in narrative form. E.g., Sire, *Naming the Elephant*, 126–29; Wright, *New Testament and the People of God*, 38–46.

recognizes that Paul has traced the story truly, but this fact does not mitigate either the story's fundamentally hermeneutic character or its being marked by the absences involved in its tracing.[10] Phenomenologically, each of these constructions is simply its own version of the story, and the versions are competing alternatives to one another. As such, to do justice to the context into which Paul wrote, his argument must be allowed to take its stand among its contemporaries precisely as a *reading* of Yahweh's disposition toward his creation.

This reading will have met with more or less favor in different contexts, but from this standpoint, it does not have a *de facto* privileged status, only a *de facto* in-focus status. A privileged status for Paul's reading is a valid and valuable lens, but it is a lens that shades out as already resolved certain kinds of historical questions, or at least shades out these questions' being asked in certain ways. Therefore, the question presently at issue is not so much "How does Paul explicate what Israel's scriptures have been trying to say about Torah obedience all along?" It is, rather, "*Given Paul's conviction that Yahweh's plan for his creation has culminated in Messiah Jesus*, how does Paul read the testimony of Israel's scriptures about Torah obedience?"[11] This confessional basis also has echoes in the later tradition and so provides a convenient transition point toward contemporary theological engagement about Torah obedience for the church's edification.[12]

Taking these two aspects of "trace" in reverse order, this essay will show how Romans rewrites what counts as proper Torah obedience. This rewriting allows Paul holistically to commend this obedience even to Gentiles as such who are members of the Christian community ("retentive tracing").[13]

10. Smith, *Who's Afraid of Postmodernism?*, 50–57.

11. This question presupposes at least some validity to retrospective descriptions of Paul as having worked "from solution to plight." E.g., Sanders, *Paul and Palestinian Judaism*, 442–47. Yet, Paul's confessional prejudgment about Jesus' messiahship defines a hermeneutic field within which Paul can—and arguably does—work the revised plight back out to the revised solution that created the field. Within the new hermeneutic field, both movements (solution to plight and plight to solution) have an inherent logic and mutually reinforce the field's validity. E.g., Acts 23:1; 24:14, 16; Gal 1:13; Phil 3:1–11; see also Gadamer, "The Hermeneutical Problem"; Kuhn, *Scientific Revolutions*; Stark, *Sacred Texts and Paradigmatic Revolutions*; Wright, *New Testament and the People of God*, 31–46; Wright, *Paul and the Faithfulness of God*, 619–1042.

12. E.g., Augustine, *Symb.*, 2.3 (NPNF1, 3:370); Augustine, *Util. cred.* (NPNF1, 3:345–66); cf. Anselm, *Proslogion*, 1 (*Anselm of Canterbury*, 84–87).

13. Of course, for Derrida, to say that "the trace is . . . the absolute origin of sense in general . . . amounts to saying that there is no absolute origin of sense in general." Derrida, *Grammatology*, 65. The trace always bears the character of something that has passed away and become absent. Consequently, due to limitations of space and as a general function of human hermeneutic and communicative effort, there must

Finally, consideration will be given to how this retheologizing connects to subsequent testimony within the Christian tradition and what way(s) it may open for similarly theological readings of Christian scripture by contemporary interpreters ("protentive tracing").

Retentive Tracing

Romans 2:13–14

In working out precisely how Paul seeks to rewrite Torah obedience, Romans 2:13 may provide a helpful starting point. There, Paul is seeking to disabuse his interlocutor and his readers of the notion that Torah-possession ultimately implies favorability of divine judgment. Judgment is "apart from the Torah" to the Greeks who do not normally have access to it, and judgment is "through the Torah" to the Jews who do normally have access to it.[14] In the end, "the hearers of the Torah will not be righteous before God, but the doers of the Torah will be justified."[15] "Hearing" itself was regularly a positive concept within Judaism.[16] In this context, however, Paul gives "hearing" a clearly negative flavor by characterizing it as *mere* hearing not united to active obedience.[17]

This text has often been read to suggest that what "the doers of the Torah" do is what's cause the doers' justification.[18] This interpretation seems

---

remain a good many untraced traces, or traces that do not appear as such because both their presence and their absence have become absent, or unfelt. Some such traces could doubtless reshape the present discussion were they to be included. Derrida, *Writing and Difference*, 12, 56–73; Gadamer, *Truth and Method*, 304, 354; Gadamer, "The Hermeneutical Problem"; Selby, *Comical Doctrine*, 37–38; Smith, *Who's Afraid of Postmodernism?*, 31–53; see also Osborne, *Hermeneutical Spiral*, 7, 412; Smith, *Jacques Derrida*, 99–102.

14. Rom 2:12; cf. Rom 2:14; Lamp, "Paul, the Law, Jews, and Gentiles," 42; Luther, *Lectures on Romans*, 45, 49; Moo, *Romans*, 145; Moo, "'Law,' 'Works of the Law,' and Legalism in Paul," 80, 82, 88.

15. Rom 2:13. The several surrounding references to an eschatological judgment scenario suggest that the grammatically non-verbal v. 13a also has a future reference. Westerholm, *Perspectives Old and New on Paul*, 267.

16. Deut 6:4; Dunn, *Romans*, 97; Lamp, "Paul, the Law, Jews, and Gentiles," 43.

17. Cranfield, *Romans*, 154; Schreiner, "Justification by Works," 145. Paul's sentiment closely resembles Matt 7:24–27, a cross-reference for which I am grateful to Robbie Castleman.

18. E.g., Moo, "Saved Apart from the Gospel?," 138–41; cf. Barrett, *Romans*, 78; Käsemann, *Romans*, 58; Sanders, *Paul, the Law, and Jewish People*, 125; Schreiner, "The Law in Paul," 48; Schreiner, "Justification by Works," 134; Schreiner, "Paul and Perfect Obedience to the Law," 278.

to cause tension between this text and other Pauline texts inside and outside Romans.[19] Consequently, some scholarship has suggested that the view of justification presented in Rom 2:1–16 is one that Paul intends to undo or short-circuit by demonstrating that there are actually no Torah keepers.[20]

Yet, two factors qualify the relationship between doing the Torah and justification that Rom 2:13 proposes. First, the Pauline corpus uses "to justify" in the passive twenty times.[21] Whenever "to justify" and "work" occur in the same Pauline clause,[22] they are coordinated in a denial that justification occurs based on works. Thus, both in 2:13 and in 6:7 (the only other instance of a passive "to justify" referring to human justification without an express agent or means), one might do well initially to suspect that these texts' implicit justifying agent is something from the list of agents affirmed elsewhere. Particularly, the initial assertion in 2:13 that hearers will not be "righteous before God" parallels the following counter-assertion that doers "will be justified." Thus, the latter clause appears elliptically to omit "before God" or some other parallel phrase, but this phrase still informs the counter-assertion in 2:13b. Because of the generally forensic context in 2:1–16, justification "before God" (the judge) is justification "by God." The one before whom the defendant stands also renders the verdict.

Second, for Paul, "to be justified" is equivalent to being "reckoned as righteous."[23] The later construction's full formulation is "to reckon (thing) *X* to (person) *Y* as (thing) *Z*."[24] Applying this cognitive rubric to "the doers of the Torah will be justified" in 2:13b, it becomes manifest that the thing to be reckoned (*X*) is left unspecified in this passive construction. Consequently, as Paul phrases v. 13b, the phrase "the doers of the Torah" identifies a class of the people who will receive justification or will have righteousness reckoned to them (term *Y*). On the other hand, this clause does not indicate the means by which these people will be justified and certainly does not indicate that this means will be the works of the Torah themselves.[25]

19. E.g., Rom 3:20; Gal 2:16.

20. E.g., Calvin, *Romans*, 95–96; Moo, "'Law,' 'Works of the Law,' and Legalism in Paul," 98; Moo, *Romans*, 142; Moo, "Saved Apart from the Gospel?," 142; Thielman, *Paul and the Law*, 172; Watson, *Hermeneutics of Faith*, 344–53; Westerholm, *Justification Reconsidered*, 19–21; Westerholm, "The 'New Perspective' at Twenty-Five," 26.

21. Rom 2:13; 3:4, 20, 24, 28; 4:2; 5:1, 9; 6:7; 1 Cor 4:4; 6:11; Gal 2:16–17 (4x); 3:11, 24; 5:4; 1 Tim 3:16; Tit 3:7.

22. Rom 3:20, 28; 4:2; Gal 2:16.

23. Cf. Rom 4:2–3.

24. Cf. Gen 15:6; Num 18:27; Ps 106:31; Prov 27:14; Calvin, *Psalms*, 4:231; Koehler and Baumgartner, *HALOT*, s.v. חשב; see also Buttrick, "Genesis 15:1–18," 396; Heidland, "λογίζομαι, λογισμός," 284–85; Piper, *Counted Righteous in Christ*, 7, 63–64.

25. Cf. Rom 3:21-31; Moo, "'Law,' 'Works of the Law,' and Legalism in Paul," 94. Cranfield, "'Works of the Law,'" 101; contra Moo, "Israel and the Law in Romans 5–11,"

Immediately following, Paul cites the example of Gentiles who do not naturally have the Torah but still "do the things of the Torah" (v. 14). One might attempt to distinguish the referent of this phrase from that of "the works of the Torah."[26] Yet, doing so removes the primary option for the meaning of "the things of the Torah," especially when these things are things people can apparently "do." Therefore, fully separating "the things of the Torah" from "the works of the Torah" seems imprudent. Instead, the phrase "the things of the Torah" immediately appears as a more general form of "the works of the Torah"[27] that retains the plural in the head nominal so that the phrase refers to "the things required by the law given to Israel"[28] in their plurality rather than as a single, collective grouping.

In contexts "where the relationship of Israel with other nations is at issue, certain laws would naturally come more into focus than others. . .circumcision and food laws in particular."[29] Yet, flattening the category of "the works of the Torah" to function as if it here includes *only* or primarily these items mutes the breadth of Paul's claims about the category. But, understanding "the things of the Torah" (≈ "the works of the Torah") in Romans 2:14 simply as "the works which the law requires" or "the works required by the law" fits well with the following singular reference to "the work of the Torah."[30] In keeping with the similar later reference to "the righteous requirement of the Torah,"[31] the singular reference in Rom 2:15 also characterizes the Torah's requirements as a summary whole.[32]

Moreover, with the clause "who manifest the work of the Torah as written on their hearts," Paul probably alludes to Jer 31 (OG 38):33 or Isa 51:7.[33] If these Gentiles are those who have had the Torah divinely written

140.

26. See Lamp, "Paul, the Law, Jews, and Gentiles," 46–47, although this specific distinction receives comparatively less attention than the one between "the work [sg.] of the Torah" and "the works [pl.] of the Torah."

27. Cf. Gathercole, "A Law unto Themselves," 34.

28. Denney, "Romans," 597.

29. Dunn, *Theology of Paul the Apostle*, 358.

30. Cranfield, "'Works of the Law,'" 94; Dunn, *Epistle to the Galatians*, 135; Moo, "Saved Apart from the Gospel?," 139–40; Stuhlmacher, *Revisiting Paul's Doctrine of Justification*, 43–44; cf. Cranfield, *Romans*, 219–20.

31. Rom 8:4.

32. Cranfield, *Romans*, 158; Cranfield, "'Works of the Law,'" 94; Schreiner, "The Law in Paul," 60–61.

33. Dunn, *Romans*, 100; Lamp, "Paul, the Law, Jews, and Gentiles," 47; Schreiner, "Justification by Works," 146; see also Cranfield, *Romans*, 158; Cranfield, "'Works of the Law,'" 94; Gathercole, "A Law unto Themselves," 37; Kasemann, *Romans*, 64; Luther, *Lectures on Romans*, 52; Moo, "'Law,' 'Works of the Law,' and Legalism in Paul," 79, 83,

in them,[34] then they do in this sense possess the Torah, although they do not possess it by their ethnic heritage (thus: ἑαυτοῖς εἰσιν νόμος ≈ "they are, among themselves, a [manifestation of the] Torah").[35] Yet, the Torah's embedding in the people's hearts apparently does not effect their entire sinlessness.[36] Rather, it provides a compass—which may still be disobeyed—to direct people's hearts toward right and pleasing action before Yahweh so that he may give a positive verdict for them at the final judgment through Messiah Jesus.[37]

Romans 2:17–29 and 3:1–20

The balance of Romans retains traces of such sentiments about Torah obedience. Especially relevant for this argument's context are the traces in 2:17–29; 3:1–20; 3:21–31; and the major section of 4:1–8:17. In 2:17–29, the primary point is negative. Given that Torah obedience identifies those whom Yahweh will vindicate at the eschatological judgment, the Jews who have the Torah "by nature" might be expected to be on reasonably sound footing.

Because of the conditionality in how the pericope opens—"If you call yourself a Jew. . . ," there is some debate about whether the interlocutor in view in 2:17–29 is ethnically Jewish or is only adopting that title (e.g., as in the case of a proselyte).[38] Space prohibits this question from being fully adjudicated here. Yet, the observation may be made fairly briefly that, for Paul, Jewish identity seems not entirely to be coterminous with the domain of "ethnicity" insofar as it, in contemporary usage, implies biological descent. Circumcision too plays a prominent role. Certainly, males who

---

96; Moo, *Romans*, 151; Pickup, "Theological Rationale of Midrashic Exegesis"; Schreiner, "Paul and Perfect Obedience to the Law," 247n2; Schreiner, "Works of Law," 232.

34. Rom 2:14; Wright, "Letter to the Romans," 442; cf. 2 Cor 3–4.

35. Rom 2:14. Even if Paul saw this statement as reflecting a Greek philosophical sentiment, the statement's significance in his argument does not therefore seem to be that the individuals involved are somehow "self-directed." Rather, the individuals who ἑαυτοῖς εἰσιν νόμος evidence the Torah's presence with them in a way that continues deconstructing the category of Jewish ethnic privilege understood as Paul describes his hypothetical interlocutor as doing (vv. 9–15). Cranfield, *Romans*, 157–58; Dunn, *Romans*, 91, 99; Gathercole, "A Law unto Themselves," 37; cf. Acts 9:15; Aristotle, *Eth. Nic.*, 1128a.31–32; Bauer et al., *Lexicon*, s.v. νόμος §2.b; Blass and Debrunner, *Greek Grammar*, §190.1; Robertson, *Grammar*, §3.11.12.d.

36. Rom 2:15.

37. Cf. Rom 2:16.

38. E.g., Rodríguez, *If You Call Yourself a Jew;* Rodríguez and Thiessen, eds., *The So-called Jew.*

were ethnically Jewish would tended to have been circumcised in all but the most Hellenizing families. There seems to have been some variety of opinions about whether and how firm a requirement was circumcision for male proselytes of ethnically Gentile descent.[39] Nevertheless, Gentile converts had the option to undergo circumcision and appear to have done so in some cases.[40] After an ethnically Gentile male's circumcision and notwithstanding his biological descent, however, he would seem to have been regarded as crossing over—within Pauline categories—from one to the other of two binary options. At that juncture, therefore, the newly circumcised individual's Gentile genetics would be effectively irrelevant in a great many cases, and in such cases, he could be regarded simply as a Jew in terms of his identity as constructed around his submission to circumcision.[41] Consequently, when Paul's dialog with this interlocutor turns explicitly to the question of circumcision in Rom 2:25–29, the significant consideration seems to be that this individual is within the category over which Paul would write the label "Jew."[42]

Thus, in pressing his case, Paul begins to take sharper aim at his fellow Jews' failure legitimately to find themselves within the class of "Torah doers." Even within Israel's scriptures, however, linkage between Jewish

39. E.g., Exod 12:48–49; Josephus, *A.J.*, 20.40–48; cf. Num 9:14.

40. E.g., Esth 8:17 OG; Gal 2:3; 5:2–3; 6:12–13; Josephus, *A.J.*, 20.38.

41. E.g., Exod 12:48–49; Jud. 14:10; Rom 11:17–24; cf. Num 9:14; Josephus, *A.J.*, 20.38–39; see also Rom 3:1–2. This assessment does not suggest that there would not have been some instances where biologically Gentile descent would not still have distanced an individual from others who were biologically Jewish. Cf. CD 14.3–6. The point is simply that cases where Gentile biology might matter seem not to be among those Paul has in view as he works with what appear to be the reasonably firm identity binaries of "Jew and physical circumcision" and "Gentile and physical uncircumcision." The possibility of transgressing these binaries from the "Gentile and physical uncircumcision" to the "Jew and physical circumcision" side of the opposition draws significant ire from Paul in Galatians. In one sense, "neither circumcision nor uncircumcision is anything" (Gal 6:15; cf. Gal 5:6). Yet, where transgressing the binary boundary is a means of identity (re)construction for an individual as standing within the faithful people of Yahweh, Paul thinks that method of identity construction stands unalterably opposed to the central messianic reality and community that has come to being in Jesus. Gal 5:2–4; Phil 3:2–11; cf. Augustine, *De mend.*, 5.8 (NPNF1, 3:261–62).

42. Dunn has suggested "we would probably not be far from the mark if we were to conclude that Paul's interlocutor is Paul himself—Paul the unconverted Pharisee, expressing attitudes Paul remembered so well as having been his own!" *Romans*, 91. To the extent that this assessment is reasonable, the several echoes of Rom 2 in Rom 7 emerge perhaps partly due to the similarity in Paul's method of approaching his subjects in those contexts (e.g., Rom 7:3 // 2:17, 22, 26; 7:6 // 2:26–29; 7:7 // 2:18; 7:8 // 1:32–2:1, 21–23; 7:10 // 2:7–10; 7:12 // 2:20; 7:14 // 2:25–29; 7:15 // 1:32–2:1, 21–24; 7:16 // 2:13, 17, 23; 7:18–19, 21 // 2:19–29; 7:22–23, 25 // 2:25–29).

descent and Torah performance is not so simple. For instance, Ps 73 (HB, ENG; 72 OG) begins, "Surely, good to Israel is God, to those who are upright of heart." The Israel to whom God shows himself beneficent are those who are "upright of heart."[43] Or, in Paul's own language, "It is not he who is manifestly [that is, in circumcision] a Jew who is one, nor is circumcision manifestly in the flesh, but he is a Jew who is one secretly [that is, without or irrespective of circumcision], and circumcision is of the heart, by means of the Spirit, not by means of the letter [that is, of the Torah in which bodily circumcision is literally prescribed]."[44] Thus, from within the categories of Israel's own scriptural tradition, Paul begins to rewrite his contemporaries' cultural scripts for key categories of "Jew," "Gentile," "circumcision," and "uncircumcision."

Of course, Jews do have advantages, but according to Paul, these advantages differ from those that might have been suspected. The Jews indeed "were entrusted with the oracles of God."[45] Yet, these "oracles" themselves are not a point of boasting or exultation but of reproach because Israel proved to be unfaithful to them.[46] Because of this disobedience, the consummate blessing of having received "the oracles of God" resulted primarily in Israel's inexcusability before God and in an ability to recognize their transgressions.[47]

Romans 3:21–31

Nevertheless, for Paul, these oracles—in another respect—are not themselves. The oracles are likely the Torah.[48] The Torah speaks to those who are under it and, through their disobedience, produces accountability, knowledge of sin, and non-justification.[49] On the other hand, the Torah—with the prophets—testifies that "God's righteousness is manifest as being distinct from the Torah . . . , and God's righteousness comes through Messiah Jesus's

43. See also Deut 10:16; 30:6; Jer 4:4; 5:10; cf. Isa 29:22–24.

44. Rom 2:28–29a; cf. Rom 4:13:25; 11:17–24; Gal 3:15–29; Phil 3:3; Col 2:11–12.

45. Rom 3:2.

46. Rom 2:17–18, 23; 3:3. Paul's exact language is "If some have been unfaithful . . ." (3:3). Judging from succeeding argument, Paul takes this protasis as definite fact and not merely as one hypothesized for the sake of argument (3:5–20). In 3:3 also, his "some" seems to be an understatement like he uses elsewhere (e.g., 9:1–5; 11:17).

47. Rom 3:2, 4b, 19–20.

48. Cf. Acts 7:38.

49. Rom 3:19–20.

faithfulness to everyone who believes."[50] Certainly, this Messiah's faithfulness manifests itself in other areas too, but principally relevant is his identity as "him whom God put forward as a sacrificial offering through [his own or the Messiah's] faithfulness by means of [the Messiah's] blood."[51] Because "all have sinned and lack God's glory, although they are being justified freely by means of his grace through the redemption that is in Messiah Jesus,"[52] Yahweh beneficently shows his own righteousness to those who believe without making socio-ethnic distinctions among them.[53]

On this basis then, Paul inquires, "Where is boasting?"[54] a theme that has already been raised.[55] His response is abrupt and shocking: "It has been excluded. Through what kind of νόμος has it been excluded? Has it been excluded through a νόμος of works? No, but it has been excluded through a νόμος of faith." Of course, νόμος is Paul's typical term for the Jewish Torah, or law, given through Moses.[56] Yet, Paul's reference here to a "νόμος of faith" has led some interpreters to think that the referent is a "principle of faith" whereby one may believe in Jesus and be saved.[57] Νόμος may indeed have this more general sense in some cases,[58] but there are good reasons to doubt the term has this sense here.

First, in his preceding paragraph, Paul represents God's righteousness as being borne witness "by the νόμος and the prophets," a direct reference to Israel's scriptural tradition.[59] Indeed, according to Paul, these very scriptures testify that the manifestation of God's righteousness is not inextricably linked to νόμος.[60] Rather, although Jews have certain advantages,[61] God's righteousness is ultimately put beneficently before them on the same footing

50. Rom 3:21–22; cf. Acts 3:14–17; 1 Cor 2:5, 8; Augustine, *Spir. et litt.*, 54 (NPNF1, 5:107); contra Dunn, *Romans*, 166–67.

51. Rom 3:25; cf. Bauer et al., *Lexicon*, ἱλαστήριον; see also Rom 3:21–22, 25, 30–31; Holmes, *SBLGNT*, Rom 3:25; Metzger, *Textual Commentary*, 449; Moo, *Romans*, 218–19n3; Schreiner, *Romans*, 199.

52. Rom 3:23–24.

53. Rom 3:22; cf. Rom 3:27–31; Jas 2:1–7.

54. Rom 3:27a.

55. E.g., Rom 2:17, 23.

56. Cf. Bultmann, *Theology of the New Testament*, 1:259.

57. E.g., ibid.; Sanders, *Paul, the Law, and Jewish People*, 33; cf. Rom 10:12–13.

58. Kleinknecht, "νόμος."

59. Dunn, *Romans*, 165–66; Jewett, *Romans*, 274–75.

60. Rom 3:21–22.

61. Rom 3:1–2.

as it is with Gentiles—namely, "through Messiah Jesus's faithfulness [and] to those [among either Jews or Gentiles] who believe."[62]

Second, Paul could theoretically introduce a "principle of faith" that should be preferred over against the Mosaic Torah construed around works. Were he to do so, however, his argument would likely need to provide some basis for this preference, particularly for members of his audience favorable to Israel's heritage.[63] Instead of taking this route in his argument, Paul inscribes Jesus firmly within the categories of "atonement" and "Passover" that emerge from the Mosaic literature, and Paul seeks to demonstrate from these texts his position about Jesus' messiahship and the nature of the community surrounding him.[64]

Consequently, the notion of a "Mosaic law of works" that is set over against a "principle of faith" fails to do justice to the argument Paul constructs in Rom 3–4. Rather, the language of "νόμος of works" and "νόμος of faith" is much better construed as related to particular interpretations of a single Mosaic Torah.[65] This Torah appears as a "Torah of works" when construed around the deeds that it prescribes. It appears—rightly in Paul's estimation—as a "Torah of faith" when construed around Yahweh's promises that give rise to human responses of belief on the one hand and to that Torah's further behavioral prescriptions on the other.[66] Nevertheless, "through this faith"—through faith in the faithful Messiah—Paul provocatively and insistently still claims "we establish the Torah."[67]

Romans 4:1—8:17

One of Paul's major aims in the large section of 4:1—8:17 is, then, to demonstrate how the Torah is established—is upheld for proper enactment—"through this faith" that he affirms.[68] For Paul, Abraham is the prototypical and logical place to begin. According to Genesis 15, Abraham had faith reckoned as righteousness before he had the works—circumcision in

62. Rom 3:22; cf. 3:21–22a, 24–26.

63. Cf. Jewett, *Romans*; Nanos, *Mystery of Romans*.

64. Rom 3:25–26; 4:1–25.

65. Rom 9:30–33; Jewett, *Romans*, 297.

66. Rom 4; 10; Augustine, *Spir. et litt.*, 21–26 (NPNF1, 4:91–95); Augustine, *Util. cred.*, 9, 12 (NPNF1, 3:351, 353).

67. Rom 3;31.

68. Deut 28:69 LXX; 2 Chron 35:19; Jer 42:14, 16; Mark 7:9; Grundmann, "στήκω, ἵστημι," 641–53; Jewett, *Romans*, 302–3.

particular—that ought to have accompanied that faith.[69] Thus, Yahweh's behavior toward Abraham shows that, although Abraham does come to be circumcised, his justification before Yahweh is a distinct matter.[70] Consequently, "this faith is nullified" if Abraham, contrary to the divine decree, is not situated by means of his faith to inherit the promises made to him (i.e., as "righteous").[71] Moreover, the divine word to Abraham in Genesis 17 promised that Abraham would be the father of "many nations."[72] By definition, therefore, "this promise is invalidated" if Gentiles—precisely as such—cannot find membership within Abraham's family.[73] Ultimately, Messiah Jesus has become the culminating fulfillment of the promise to Abraham and is the one through whom this family extends to include Gentiles.[74]

So far so good, but how is it that "we establish the Torah"—seemingly in its entirety—within this context? Romans 5–7 answers this question along several intersecting lines:

1. Messiah Jesus has died and risen again. His death breaks the hold that death has even over God's enemies, and the breakage becomes manifest as these enemies come to ally themselves with him.[75]
2. Those who cast their lot in with (οἱ πιστεύοντες) this Messiah in baptism become partakers of his death and resurrection.[76]
3. By becoming united with Messiah Jesus's death, those who believe in him die with respect to "the old person."[77] That is, their identity is decoupled from the "body of sin" by which they previously actualized the covenantal curses that resulted in death.[78] Correspondingly, by becoming united with Messiah Jesus's resurrection, those who believe in him also become united with the "body of the Messiah" by which covenantal blessings are climactically actualized for them and result in life.[79]

69. Rom 4:3–5, 9–12.
70. Cf. Rom 2:13; 3:21.
71. Rom 4:14.
72. Rom 4:17.
73. Rom 4:14.
74. Rom 4:24–25.
75. Rom 5:5–21.
76. Rom 6:1–5.
77. Rom 6:5.
78. Rom 6:6.
79. Rom 7:4, and the broader section of Rom 6:6—7:25.

4. Within this matrix and by the presence of Spirit, those who have come to be included in the Messiah also truly and properly fulfill the Torah as the Spirit animates both them and it,[80] although they do not always do so perfectly and sometimes need repentance.

This fulfillment occurs through Jesus, in whom his followers come to be included. Yet, it is not simply a theological reality but one that affects the practical behavior of those who are included in Jesus and who are, as such, members of his body.[81] Within the Pauline corpus, individual Christians' obedience—even Gentile Christians—sometimes matches more closely what contemporary readers might consider to be a "literal" reading of the Torah.[82] In other cases, Paul's approach seems much more "figural."[83] Within Romans, the two reading strategies collide not least in how Paul adjudicates the relationship between circumcision and Gentiles' inclusion in Abraham's family. On the one hand, Paul is committed to identifying the ἔθνη with uncircumcised Gentiles. Yahweh promised Abraham would be "father of many ἔθνη."[84] Consequently, as Paul works out how Abraham becomes the father of uncircumcised Gentiles, he treats circumcision figurally so that it remains a marker of Abraham's family but becomes one in which Gentiles as such may participate.[85]

The arbitrator between the two styles of reading is not either one of these styles themselves, nor is it likely advisable to characterize one or the other as Paul's "default" approach and the other as one he leverages in "exceptional" cases.[86] Rather, Paul's hermeneutic loadstone is the divine fidelity and righteousness that have come to bear in Messiah Jesus. No scripture can

80. Rom 8:2–4, 6–8.

81. Rom 6:1—7:5; 8:1–17; cf. John 15:1–17. I am grateful to Robbie Castleman for suggesting the Johannine cross-reference.

82. E.g., Rom 13:9; 15:10; 1 Cor 5:13; Eph 4:26; 6:2; cf. Rom 12:20; 15:11; 1 Cor 1:31; 2 Cor 6:17; 10:17; Eph 4:25; 2 Tim 2:19. Strictly literal interpretation is quite rare in the Pauline corpus (e.g., Gal 3:17; cf. Gen 15:13; Exod 12:40–41). Most often, even when interpretations are comparatively more literal, figuration has clearly already begun. Scriptural texts are treated as addressing the audience's contemporary situation, thereby treating the past, in these instances, as a figure of the present. Cf. Nicholas of Lyra, *Mystical Interpretation*; Childs, *Old Testament Theology*, 153; see also Stark, "Figuring Things Out," 57–58. Hence, the difference between how Paul reads one text or another is often not the either-or of literal-figural tension. More typically, it is a difference in degrees or kinds of figuration. Cf. Gadamer, *Truth and Method*, 306–36.

83. E.g., 1 Cor 9:8–12; 2 Cor 3:4–4:6; Gal 4:21–31.

84. Rom 4:17–18, quoting Gen 17:5.

85. E.g., Rom 2:25–29; 1 Cor 7:19; Eph 2:11; Phil 3:3; Col 2:11.

86. Cf. Kuhn, *Scientific Revolutions*; Lewis, "Evil and God."

fail to speak to the church,[87] and in the revelation of Jesus' messiahship, Paul finds the bar to which all proper readings of scripture for the church must be held.[88] Readings must, therefore, pass this bar to speak validly to the church that has been formed under this Messiah's authority and as his body.

Protentive Tracing: Reception-Historical Soundings and Ressourcement

Finally, Romans' traces of Torah obedience protentively give rise to particular reception-historical effects. In turn, these historically effected (*wirkungsgeschichtlich*) traces protend possibilities for productive play in the church's engagement with its scriptures' legal material. First and by way of dispelling the "let's all practice the Torah in order to earn favor with God and cause him to act beneficently toward us" bogeyman,[89] Romans insists on the importance of performing the Torah. It does so under a reading much different to what many Second Temple Jews would have proposed.[90] Romans also insists on Yahweh's graciousness in beneficently acting toward those who receive his favor. The bogeyman's suggestion is arguably one with which Paul was not directly contending, but it is one to which Romans protends a response. For instance, Augustine suggests, "To a man who holds such views [as the Pelagians], it is perfect truth to say: It is His own gifts that God crowns, not your merits—if, at least, your merits are of your own self, not of Him. If, indeed, they are such, they are evil and God does not crown them; but if they are good, they are God's gifts. . . . If, then, your good merits are God's gifts, God does not crown your merits as your merits, but as His

87. Rom 15:4; cf. 1 Cor 10:11; Barrett, *Romans*, 247–48; Calvin, *Romans*, 516–17; Mounce, *Romans*, 260; Newman and Nida, *Romans*, 272.

88. Rom 1:1–5, 16–18; 3:21–26; 9:30–33; 10:4; cf. Gal 1:3–4; 5:6; 6:15.

89. This bogeyman quite arguably does not represent either significant areas within Second Temple Judaism or Roman Catholicism. Doubtless, however, there may be areas where it does apply more properly. Yet, danger from this angle has been regularly and strongly felt within Protestant and other Evangelical circles, and it does need to be addressed seriously for those contexts. By comparison, if a householder is confronted in the middle of the night with a heavily armed intruder, the householder is not—and quite rightly not—likely to be much comforted by recognizing that the intruder is actually six inches shorter than initially imagined. Similarly, the danger of a cheaply mercantile spirituality arguably does not derive from the kinds of historical antecedents that have tended to be supposed for it. Nevertheless, it can certainly be recognized as a genuine danger that bears a careful response, although space constrains the attention that can be given to the matter here. Cf. Lewis, "Jesus Christ," 182.

90. Cf. Eph 3:4–6.

own gifts."[91] Again, the bogeyman's categories and, perhaps much more so Augustine's, are not precisely Paul's. Nevertheless, Romans exhibits protentive traces that move along these lines.

Augustine also well knows both that there is a "law of works" and a "law of faith" and that the difference between the two lies not in their fields of operation, as if Judaism had a "law of works" and Christianity a "law of faith."[92] Rather, one and the same law has within itself a dual aspect, even as both aspects have the same textual contents (e.g., both prohibit coveting).[93] On Augustine's understanding, the distinction between the two is rather that:

> What the law of works enjoins by menace, that the law of faith secures by faith. The one says, "Thou shalt not covet;" the other says, "When I perceived that nobody could be continent, except God gave it to him; and that this was the very point of wisdom, to know whose gift she was; I approached unto the Lord, and I besought Him." [Wis 8:21]. . .[B]y the law of works, God says to us, Do what I command thee; but by the law of faith we say to God, Give me what Thou commandest. Now this is the reason why the law gives its command,—to admonish us what faith ought to do, that is, that he to whom the command is given, if he is as yet unable to perform it, may know what to ask for; but if he has at once the ability, and complies with the command, he ought also to be aware from whose gift the ability comes. . . . [Thus,] a man is not justified by the precepts of a holy life, but by faith in Jesus Christ,—in a word, not by the law of works, but by the law of faith; not by the letter, but by the spirit; not by the merits of deeds, but by free grace.[94]

To be sure, one must try to avoid mixing Augustine's distinct emphases (e.g., ability, enablement, merit) with those more endemic to Paul's argument considered in itself (e.g., scripture, interpretation, Jews, Gentiles, messiahship). Yet, neither does Augustine's theological exegesis seem to emerge simply out of his own head or from a crude "prooftexting" approach to Paul. For Paul, Jesus' followers find Torah fulfilled in themselves precisely because of the Spirit's activity.[95] Considered apart from this activity, apart from the

91. Augustine, *Grat.*, 15 (NPNF1, 5:450).

92. Rom 3:27–28; Augustine, *Spir. et litt.*, 21 (NPNF1, 5:91–92).

93. Augustine, *Spir. et litt.*, 21 (NPNF1, 5:92); cf. Augustine, *Serm.*, 31.1 (NPNF1, 6:352); Bonhoeffer, *Discipleship*, 135–41; Von Rad, *Studies in Deuteronomy*, 66–67.

94. Augustine, *Spir. et litt.*, 22 (NPNF1, 5:92); see also Augustine, *Fid. symb.*, 23 (NPNF1, 3:331–32); Augustine, *Spir. et litt.*, 13 (NPNF1, 5:88).

95. Rom 8:1–17; cf. Augustine, *Spir. et litt.*, 26, 29 (NPNF1, 5:94–95).

new reality they have come to inhabit in Jesus and, consequently, still as connected to the old and dying person, a plea for help from free divine condescension is certainly fitting.[96] Thus, the notes Augustine plays are Pauline notes, but the tune is a bit different since Augustine plays some parts more loudly and bypasses others.

Christians' performances are real performances, and these do actually constitute fulfillments of the Torah. Circumcision is received, purity regulations are kept, neighbors are loved, and yet Jews remain Jews, and Gentiles remain Gentiles.[97] Only, "the law, which was not fulfilled in the requirement of the letter, was fulfilled in the liberty of grace. In the same way, everything in the law that was prophetic of the Saviour's advent, whether in words or in typical actions, became truth in Jesus Christ. For 'the law was given by Moses, but grace and truth came by Jesus Christ.'"[98] The Christian's performances are made—and only made successfully—within the domain of "the new person" within the Christian's identity as constructed around and empowered by the Messiah and the Spirit.[99] Thus, Yahweh's vindication of such individuals at the last day really will take their works into account, and he will make his judgment accordingly.[100] Even so, Yahweh's granting this verdict in their behalf graciously validates the powerful presence among them of the Messiah and the Spirit.[101]

Thus, Romans holds out several options for constructing what seems consistently to be the same Torah. One may construct it around its Jewish recipients, the works it prescribes in its literal sense, and the familiarity with sin and punishment that it produces for the disobedient.[102] Or, one may construct it around those who are able to fulfill it, faith in Yahweh's promises, and the familiarity with righteousness and blessing that it produces for the obedient.[103] Despite protestations to the contrary, the same Torah

96. Rom 6:5—7:6; 7:24–25.

97. E.g., Rom 2:25–29; 13:9; 1 Cor 7:17–24; 2 Cor 6:14—7:1; Col 2:11–12; cf. Mark 7:14–23; Acts 10:9–29; see also Heb 4:9; Augustine, *De mend.*, 5.8 (NPNF1, 3:461–62); Augustine, *Enarrat. Ps.*, 48.10, 76.1, 114.6 (NPNF1, 8:167, 355, 551); Augustine, *Faust.*, 19.9–10 (NPNF1, 4:242–43).

98. Augustine, *Faust.*, 19.8 (NPNF1, 4:242).

99. Paul does not refer to "the new person" as such in Romans, but the category does seem operative in Rom 6–8. Cf. Eph 2:15; 4:24; see also 2 Cor 5:17; Gal 6:15.

100. Augustine, *Ep.*, 214.1 (NPNF1, 5:437).

101. Cf. ibid.; Augustine, *Grat.*, 7.17 (NPNF1, 5:450–51); Augustine, *Spir. et litt.*, 44–45 (NPNF1, 5:101–2).

102. Rom 2:26a; 3:2, 20, 27–28; 4:13–16; 5:13, 20; 6:15; 7:1–9, 14, 16, 21, 23, 25; 8:2–3, 7; 9:31–32; 10:5.

103. Rom 2:26b–27; 3:27, 31; 7:3b–5, 7, 12, 14, 16, 21–23, 25; 8:2–4; 9:31–32; 10:4; 13:8, 10.

seems to be in view throughout.[104] What "makes" the difference in more senses than one is a matter of construction, or interpretation. Differing interpretations cause the Torah's reception to end up in different places. The Torah of works ends up in non-performance and the wrathful execution of Yahweh's righteousness on the disobedient, but the Torah of faith ends up with the Messiah as the manifestation of Yahweh's beneficent righteousness for everyone who believes.[105]

So far, this description—to the extent that it adequately reflects Romans' testimony—is simply a matter of descriptive Pauline theology and tracing a small slice of this theology's later reception. Having made his argument in Romans as he did, Paul seems to have felt that this approach would have had sufficient persuasive clout even with members of his audience who might tend to have questions (even if friendly ones) about it. The letter's strategy for reading the Torah and how this strategy contributes to the balance of the letter's rhetoric are certainly connected to the Roman Christians' perception of Paul's apostolic authority. Yet, Paul apparently does not expect his audience to accept his argument "because he says so." Rather, he expects it to stand as a legitimate reading of Israel's scriptures.

To the extent that Romans continues to speak authoritatively to the church on a basis wider than simply the sentimentalizing influence of its connection to Paul (e.g., in some cases almost approximating a disposition of "Paul spoke magic words that we should revere without caring too much for the sense they make"), its rhetoric and reading strategy also implicitly continue to find affirmation. To be sure, attempting to move from observation and description to affirmation and practice is a transition that entails its own difficulties and pitfalls. Nevertheless, it is but another instance of same kind of movement the contemporary church regularly makes. Some communions make this movement with much less historically effected friction than others. Yet, latent within a cherishing and celebration of Pauline theology is an appreciation for the strategy of engagement with Israel's scriptures that Pauline theology entails.

Certainly, appreciation may sometimes be puzzled appreciation as with one spouse to another who has done something confusing and about which further explanation needs to be sought. Or, appreciation may be adaptive as when a pianist performing Beethoven's *Für Elise* finds it so compelling as not only to represent the piece faithfully but also to put a distinctive expression to it. In either case, the appreciation remains, and practice follows. So

104. Augustine, *Spir. et litt.*, 21 (NPNF1, 5:91–92).

105. Rom 1:17–18; 4:15; 9:31–32; 10:5; Augustine, *Spir. et litt.*, 22 (NPNF1, 5:92); cf. Augustine, *Util. cred.*, 9, 12 (NPNF1, 3:351, 353).

too within Pauline theology, appreciation and celebration logically should inform following practice not simply with respect to deeds of piety toward the rest of creation but also in the way the church continues engaging the sacred texts it has inherited. The church must play the score it has received faithfully so that the score remains itself; the church must also make sense out of that score for its own context where players for some parts might be difficult to find or some of the tools necessary for that part might appear no longer to be available.[106]

As for Paul, so too for the church that wishes to engage its inherited scriptures in a faithful and lively manner—the divine revelation and the church's confession of Jesus' messiahship are the church's hermeneutic loadstone. Certainly, there remains a large and necessary field in which descriptive-historical work on Jewish scripture needs to be performed. Without such work, the church has two main kinds of choices. One choice is to leave the Jewish scriptures alone by themselves as largely irrelevant. The other is to see in them only the church's own reflection.[107] Marcion tried the first. More orthodox Christianities have sometimes tried the second. Both have justly been found wanting.[108] Rather, for the church to receive its inherited scriptures as authoritative and lively, these scriptures must speak in the area where the church hears the divine word. This area is the rule of faith, the rule of the new creation, the rule determined by Jesus's messiahship, and while standing in this area under the word, the church becomes most truly itself.[109]

Conclusion

In conclusion, Romans retraces Torah obedience in fresh terms. This sketch prominently includes Jesus' death and resurrection and the Spirit's enlivening presence. Yet, inasmuch as writing is largely defined by what is not written—the marks made distinguishable by what is not marked, by the remaining "white space"—so also is this obedience identifiably inscribed by the allegorical absence of distinctively Jewish practices and the judicial absence of credit to those who obey. The obedient do indeed benefit, but

106. Cf. Childs, "Biblische Theologie," 22.

107. Cf. Gadamer, *Truth and Method*; Gadamer, "The Hermeneutical Problem"; Kuhn, *Scientific Revolutions*.

108. E.g., Irenaeus, *Haer.*; Block, *The Gospel According to Moses*; Gunneweg, *Vom Verstehen des Alten Testaments*; Sandys-Wunsch and Eldredge, "Gabler"; Wright, *Justification*.

109. Childs, *Biblical Theology in Crisis*, 99; Käsemann, *New Testament Questions*, 261; cf. Childs, *Old Testament Theology*, 60.

they benefit by being partakers of the one body of the faithful Messiah in and through whom all Yahweh's promises to Abraham come to fulfillment. Within this obedience, ethnic and credit-side ledger markers pass under erasure. Much of Paul's argument portrays them as only ever having been a mirage in the first place. The narrative within which Abrahamic parentage and inheritance are to be inscribed orbits around the faith that Abraham exhibited and that Yahweh validated.

With Paul having (re)inscribed the context in this manner, Yahweh's promise to Abraham of offspring among many nations requires, by definition, the inclusion of Gentiles within the covenant community. Being included in this community, these Gentiles too are subject to the covenant charter, and Yahweh's climactic act in and through Messiah Jesus establishes the definitive context within which both Jews and Gentiles fulfill the covenant charter's stipulations. Precisely for Gentiles to remain Gentiles and actualize the fulfillment of Yahweh's promise to Abraham, however, there are certain stipulations in the charter that must not be impressed upon Gentiles in these stipulations' literal sense. Doing so would be urging Gentiles to Judaize. Thus, for the church, Israel's Torah has received its germinative setting in death (*Sitz im Tod*) and its verdant setting in life (*Sitz im Leben*) in Jesus' own death and resurrection. By virtue of this fact too, the line between the Torah and legitimately figural-theological engagement with it for the church's edification has itself been most pointedly unwritten.

Bibliography

Anselm of Canterbury. *Anselm of Canterbury: The Major Works*. Edited and translated by Brian Davies and G. R. Evans. Oxford World's Classics. Oxford: Oxford University Press, 1998.

Barrett, C. K. *The Epistle to the Romans*. 2nd ed. Black's New Testament Commentaries 6. London: Hendrickson, 1991.

Bauer, Walter, et al., eds. *A Greek-English Lexicon of the New Testament and Other Early Christian Literature*. Translated by Frederick W. Danker. 3rd ed. Chicago: University of Chicago Press, 2000.

Blass, Friedrich, and Albert Debrunner. *A Greek Grammar of the New Testament and Other Early Christian Literature*. Edited and translated by Robert Walter Funk. Chicago: University of Chicago Press, 1961.

Block, Daniel I. *The Gospel According to Moses: Theological and Ethical Reflections on the Book of Deuteronomy*. Eugene, OR: Cascade, 2012.

Bonhoeffer, Dietrich. *The Cost of Discipleship*. Edited by Irmgard Booth. Translated by R. H. Fuller. Rev. ed. New York: Macmillan, 1963.

Bultmann, Rudolf. *Theology of the New Testament*. Translated by Kendrick Grobel. 2 vols. Waco, TX: Baylor University, 2007.

Buttrick, David G. "Genesis 15:1–18." *Interpretation* 42.4 (1988) 393–97.

Calvin, John. *Commentary on the Book of Psalms*. Translated by James Anderson. 5 vols. Calvin's Commentaries. N.p.: n.p., 1845.

———. *Commentary on the Epistle of Paul the Apostle to the Romans*. Edited and translated by John Owen. Calvin's Commentaries. N.p.: n.p., 1849.

Childs, Brevard S. *Biblical Theology in Crisis*. Philadelphia: Westminster, 1970.

———. "Biblische Theologie und christlicher Kanon." In *Zum Problem des biblischen Kanons*, edited by Ingo Baldermann, 13–27. Jahrbuch für biblische Theologie 3. Neukirchen-Vluyn, Germany: Neukirchener, 1988.

———. *Old Testament Theology in a Canonical Context*. 1st ed. Philadelphia: Fortress, 1986.

Cranfield, C. E. B. *A Critical and Exegetical Commentary on the Epistle to the Romans*. Edited by J. A. Emerton, C. E. B. Cranfield, and G. N. Stanton. Rev. ed. 2 vols. International Critical Commentary. New York: T. & T. Clark, 1975.

———. "'The Works of the Law' in the Epistle to the Romans." *Journal for the Study of the New Testament* 43.1 (1991) 89–101.

Denney, James. "St. Paul's Epistle to the Romans." In *Acts of the Apostles, Romans, First Corinthians*, edited by W. Robertson Nicoll, 555–725. The Expositor's Greek Testament 2. Peabody, MA: Hendrickson, 2002.

Derrida, Jacques. *Of Grammatology*. Translated by Gayatri Chakravorty Spivak. Corrected ed. Baltimore: Johns Hopkins University, 1997.

———. *Writing and Difference*. Translated by Alan Bass. Routledge Classics. London: Routledge, 1978.

Dunn, James D. G. *The Epistle to the Galatians*. Black's New Testament Commentaries 9. Peabody, MA: Hendrickson, 1993.

———. *Jesus Remembered*. Christianity in the Making 1. Grand Rapids: Eerdmans, 2003.

———. *Romans*. Word Biblical Commentary 38. Dallas, TX: Word, 1988.

———. *The Theology of Paul the Apostle*. Grand Rapids: Eerdmans, 1998.

Gadamer, Hans-Georg. "The Universality of the Hermeneutical Problem." In *Philosophical Hermeneutics*, edited and translated by David E. Ligne, 1st paperback ed., 3–17. Berkeley, CA: University of California Press, 1977.

———. *Truth and Method*. Edited and translated by Joel Weinsheimer and Donald G. Marshall. 2nd ed. New York: Continuum, 2006.

Gathercole, Simon J. "A Law unto Themselves: The Gentiles in Romans 2.14–15 Revisited." *Journal for the Study of the New Testament* 85 (2002) 27–49.

Grundmann, Walter. "στήκω, ἵστημι." Edited by Gerhard Kittel. Translated by Geoffrey W. Bromiley, Gerhard Friedrich, and Ronald E. Pitkin. *Theological Dictionary of the New Testament*. Grand Rapids: Eerdmans, 2006.

Gunneweg, Antonius H. *Vom Verstehen des Alten Testaments: Eine Hermeneutik*. 2nd ed. Grundrisse zum Alten Testament 5. Vandenhoeck und Ruprecht, 2011.

Heidland, H. W. "λογίζομαι, λογισμός." Edited by Gerhard Kittel. Translated by Geoffrey W. Bromiley, Gerhard Friedrich, and Ronald E. Pitkin. *Theological Dictionary of the New Testament*. Grand Rapids: Eerdmans, 2006.

Holmes, Michael W., ed. *The Greek New Testament: SBL Edition*. Atlanta: Society of Biblical Literature, 2010.

Jewett, Robert. *Romans: A Commentary*. Hermeneia. Minneapolis: Fortress, 2007.

Käsemann, Ernst. *Commentary on Romans*. Translated by Geoffrey W. Bromiley. Grand Rapids: Eerdmans, 1980.

———. *New Testament Questions of Today*. Translated by W. J. Montague and Wilfred F. Bunge. Philadelphia: Fortress, 1969.

Kleinknecht, Hermann. "νόμος; in the Greek and Hellenistic World." In vol. 4 of *The Theological Dictionary of the New Testament*, 1023–35. Edited by Gerhard Kittel and Gerhard Friedrich. Translated by Geoffrey W. Bromiley. 10 vols. Grand Rapids: Eerdmans, 1964–1976."

Koehler, Ludwig, and Walter Baumgartner. *The Hebrew and Aramaic Lexicon of the Old Testament*. Study Guide ed. 2 vols. Boston: Brill, 2001.

Kuhn, Thomas S. *The Structure of Scientific Revolutions*. 3rd ed. Chicago: University of Chicago Press, 1996.

Lamp, Jeffrey S. "Paul, the Law, and Gentiles: A Contextual and Exegetical Reading of Romans 2:12–16." *Journal of the Evangelical Theological Society* 42.1 (1999) 37–51.

Lewis, C. S. "Evil and God." In *God in the Dock: Essays on Theology and Ethics*, edited by Walter Hooper, 21–24. Grand Rapids: Eerdmans, 1970.

———. *Mere Christianity*. HarperCollins ed. San Francisco: HarperCollins, 2001.

———. "Rejoinder to Dr Pittenger." In *God in the Dock: Essays on Theology and Ethics*, edited by Walter Hooper, 177–83. Grand Rapids: Eerdmans, 1970.

Luther, Martin. *Lectures on Romans*. Translated by Wilhelm Pauck. Library of Christian Classics. Philadelphia: Westminster, 1961.

Metzger, Bruce M. *A Textual Commentary on the Greek New Testament*. 2nd ed. Stuttgart: United Bible Societies, 1994.

Moo, Douglas J. *The Epistle to the Romans*. Edited by Gordon D. Fee. New International Commentary on the New Testament. Grand Rapids: Eerdmans, 1996.

———. "Israel and the Law in Romans 5–11: Interaction with the New Perspective." In *The Paradoxes of Paul*, edited by D. A. Carson, Peter Thomas O'Brien, and Mark A. Seifrid, 185–216. Justification and Variegated Nomism: A Fresh Appraisal of Paul and Second Temple Judaism 2. Grand Rapids: Baker, 2001.

———. "'Law,' 'Works of the Law,' and Legalism in Paul." *Westminster Theological Journal* 45.1 (1983) 73–100.

———. "Romans 2: Saved Apart from the Gospel?" In *Through No Fault of Their Own?: The Fate of Those Who Have Never Heard*, edited by William V. Crockett and James G. Siqountos, 137–45. Grand Rapids: Baker, 1991.

Mounce, Robert H. *Romans*. New American Commentary 27. Nashville: Broadman and Holman, 1995.

Nanos, Mark D. *The Mystery of Romans: The Jewish Context of Paul's Letter*. Minneapolis: Fortress, 1996.

Newman, Barclay M., and Eugene A. Nida. *A Handbook on Paul's Letter to the Romans*. United Bible Societies Handbook Series. New York: United Bible Societies, 1973.

Osborne, Grant R. *The Hermeneutical Spiral: A Comprehensive Introduction to Biblical Interpretation*. 1st ed. Downers Grove, IL: InterVarsity, 1991.

Pickup, Martin. "New Testament Interpretation of the Old Testament: The Theological Rationale of Midrashic Exegesis." *Journal of the Evangelical Theological Society* 51.2 (2008) 353–81.

Piper, John. *Counted Righteous in Christ: Should We Abandon the Imputation of Christ's Righteousness?* Wheaton, IL: Crossway, 2002.

Robertson, A. T. *A Grammar of the Greek New Testament in the Light of Historical Research*. New York: Hodder and Stoughton, 1914.

Rodríguez, Rafael. *If You Call Yourself a Jew: Reappraising Paul's Letter to the Romans.* Eugene, OR: Wipf & Stock, 2014.

———, and Matthew Thiessen, eds. *The So-called Jew in Paul's Letter to the Romans.* Minneapolis: Fortress, 2016.

Sanders, E. P. *Paul and Palestinian Judaism: A Comparison of Patterns of Religion.* Minneapolis: Fortress, 1977.

———. *Paul, the Law, and the Jewish People.* Philadelphia: Fortress, 1983.

Sandys-Wunsch, John, and Laurence Eldredge. "J. P. Gabler and the Distinction Between Biblical and Dogmatic Theology: Translation, Commentary, and Discussion of His Originality." *Scottish Journal of Theology* 33.2 (1980) 133–58.

Schaff, Philip, ed. *Nicene and Post-Nicene Fathers, First Series.* 14 vols. Grand Rapids: Eerdmans, 1978.

Schreiner, Thomas R. "The Abolition and Fulfillment of the Law in Paul." *Journal for the Study of the New Testament* 35 (1989) 47–74.

———. "Did Paul Believe in Justification by Works?: Another Look at Romans 2." *Bulletin for Biblical Research* 3 (1993) 131–58.

———. "Paul and Perfect Obedience to the Law: An Evaluation of the View of E. P. Sanders." *Westminster Theological Journal* 47.2 (1985) 245–78.

———. *Romans.* Edited by Moisés Silva. Grand Rapids: Baker, 1998.

———. "'Works of Law' in Paul." *Novum Testamentum* 33.3 (1991) 217–44.

Selby, Rosalind M. *Comical Doctrine: An Epistemology of New Testament Hermeneutics.* Paternoster Biblical Monographs. Milton Keynes, United Kingdom: Paternoster, 2006.

Sire, James W. *Naming the Elephant: Worldview as a Concept.* Downers Grove, IL: InterVarsity, 2004.

Smith, James K. A. *Jacques Derrida: Live Theory.* London: Continuum, 2005.

———. *Who's Afraid of Postmodernism?: Taking Derrida, Lyotard, and Foucault to Church.* The Church and Postmodern Culture. Grand Rapids: Baker Academic, 2006.

Spivak, Gayatri Chakravorty. Translator's Preface to *Of Grammatology*, by Jacques Derrida. Corrected ed. Baltimore: Johns Hopkins University, 1997.

Stark, J. David. "Figuring Things Out: Lyrical Resourcement for Figural Readings of Biblical Literature in the Contemporary Academy." *Journal of Faith and the Academy* 8.1 (2015) 47–60.

———. *Sacred Texts and Paradigmatic Revolutions: The Hermeneutical Worlds of the Qumran Sectarian Manuscripts and the Letter to the Romans.* Jewish and Christian Texts in Contexts and Related Studies 16. New York: Bloomsbury T. & T. Clark, 2013.

Stuhlmacher, Peter. *Revisiting Paul's Doctrine of Justification: A Challenge to the New Perspective.* Edited by Peter Stuhlmacher. Downers Grove, IL: InterVarsity, 2001.

Thielman, Frank. *Paul and the Law: A Contextual Approach.* Downers Grove, IL: InterVarsity, 1994.

Von Rad, Gerhard. *Studies in Deuteronomy.* Translated by David Stalker. Studies in Biblical Theology 9. London: SCM, 1953.

Watson, Francis. *Paul and the Hermeneutics of Faith.* New York: T. & T. Clark, 2004.

Westerholm, Stephen. *Justification Reconsidered: Rethinking a Pauline Theme.* Grand Rapids: Eerdmans, 2013.

———. *Perspectives Old and New on Paul: The "Lutheran" Paul and His Critics*. Grand Rapids: Eerdmans, 2004.

———. "The 'New Perspective' at Twenty-Five." In *The Paradoxes of Paul*, edited by D. A. Carson, Peter Thomas O'Brien, and Mark A. Seifrid, 1–38. Justification and Variegated Nomism: A Fresh Appraisal of Paul and Second Temple Judaism 2. Grand Rapids: Baker, 2001.

Wright, N. T. *Justification: God's Plan and Paul's Vision*. Downers Grove, IL: InterVarsity, 2009.

———. "The Letter to the Romans." In *Acts, Introduction to Epistolary Literature, Romans, 1 Corinthians*, edited by Leander E. Keck, et al., 393–770. New Interpreter's Bible 10. Nashville: Abingdon, 2002.

———. *The New Testament and the People of God*. Christian Origins and the Question of God 1. Minneapolis: Fortress, 1992.

———. *Paul and the Faithfulness of God*. Christian Origins and the Question of God 4. Minneapolis: Fortress, 2013.

4

"Necessary but Not Sufficient"

The Role of History in the Interpretation of James as Christian Scripture

Darian Lockett

How important is history for interpreting the Old and New Testaments as Christian Scripture? This hermeneutical question is timely especially with the rise of the theological interpretation of Scripture movement and attendant discussions (debates) over what counts as theological interpretation.[1] Jon Levenson once said:

> The contextualization of biblical documents in the cultures in which they were written is not only the hallmark of historical criticism; it is also inevitable. . . . The question is not whether we make historical judgments; the question can only be whether we do so poorly or well . . . .[2]

In Levenson's estimation, every interpretive approach—even the theological interpretation of Scripture—includes making historical judgments;

1. I would like to thank Carl Mosser, Matthew Harmon, and Jason Smith for their critical and insightful comments on an earlier draft of this essay.

For introductions to theological interpretation see Treier, *Introducing Theological Interpretation*; Treier, "Biblical Theology and/or Theological Interpretation of Scripture?"; Fowl, *Theological Interpretation of Scripture*. For varying levels of appreciation and critique see Trimm, "Evangelicals, Theology, and Biblical Interpretation"; Carson, "Theological Interpretation of Scripture"; Poirier, "'Theological Interpretation' and its Contradistinctions"; and Barton, *The Nature of Biblical Criticism*, especially 176–77.

2. Levenson, "Hebrew Bible, the Old Testament, and Historical Criticism," 110–11.

however, the key point is whether such judgments are rendered well or poorly. Thus it is not *whether* one uses history in interpretation, but *how* history is used and understood.

With this in mind, John Webster has argued with great energy that when interpreters attempt to understand the Old and New Testaments they should first be mindful of what the Bible *is*. He notes that, "proposals about 'theological interpretation' of the Bible commonly lack an ontology of Scripture." Webster continues, by noting when theological interpretation reads for "certain theological themes . . . , or perhaps, a matter of reading under the tutelage of the church's traditions of interpretation, or of reading virtuously . . . [these] will only prove fruitful if grounded in a theological account of what Scripture is."[3] When there is confusion over what Scripture is—its theological ontology—there will be confusion over how to read and interpret it. Webster argues, "Affirmations about the natural history of the biblical texts go wrong, not in claiming necessity for themselves *but in claiming sufficiency*."[4] When the natural or historical elements of Scripture are taken as sufficient in themselves for determining meaning, the interpretive endeavor goes wrong. Similarly, Hank Voss notes, "By carefully listening to each human author, theological interpreters are more accurately able to hear the divine voice speaking through the canon as a whole. Thus evangelical TE [theological exegesis] does not denigrate GHE [grammatical-historical exegesis], but seeks to recover alongside of it the historic emphasis of the church on the divine voice speaking in Scripture as a whole."[5] The spatial analogy rings true—grammatical-historical and theological methods should lay alongside one another rather than one serving as foundational to the other.

The present point is that whereas grammatical-historical interpretation of the Bible is necessary, it cannot be the sole method used to understand and read Christian Scripture. The major short-coming of the grammatical-historical approach is that it is too often seen as interpretation *in toto*, with its practitioners failing to move on to other interpretive tasks owing to the assumption that the meaning of the text has already been established through historical-grammatical reconstruction of the author's intention.[6] The argu-

3. Webster, *Domain of the Word*, 32–33. See especially his argument that a biblical ontology is necessarily prior to hermeneutics (viii).

4. Ibid., 40 (emphasis added).

5. Hank Voss, "From 'Grammatical-historical Exegesis' to 'Theological Exegesis,'" 145. He concludes: "In this essay I have argued that theological exegesis (TE), rather than grammatical historical exegesis (GHE) alone, will best serve the global church" (152).

6. I am grateful to Carl Mosser for this language.

ment forwarded here is that a strictly grammatical-historical methodology for reading the Bible fails to read the text as Christian Scripture and, consequently, such historically focused scholarship is in real danger of eclipsing further, *equally necessary*, tasks in interpreting the Bible.

Using the Epistle of James as a test case, this essay will consider the degree to which historical details such as author, genre, and audience end up aiding the interpretive task. Whereas such details are hermeneutically meaningful—they are necessary—such information alone is inadequate for interpreting the text. Specifically, such an approach falls short especially when methodologically treating such grammatical-historical details as sufficient in and of themselves. After demonstrating the limitation of such a study with regard to James, this essay briefly suggests that reading James canonically—that is, reading James within the context of its near canonical neighbors—should not only supplement grammatical-historical reading but rather be elevated alongside of it. For present purposes, interpreting James in canonical context is considered a form of "theological interpretation." But before considering James as a test case, the essay first turns to a description of the grammatical-historical method as generally practiced by evangelical scholars. There is not space to offer a comprehensive description of the history and development of the grammatical-historical method or to consider the various ways in which it is put to use by evangelical scholars. Furthermore, though important, we will not draw much of a distinction between grammatical-historical and historical-critical exegesis. For clarity, and brevity, after some general, orienting comments, the grammatical-historical method as described by Craig Blomberg will serve as a foil for comparison with James in canonical context.[7]

Grammatical-Historical Interpretation

Grant Osborne notes: "Since Christianity is a historical religion, the interpreter must recognize that an understanding of the history and culture within which the passage was produced is an indispensable tool for uncovering the meaning of that passage."[8] Even more pointedly Gordon Fee and Douglas Stuart, in their widely used primer on evangelical hermeneutics argue, "On this one thing, however, there must surely be agreement. *A text*

7. For a discussion of history and biblical hermeneutics see Rae, *History and Hermeneutics*; and for a recent survey of historical criticism as a method for biblical interpretation see Harrisville, *Pandora's Box Opened*.

8. Osborn, *The Hermeneutical Spiral*, 158.

cannot mean what it never meant."[9] For E. D. Hirsch it is specifically discerning the historical author's intention that uncovers the meaning of the text: "all valid interpretation of every sort is founded on the recognition of what an author meant."[10]

Craig Blomberg clarifies the relationship between the historical author's intention and the meaning of the text:

> What is described as discerning "authorial intent," moreover, is often really shorthand for discerning the most likely meaning of a given text in light of all that we can recover about its original author(s), audience(s) and the historical and cultural milieus in which they lived.[11]

Broadly representative of evangelical hermeneutical practice, Blomberg argues that grammatical-historical interpretation is first, grammatical in that "it insists on a careful study of words, grammatical forms, sentence parts, sentences and multisentence structures as they relate to each other."[12] It is also historical in that it "analyzes the historical setting in which a given communicative act occurs" which takes into account "whatever knowledge the author and audience share about past or present events, customs and practices, culture and society, and so on . . . ." Further, these features—grammar and history—are important because both are used to analyze the

> formation of documents, including earlier written sources, oral forms of communication and whatever distinctive emphases the author of the document may have added to the tradition he or she inherited. Such analysis can also lead to judgments about the reliability of the document being assessed.[13]

Blomberg goes on to note what the grammatical-historical approach does *not* seek to accomplish. The grammatical-historical approach does

9. *How to Read the Bible for All its Worth*, 30. Peter Leithart notes, "E. D. Hirsch has, in the last few decades, been the primary (almost the only) exponent of the view that textual meaning is the meaning intended by the author, and that this meaning is stable through time" (*Deep Exegesis*, 35). Leithart goes on to provide a very helpful discussion of typology and textual meaning which is appreciative yet critical of Hirsch's focus on stable, authorial meaning. See also the introductory discussion in Brown, *Introduction to Biblical Hermeneutics*, especially chapters 4 and 5.

10. Hirsch, *Validity*, 126. Famously, Hirsch distinguished between unchanging "meaning" (intended results and desired consequences) and constantly changing "significance" (unintended results and arbitrary applications) (8, 62–63).

11. Blomberg, "The Historical-Critical/Grammatical View," 31.

12. Ibid., 39.

13. Ibid.

not focus on implied authors or readers, nor is it satisfied with an appreciation of the coherent narrative-world internal to the text on its own. The grammatical-historical approach does not make synthetic conclusions regarding theological concerns in the text. That is, a grammatical-historical reading does not systematize theological concerns across books let alone across Testaments. Furthermore, it is not concerned with "the 'afterlife' of texts via the history of their interpretation through the centuries, nor is it particularly interested in the 'history of the effects' of the passage on other disciplines."[14] Blomberg is clear that grammatical-historical interpretation does not "read New Testament meaning back into Old Testament texts." And "tends not to raise questions of contemporary significance, application or contextualization, or locate a biblical passage in the flow of redemptive history . . . ."[15] Finally, he argues that grammatical-historical interpretation is not concerned with "later stages of canonical development, when interpreters read those books alongside other canonized books." Grammatical-historical interpretation, for example, will not consider the hermeneutical implications of either the content or arrangement of the Christian canon in its final form. For Blomberg "[s]uch questions are legitimate, but if some of the answers to those questions contradict the interpretation of the texts on their own integrity, the former must be eschewed in favor of the latter."[16] In other words, insights derived from other approaches that are not first grounded by the results of grammatical-historical investigation are to be rejected.

In the end, Blomberg is careful to indicate that he does not think the grammatical-historical hermeneutic is the only approach; however, he says, "I am convinced that all of the other approaches *must build on* the historical-critical/grammatical approach *in order to function legitimately*."[17] Note the insistence on the logical priority of the grammatical-historical method.

14. Ibid., 40.

15. Ibid.

16. Ibid., 41. Implicitly, Blomberg claims that issues of canon (selection and arrangement) are, historically speaking, anachronistic—that is, the later fact of canon cannot provide hermeneutical guidelines beyond the parameters set by grammatical-historical inquiry. Especially in light of Christian theological convictions regarding reading Scripture—namely, considering what Scripture *is* (God's divine self-communication) as well as what Scripture *does*—Blomberg's position seems to deny implicitly much of what (Evangelical) Christian reading of Scripture insists upon (e.g., canon, Scripture interpreting Scripture, ect.).

17. Ibid., 28 (emphasis added). Elsewhere Blomberg argues: "I said at the outset of this chapter that I was *not* trying to defend the historical-critical/grammatical method as the sole legitimate approach among the five hermeneutical approaches that this book presents but that I *would* argue for its logical priority" (41).

Blomberg's approach does not dispense with the divine author, which itself is a key point at which his historical-grammatical approach differs from standard historical-criticism. Yet at the same time the meaning of the text of Scripture, according to the grammatical-historical method, is anchored to or grounded in the historical context, namely, the historical meaning of words and grammatical structures as the original author intended them.

Though the grammatical-historical approach is necessary for proper interpretation it cannot function in exclusion of theological convictions regarding Christian Scripture. Stated clearly, history *per se*, and the grammatical-historical approach that depends upon it, must be defined theologically because, as noted above by Webster, this takes into account what Scripture *is*. Murray Rae argues convincingly for a theological redefinition of history:

> We may say, therefore, that the Bible is a theological account of history. It is an account that is shaped by the conviction that all that takes place does so within the context of God's providential care for the created order. That this is a theological account, employing categories particular to its own concerns, does not render it illegitimate as history . . . .

Rae continues,

> As such, every telling of the story of history involves the selection and interpretation of evidence according to the historian's convictions about the meaning and purpose of the whole. There is no good reason to suppose that a purely secular account of history, in which divine action is dispensed with as an explanatory category, brings the historian closer to the truth.[18]

Whereas one might expect Blomberg and other evangelical interpreters would generally agree with Rae's point here, the manner in which the grammatical-historical approach is used seems to minimize the theological aspects (or divine intention) of the text.

With Blomberg's implicit understanding of history put forward in his version of the grammatical-historical approach, we now turn to James as a test case. How important is history, as defined by the grammatical-historical approach, for interpreting the Letter of James?

18. Rae, *History and Hermeneutics*, 49–50.

James as a Test Case

According to the grammatical-historical hermeneutic, one must discern the historical author's intention in order to discover meaning. Again, for Blomberg, this is "really shorthand for discerning the most likely meaning of a given text in light of all that we can recover about its original author(s), audience(s) . . . ." Turning to James, however, knowledge of the author is sparse at best.

The Author of James

The author, according to James 1:1 is "James, a servant of God and of the Lord Jesus Christ." Few question that this James is none other than James, the brother of Jesus, who was the leader of the earliest followers in Jerusalem.[19] Yet internal, direct evidence—evidence from the letter itself—regarding the author of James is limited. From the prescript we find the most straightforward self-description of the author. Here the author claims the identity of "James." Almost all scholars have observed that the simple designation of James must refer to an individual who would have been sufficiently well-known in the early Christian movement and one specifically the addressees would have automatically known and accepted as an authority. Beyond 1:1 there are oblique references to the character and identity of the author surfacing in phrases such as: "our Lord Jesus Christ" (2:1), "our father" referring to Abraham (2:21), and "we who teach" (3:1). The author self-identifies as a Jewish follower of Jesus the Messiah and considers himself a teacher of the community with some authority.

The Genre and Audience of James

Because choice of genre is never accidental and is appropriate to the communicative intention of the author, one might deduce more regarding the historical author of the letter by determining the particular genre in which he wrote. Martin Dibelius is famous for having argued that James belongs to a type of writing called paraenesis, a collection of unoriginal maxims or proverbs designed to give moral instruction. Paraenesis is characterized by a loose collection of aphorisms and essays held together by catchwords. There are clear examples of proverbs (2:13, 26; 3:12, 18 etc.), essays (2:1–13; 14-26; 3:1–12; 3:13—4:10), and catchwords (greeting/joy 1:1 and 1:2; lacking/

19. Blomberg and Kamell, *James*, 27–28 among others.

lacking in 1:4 and 1:5, etc.) in James. And as a prominent feature of paraenesis, James contains many imperatives. Dibelius argued that such literature generally lacks literary coherence, theological content, and social location, yet a majority of scholars have questioned each of these conclusions regarding paraenesis both in general and as applied to James specifically.

Whereas there are compelling arguments demonstrating that James does contain both coherent structure and clear theological content, Dibelius was generally correct to stress the lack of social location in the letter.[20] He concluded that there was no particular historical-cultural situation behind the text at all. And though recent research by Leo Perdue, James Gammie, and Karl-Wilhelm Niebuhr has reassessed the lack of coherence and theological content in paraenesis generally, even these scholars have been hard pressed to demonstrate anything beyond a general social-historical setting for this kind of writing.[21]

As wisdom paraenesis lacking specific historical and social context, many have noted the hypothetical character of James. Luke Timothy Johnson observes that "[t]he way to the real readers is blocked above all by the general character of James's moral exhortation. He is certainly detailed enough, but his lively vignettes appear as situations that might apply to all communities, rather than a single church."[22] Peter Davids finds that there is neither a

> definite crisis in the epistle such as those which called forth 1 Thessalonians or 1 Corinthians nor a specific persecution such as those which called forth 1 Pet. 4:12 and (probably) the book of Revelation . . . .[23]

Luke Timothy Johnson adds with a hint of exasperation:

> What, if anything, can be determined from the Letter of James about the social world of its author or readers? Can the letter of James be rooted in history at all? If so, by what means or with what benefit to the understanding of the letter? On the one hand, we are offered hope because James is so obviously enmeshed in the realities of life and practical wisdom. On the other hand, our hope is qualified by the realization that James's no-nonsense

20. For example, Bauckham, *James*; Moo, *Letter of James*; McKnight, *Letter of James*; and Lockett, "Structure or Communicative Strategy."

21. Perdue, "The Social Character"; Gammie, "Paraenetic Literature"; Niebuhr, *Gesetz und Paränese*.

22. Johnson, *Brother of Jesus*, 37.

23. Davids, *Epistle of James*, 29–30.

> practicality is never clothed with the sort of specific information we desire.[24]

Finally, Richard Bauckham most concisely articulates both the scholarly desire to uncover the historical-cultural setting of James alongside the letter's resistance to such reconstruction.

> The seemingly irrepressible desire of modern historical criticism of the New Testament to specify the contexts of the original audiences of the New Testament texts as closely as possible must be resisted, since the character of James as an encyclical contradicts it. We must take seriously the implication that James addresses not specific but typical situations, such as he knows it is quite likely his readers in many parts of the Diaspora might encounter, and rebukes typical failings, such as he might think likely to occur in many Jewish Christian communities in the Diaspora.[25]

As we shall consider further, though James is clearly fashioned as a letter, the main body is written in the form of wisdom paraenesis—a genre that is not concerned to foreground a specific historical-cultural context.

In addition to the genre of the letter, the content of James also indicates its generalized and hypothetical character, especially with respect to the letter's audience. The text opens with a stereotypical form of epistolary greeting: "James . . . , To the twelve tribes . . . : Greetings" (1:1). This prescript includes the "parties formula" ("A to B") and a salutation ("Greetings") typical of all Greek letters.[26] But James is not a personal letter addressed to a small group; it is rather "an official letter or encyclical [which] . . . addresses . . . the Jewish Diaspora."[27] Many have noted that the text does not contain any personal greetings, travel plans, or prayer requests for specific situations, some of which would be expected in a typical Christian letter. These conspicuous omissions have led some to deny James as a real letter

24. *Brother of Jesus*, 104–5. See also the similar comments by Dibelius and Greeven, *James*, 128–30.

25. Bauckham, *James*, 26. Also, Bauckham notes: "Taking seriously the epistolary situation which the letter of James claims for itself means resisting the tendency in some scholarly work on James to envisage a specific 'community of James'—whether a single Christian community or a group of such communities—which the work has in view as its audience . . . " (25).

26. Ibid., 11; Stowers, *Letter Writing*, 21; Bauckham, "Pseudo-Apostolic Letters," 473.

27. Ibid., 13. Several scholars identify similarities between James and Jewish encyclicals: Niebuhr, "Jakobusbrief im Licht frühjüdischer Diasporabriefe"; Wachob, *The Voice of Jesus*, 6–8.

at all. Though the content of James does not represent a type of personal letter between family or friends it still may be considered a letter in its own right—James at least contains the one formal criterion of an epistle, namely, the letter-opening.

Rather than a so-called "personal" letter, some have compared the Letter of James to a "diaspora letter." There was a tradition of official letters sent from the Jewish leadership in Jerusalem to diaspora communities in Babylon (Jer 29:1–28; Ep Jer), Egypt (2 Macc 1:1–9, 10; 2:18), and from Baruch "to the nine and a half tribes which were across the river" (*2 Bar* 78–86; cf. *4 Bar* 6:19–23). There are also references to messengers going out from the temple authorities in Jerusalem to Syria communicating the correct dates for the festivals (*Roš Haš* 1.3–4; cf. Acts 15:24–29; 28:21). These diaspora letters were written from a central religious authority in Jerusalem to geographically removed communities, usually with the intent of encouraging them not to assimilate to their surrounding cultural context and to disseminate official information. As these Jewish diaspora letters, James too could be a work addressed from a leader in Jerusalem to those living outside Palestine with the intent of bringing exhortation and encouragement to persevere in the face of trial. Thus the letter could be considered an encyclical written to the messianically renewed people of God living in the diaspora.[28] "By contrast with the major Pauline letters," Bauckham notes, "it is remarkable that, after 1:1, James makes no factual statement about his addresses at all. Everything is hypothetical."[29]

Immediately following the letter introduction, where one would expect to find a personal greeting or a specific prayer of thanksgiving for the audience, James 1:2 rather opens with a generalized situation: "whenever you face any kind of trial . . . ." Again, lacking specific greetings and reference to any specific trial or suffering, the opening admonition is broadly applicable to a variety of potential readers. Here, as in much of the letter, James' wisdom is both practical and portable.

In addition to a generalized description of the audience, one finds equally hypothetical descriptions of groups in the text. Though some have argued for the "rich" in James as a specific group of enemies of the community, the text rather envisions any such "group(s)" as hypothetical.[30] Once

28. See the discussion in both Bauckham, *James*, 11–28, and Cheung, *Genre, Composition and Hermemeutics*, 51–52.

29. Bauckham, *James*, 26–27. Despite this caution, McKnight consistently argues for a specific social-historical situation of James' audience within which to read the letter (*Letter of James*, 76, 84, 94, 104–5); see also, Witherington, *Letters and Homilies*, 401–5; and Brosend, *James and Jude*, 31.

30. For the "rich" as enemies or "outsiders" see Wall, *Community*; and Penner, *James*

again the interpreter is faced with the letter's persistently broad reference. Luke Timothy Johnson articulates the struggle to identify particular groups or "communities" in James whether enemies or not. He notes: "When the text itself reveals little specific information about its social world, the investigator becomes more dependent on theoretical models concerning social groups and their development," and the hypothetical nature of James "raises severe doubts concerning the usefulness of the search."[31] The language of rich/poor is highly stylized typical Jewish prophetic denunciation as found in the Old Testament.[32] Rather than making reference to specific groups, it is more likely that the author takes up the typical categories of rich and lowly out of a concern for the readers to adopt the values and actions of the poor and lowly over against those of the rich (2:2–9) and proud (4:7–10).

Moving systematically through the text, one continues to find highly generalized scenarios that speak beyond their immediate historical-cultural situation. In James 2:2–3 we find a sketch of a hypothetical situation where the poor suffer discrimination at the hands of the gathered community in contrast to the preferential treatment of the rich. Rather than a particular situation the "example of discrimination is drawn from experience in Diaspora synagogues."[33] The rhetorical point to score is not that there is a particular instance of discrimination, but that such social and economic imbalance, and discrimination based upon that imbalance, is typical of the communities to which the letter is addressed.

In 2:2–7 the audience is neither wholly identified with the man wearing a "gold ring and in fine clothes" nor with the "poor" man "in dirty clothes," but rather James addresses his audience as a third (perhaps majority) group, neither rich nor poor. Again, the entire passage is hypothetical or, as Peter Davids notes, is "simply a parabolic narrative used to introduce a teaching, not an actual report of historical occurrences."[34] Wesley Wachob notes, "if we may accept what cultural anthropologists tell us about the patron-client system that permeated the Greco-Roman world during that period, then the incident envisioned looks typical rather than unusual" and thus need not refer to a specific situation for "[t]he issue of favoring the wealthy over the poor in judicial proceedings is, in fact, a conventional subject in ancient sources."[35]

---

and Eschatology.

31. *Brother of Jesus*, 103. In general, see the critique of the sociology of the "sect" as it is used in NT studies, Barton, "Early Christianity."

32. Penner, *James and Eschatology*, 271; Moo, *Letter of James*, 35.

33. Painter and deSilva, *James and Jude*, 90.

34. Bauckham, *James*, 30.

35. Wachob, *Voice of Jesus*, 75–76.

Likewise, in 2:14–16 the addressees are offered a hypothetical situation where a brother or sister comes to the readers lacking basic food and clothing. Again, the readers are not identified with the group of needy brothers and/or sisters, nor does the text explicitly indicate that the community is primarily made up of such "poor" brothers and sisters only that there are brothers and sisters in need.[36] Continuing in chapter 2, the author uses a diatribal style where he introduces imaginary opponents through whom dissenting voices are presented. Bauckham notes that the author "does not even refer to [these voices of dissent] as 'someone among you' (as we might expect form 3:13; 5:13-14, 19) but merely as 'someone' (2:14, 18)." This is, again, indicative of the overarching hypothetical style of the letter. Bauckham concludes: "Of course, he must expect what he writes in chapter 2 to be relevant to many of his readers (nothing in an encyclical need be equally relevant to all readers), but only in general terms."[37]

In chapter four the author asks: "Where do battles and disputes among you come from?" But even this question concerning social strife need not presuppose any knowledge of some specific situation of conflict in any particular community. Later in the same chapter, the author notes the contest of loyalties between those who are "friends of the world" and others who are friends of God. But again, the conflict between those loyal to the surrounding society and those who are loyal to God might be expected in any and all Christian communities or at least in most communities his letter might reach. Again, Bauckham notes: "When he turns to address and to denounce the wealthy . . . he simply envisages the two categories of wealthy people to be found everywhere, merchants (4:13–15) and wealthy landowners (5:1–6), and castigates the sins for which each class was notorious. All is manifestly typical or hypothetical."[38]

Therefore, in both genre and content the Epistle of James is consistently hypothetical and generalized, especially with respect to its audience. Because James is an encyclical addressed to any Jewish Christian community anywhere in the diaspora, it is unlikely that any particular event or specific local crisis initiated the letter's composition. Rather than offering teaching that meets the needs of a particular moment, the Epistle of James offers instruction that the author envisions as useful for Jewish Christians in the diaspora anywhere and at any time—thus envisioning a broad—yet not indeterminate—audience and situation.[39] Rather than rendering the gram-

36. *Pace* Wall, *Community*, 13–14, 54–57; and Maynard-Reid, *Poverty and Wealth*.

37. Bauckham, *James*, 27.

38. Ibid.

39. Ibid., 28.

matical-historical method irrelevant, James' less specific historical-cultural context suggests the need for more not fewer methods of interpretation.

Canonical Context: James and 1 Peter

The interpretive payoff derived from a grammatical-historical investigation into the social context of James reveals meaningful (that is, necessary, if minimal) information for understanding the letter; however, if one's interpretive methodology insists on this as the only or primary avenue to identify the meaning of James one is left with a letter written to first-century Jewish Christians with little warrant for contemporary (non-Jewish) Christians to read the text. The generalized character of the epistle likely enabled a broader field of communication for the author as several audiences would have been able to read and understand the text as "for them" in some way or other. Yet, beyond this general address, the present observation is that the limited nature of such a grammatical-historical examination should press the reader to incorporate other tools—theological and canonical—alongside grammatical-historical tools.

Though the Epistle of James was not immediately included into the canon of New Testament, it was eventually recognized.[40] Whereas grammatical-historical information about the addressees of James indicates that his audience was likely Jewish Christ-followers, as part of the New Testament canon this text has been understood to address all Christ-followers—a conclusion which stands in contrast to the grammatical-historical assertion that a text can never mean today what it never meant to the original audience. How might Gentile Christ-followers in various locations (none of which are considered in the diaspora) read the Epistle of James as addressed to them? Bauckham articulates this question well: "When James is read within its canonical context in the New Testament, does it still address only Jewish Christians or can it be heard also by Gentile Christians as addressed to them?"[41] Implicitly, James' recognition within the New Testament canon suggests that the letter "was understood to address Gentile as well as Jewish Christians."[42]

Although the canonical relationships that stand out for the Letter of James are primarily the Torah and Old Testament wisdom,[43] there are

40. See, for example Lockett, "Why Have We Stopped," and Lockett, *Letters from the Pillar Apostles*, chapter 3.

41. Bauckham, *James*, 28.

42. Ibid., 112–13.

43. Bauckham (*James*, 140–41) notes: "The relationships with other parts of the

also hermeneutically important canonical connections with other New Testament texts including some of the other Catholic Epistles. The New Testament canon becomes a hermeneutically important context within which to read and understand the Epistle of James. Interestingly, Bauckham argues for the importance of the canonical context of James within the Catholic Epistles—that is, the interpretive significance of both the content and ordering of the seven letters of the Catholic Epistles:

> If we read the catholic epistles in the order which at an early date came to be the accepted canonical order, with James in first place and 1 Peter immediately following, then we read first a letter addressed only to Jewish Christians as the twelve tribes in the Diaspora and then a letter apparently addressed only to Gentile Christians as 'exiles of the diaspora', to whom defining descriptions of Israel as God's people are applied. One effect is to portray the inclusion of Gentiles in the eschatological people of God, which retains through its Jewish Christian members its continuity with Israel and yet is also open to the inclusion of those who had not hitherto been God's people (1 Pet. 2:10). The inclusion of Gentiles in the eschatological people of God is thus portrayed in the catholic letters in their own way just as clearly as in the Pauline corpus, reminding us that this was not confined to the Pauline mission but also happened, for example, in the church of Rome quite independently of Paul but in relationship with the mother church in Jerusalem. . . . Gentile Christians, finding themselves addressed as 'exiles of the diaspora,' are encouraged to find James' letter to the twelve tribes in the Diaspora also addressed to them by virtue of their grafting into the root of Israel (Rom. 11:17). It is theirs too, not as a Gentile appropriation of the Jewish inheritance but as the root into which they have been grafted.[44]

Here, Bauckham is reading the canonical order of the Catholic Epistles as significant to their meaning, not just their application.

David Nienhuis and Robert Wall also note the similarities between James and 1 Peter. In the opening section of each letter they both bear "a prescript locating recipients in a Diaspora (Jas. 1:1; 1 Pet. 1:1) and then immediately [each letter] calls believers to rejoice in 'various trials' (*poikilois*

---

canon of Scripture in which the letter of James itself invites us to place it are primarily with the Old Testament, especially Torah and wisdom. Addressing Jewish Christians James reads the Scriptures of Israel in the way that they address the Messianically renewed Israel."

44. Ibid., 156–57.

peirasmois) because of the role testing plays in producing genuine faith (*to dokimion hymōn tēs pisteōs*, Jas. 1:2–3; 1 Pet 1:6–9)." Nienhuis and Wall continue, "Soon thereafter James quotes, and 1 Peter alludes to, Isaiah 40 (Jas. 1:10–11; 1 Pet 1:24–25), and then each speaks of the believer's birth by a word from God (Jas. 1:18; 1 Pet 1:23)." After this analysis they conclude that such "close parallels (compare Jas. 4:6–10 with 1 Pet 5:5–9 and Jas. 5:20 with 1 Pet 4:8) clearly indicate that James and Peter are in theological agreement."[45] All of these parallels lead Nienhuis and Wall to interpret James and 1 Peter as two component parts of the Catholic Epistle collection such that their meaning is dependent upon their canonical interrelation. When James is read alongside 1 Peter it is able more fully to address the Christian church, that is, to both Jewish *and* Gentile Christians.[46]

Canonical Context: James and Jude

As an example of a further canonical connection within the Catholic Epistles one may consider the connection between James and Jude. Jude's opening address reads: "Jude, a servant of Jesus Christ and brother of James" (1), which at once both draws attention to the family relationship between Jude and James as brothers of Jesus and also effectively cues readers to think back to the letter of James. Interestingly, in Eusebius we find the first clear reference to the "Catholic Epistles" which at the same time suggests a particular relationship between James and Jude.[47] Following an elaborate record of the martyrdom of James, the Lord's brother, Eusebius notes:

> Such is the story of James, whose is said to be the first of the Epistles called Catholic [ἡ πρώτη τῶν ὀνομαζομένων καθολικῶν ἐπιστολῶν]. It is to be observed that its authenticity is denied [ἰστέον δὲ ὡς νοθεύεται μέν], since few of the ancients quote it, as is also the case with the Epistle called Jude's, which is itself one of the seven called Catholic [τῶν ἑπτὰ

45. Nienhuis and Wall, *Reading*, 253–54.

46. I have attempted to offer a more thorough account of the canonical interrelationships between the Catholic Epistles in *Wisdom of the Pillar Apostles*.

47. Painter and deSilva note: "In saying 'first of the Epistles named Catholic,' Eusebius provides the first known reference to the Catholic Epistles . . . " (*James and Jude*, 10). But he denies this is a specific reference to a collection *per se*: "The Catholic Epistles are not classified as a collection but rather are listed as individual books. . . . Although 1 Peter and 1 John are listed among the recognized books (3.25.1–2), each is attested as a single work by Papias (Eusebius, *Hist eccl* 3.39.17) and Irenaeus (Eusebius, *Hist. eccl.* 5.8.7; Irenaeus, *Haer* 4.9.2; 16.5; 5.7.2; also 1.16.3; 3.16.5, 8), not as Catholic Epistles or as part of a Petrine or Johannine collection" (11).

> λεγομένων καθολικῶν]; nevertheless we know that these letters have been used publicly with the rest [μετὰ τῶν λοιπῶν] in most churches. (*Hist eccl* 2.23.24–25)

Clearly both James and Jude are considered as members of a larger collection of letters called "Catholic," and further, Eusebius indicates that James stood at the front of the collection. Though James' authenticity was disputed due to lack of attestation by the "ancients," both James and Jude nevertheless were "used publicly with the rest in most churches."

John Painter notes that, "James and Jude, the brothers of Jesus, form an inclusion around the [Catholic Epistle] collection," that is, the two brothers of Jesus "form [. . .] the bookends of this collection."[48] And thus,

> That would explain why Eusebius, when he names James as the first of the seven CE, also names Jude, and no other from the collection. To name the first and the last was to identify this collection. This might have been necessary, given that references to a catholic epistle was used in a nonspecific way in earlier sources.[49]

Furthermore, there is an intriguing connection between the ending of James and the ending of Jude. The final exhortation of James, situated just after a discussion of prayer, brings the letter to an abrupt end (almost a non-ending): "My brothers, if anyone among you wanders from the truth and someone brings him back, let him know that whoever brings back a sinner from his wandering will save his soul from death and will cover a multitude of sins" (Jas 5:19–20). Likewise, the final exhortation of Jude (and the Catholic Epistles as a whole) echoes James' call for redeeming an erring brother. "And have mercy on those who doubt [dispute]; save others [them] by snatching them out of the fire; to others [them] show mercy with fear, hating even the garment stained by the flesh" (Jude 22–23). Though the textual and exegetical issues are legion, this final passage just before Jude's benediction could likely be taken as an exhortation to show mercy to the intruders who have been upsetting the faith of the community.[50]

48. Painter, "The Johannine Epistles as Catholic Epistles," 248–49.

49. Ibid., 458 n. 11. Childs argued that the term "catholic epistle" never referred to a (more) "canonical" letter, that the label was not canonically significant in this way; however, contrary to Wall and Nienhuis, this does not mean that Childs denied that the term "Catholic Epistles" referred to a discrete collection of letters within the New Testament canon (see Lockett "Are the Catholic Epistles a Canonically Significant Collection," 74–76).

50. See Lockett, "Objects of Mercy."

Attending to the canonical context of James—reading James along with its near neighbors in the final form of the canon—is a necessary step in understanding the meaning of James as Christian Scripture. Thus, rather than an approach secondary to grammatical-historical investigation—or as a reality anachronistic to the meaning of the New Testament texts themselves—the canonical context is equally necessary for a right understanding of the Epistle of James as Christian Scripture.

Conclusion

The aim of the above reflection is not to claim that the grammatical-historical approach is unimportant or inconsequential; rather, the goal is to demonstrate that interpretation is left incomplete if the grammatical-historical approach operates on its own. With priority given to grammatical-historical hermeneutic there is a danger of foreshortening the interpretive task—readers will actually miss the meaning of the text.[51] The suspicion for some practitioners of the grammatical-historical approach is that history is granted a foundational ("logically prior") role because history itself is viewed as theologically/philosophically neutral and semi-objective. The unstated implication is that history can play its foundational role because it somehow gives the interpreter clear and unambiguous facts about (access to) the author's intentions and therefore the meaning of the text. This view is problematic for three reasons.

First, history is not a neutral category. Though Blomberg recognizes that history can be used as either tool or weapon, the way in which he defines the grammatical-historical hermeneutic demonstrates an assumed objectivity regarding history.[52] The implied objectivity of history is expressed in the notion that the interpreter can preform objective historical analysis without theological convictions operating in the background. However, theological convictions about what Scripture *is* should instead influence how one understands history's definition and function in interpretation.

In light of, or perhaps because of, this view of history, second, is a concern that grammatical-historical analysis is taken as the sum total or

51. Leithart similarly notes: "We can reconstruct a fixed historical event form remaining sources, and we can reconstruct the original meaning of a text form the available evidence. When we have explored this dimension of the meaning of a text, though, we are only beginning to explore the text's full meaning. It is a necessary beginning, but it is not the end. Interpretation is never simply paraphrase" (*Deep Exegesis*, 46).

52. Blomberg rightly emphasizes the influence of Ernst Troeltsch's three principles of criticism that continue to animate much of modern historical-critical work ("Historical-Critical/Grammatical View," 27–29).

perhaps the first and only *necessary* step in textual interpretation. It is necessary to investigate the "natural properties" of the text—its grammar, genre, and compositional context. Yet, this essay shares Webster's concern:

> For a Christian theological account of Scripture, the problem . . . is a matter not so much of what is affirmed but what is denied. The problem, that is, is not the affirmation that the biblical texts have a "natural history", but the denial that the texts with a "natural history" may function within the communicative divine economy, and that such a function is ontologically definitive of the text.[53]

Taking account of the text's "natural history" is necessary but not sufficient. A grammatical-historical hermeneutic must take up theological and canonical insights alongside of the historical and lexical.

Finally, Augustine noted long ago in reading Christian Scripture that signs (words of Scripture) point to things (the truth of Scripture). Grammatical-historical interpretation, as defined by Blomberg, runs the risk of confusing sign with thing. In other words, the grammatical-historical approach is prone to conflate the "signs" (words of Scripture) with the "thing" itself (the truth of Scripture). That is, the natural meaning of human words and customs become the focal point of textual meaning where human authors, along with their intentions, demarcate the limits of textual meaning and thus run the risk of reducing the truth of God (the thing signified) to the mere historical/human words (signs). "To simplify matters rather drastically" John Webster notes, "a dominant trajectory in the modern development of study of the Bible has been a progressive concentration on what Spinoza called interpretation of Scripture *ex ipsius historia*, out of its own history." This historical emphasis, starting with Spinoza, understands "the natural properties of the biblical text and of the skills of interpreters are elements in an immanent economy of communication." Webster continues:

> The biblical text is a set of human signs born along on, and in turn shaping, social, religious and literary processes; the enumeration of its natural properties comes increasingly to be not only a necessary but a sufficient description of the Bible and its reception.[54]

Herein is the problem. Meaning is reduced to an enumeration of the text's natural properties. Recognizing that the words of Scripture (sign) refer not only to historical realities, but ultimately to God's true self-revelation

53. Webster, *Holy Scripture*, 19.

54. Webster, *Domain of the Word*, 5.

(thing) would force hermeneutical realignment within the grammatical-historical approach.[55]

The historical author's intention is necessary, yet is not sufficient for understanding the meaning of Christian Scripture.[56] The Epistle of James speaks in a way that both gives room for and envisions readers who are more remote from the text's original readers (both geographically and chronologically). As the letter, in a sense, speaks beyond its historical-cultural audience, James must be read in its canonical and theological context alongside its grammatical-historical context in order to interpret the letter as Christian Scripture.

Working with Hirsch's concept of "transhistorical intention,"[57] namely where an author intends to address readers in contexts other than the author's own, Kevin Vanhoozer notes the possibility for Scripture to speak beyond its original readers. Vanhoozer argues: "My thesis is that the 'fuller meaning' of Scripture—the meaning associated with divine authorship—emerges only at the level of the whole canon."[58] And he concludes:

> *If we are reading the Bible as the Word of God, therefore, I suggest that the context that yields this maximal sense is the canon, taken as a unified communicative act.* The books of Scripture, taken individually, may anticipate the whole, but the canon alone is its *instantiation*. If God is taken to be the divine author . . . then it is the canon as a whole that becomes the communicative act that needs to be described.[59]

55. Webster poses a helpful analogy: "There is a parallel here with the elements in the Lord's Supper. Bread and wine are signs in the economy of salvation; by them the ascended Christ distributes the benefits of his saving achievement, comforting and nourishing his people by his presence. These functions do not detract from the created materiality of the elements, but indicate, rather, that such created realities are taken up into the divine service. So also Holy Scripture: prophetic and apostolic words are no less creaturely for being servants of the divine Word; indeed, their creaturely nature is therein fulfilled. It is a bad dualist habit which assumes that scriptural texts are most basically products of a religious-cultural world to be investigated as such, and only secondarily describable as prophetic and apostolic testimony" (*Domain of the Word*, 121).

56. See Poythress, "Dispensing with Merely Human Meaning"; and Toom, "Was Augustine and Intentionalist?".

57. Hirsch, "Transhistorical Intentions."

58. Vanhoozer, *Is There a Meaning in This Text?*, 264. Furthermore, Leithart provocatively argues that texts can have "transhistorical meaning" that is not necessarily tided to an author's "transhistorical intention" (see *Deep Exegesis*, chapter 2). I owe this insight and expression to Carl Mosser.

59. Vanhoozer, *Is There a Meaning in This Text?*, 265.

Thus, both "fuller meaning" and discernment of the divine author's meaning are founded upon reading Scripture in light of the canon.

Theological convictions regarding Scripture will reorient, though never reject, the hermeneutical importance of the historical author and the historical context of a text. The above discussion raises the issue of whether James should be read in isolation from the rest of its canonical neighbors, taking its unique historical situation as the single, determinative context for its interpretation, or whether the fact that James is placed within the discrete collection (Catholic Epistles) specifically and its placement within the New Testament generally should constitute a further (and necessary) context within which it is interpreted. To be clear, the question here raises the issue of whether subsequent judgments regarding canon *clarify* or *obscure* the meaning of these texts. This essay concludes that theological judgments regarding the canonical context of Scripture are necessary for rightly understanding the meaning of the text. In short, the theological description and canonical context of Scripture is not somehow anachronistic or secondary to its historical context. Therefore, theological and canonical concerns must take equal priority alongside of grammatical-historical concerns in the exegetical process in order to interpret James (or any other biblical text) as Christian Scripture.

Bibliography

Barton, John. *The Nature of Biblical Criticism*. Louisville: Westminster John Knox, 2007.

Barton, Stephen C. "Early Christianity and the Sociology of the Sect," in *The Open Text: New Directions for Biblical Studies?*, edited by Francis Watson, 140–62. London: SCM, 1993.

Bauckham, Richard. *James: Wisdom of James, Disciple of Jesus the Sage*. London: Routledge, 1999.

———. "Pseudo-Apostolic Letters," *Journal of Biblical Literature* 107 (1988) 469–94.

Blomberg, Craig L. "The Historical-Critical/Grammatical View." In *Biblical Hermeneutics: Five Views*, edited by Stanley E. Porter and Beth M. Stovell, 27–47. Downers Grove, IL: InterVarsity, 2012.

Blomberg, Craig L., and Mariam J. Kamell. *James*. ZECNT. Grand Rapids: Zondervan, 2008.

Brosend, William. *James and Jude*. NCBC. Cambridge: Cambridge University Press, 2004.

Brown, Jeannine K. *Introduction to Biblical Hermeneutics: Scripture as Communication*. Grand Rapids: Baker Academic, 2007.

Carson, D. A. "Theological Interpretation of Scripture: Yes, But . . . ." In *Theological Commentary: Evangelical Perspectives*, edited by R. Michael Allen, 187–207. London: T. & T. Clark, 2011.

Cheung, Luke L. *The Genre, Composition and Hermeneutics of James*. Carlisle: Paternoster, 2003.

Davids, Peter H. *The Epistle of James*. NIGTC. Grand Rapids: Eerdmans, 1982.

Dibelius, Martin and H. Greeven. *James: A Commentary on the Epistle of James*. Translated by M. Williams. Philadelphia: Fortress, 1976.

Fee, Gordon D., and Douglas Stewart. *How to Read the Bible for All It's Worth*. 3rd ed. Grand Rapids: Zondervan, 2003.

Fowl, Stephen E. *Theological Interpretation of Scripture*. Eugene, OR: Wipf & Stock, 2009.

Gammie, John G. "Paraenetic Literature: Toward the Morphology of a Secondary Genre." *Semeia* 50 (1990) 41–81.

Harrisville, Roy A. *Pandora's Box Opened: An Examination and Defense of Historical-Critical Method and Its Master Practitioners*. Grand Rapids: Eerdmans, 2014.

Hirsch, E. D. "Transhistorical Intentions and the Persistence of Allegory." *New Literary History* 25 (1994) 549–67.

———. *Validity in Interpretation*. New Haven: Yale, 1967.

Johnson, L. T. *Brother of Jesus, Friend of God: Studies in the Letter of James*. Grand Rapids: Eerdmans, 2004.

Laws, S. *A Commentary on the Epistle of James*. HNTC. San Francisco: Harper & Row, 1980.

Leithart, Peter. *Deep Exegesis: The Mystery of Reading Scripture*. Waco, TX.: Baylor University Press, 2009.

Levenson, Jon D. *The Hebrew Bible, the Old Testament, and Historical Criticism: Jews and Christians in Biblical Studies*. Louisville: Westminster John Knox, 1993.

Lockett, Darian R. "Are the Catholic Epistles a Canonically Significant Collection? A Status Quaestionis." *Currents in Biblical Research* 14 (2015) 62–80.

———. *Letters from the Pillar Apostles: The Formation of the Catholic Epistles as a Canoncial Collection*. Eugene, OR.: Pickwick, 2016.

———. "Objects of Mercy in Jude: The Prophetic Background of Jude 22–23." *Catholic Biblical Quarterly* 77 (2015) 322–36.

———. "Structure or Communicative Strategy?: The 'Two Ways' Motif in James' Theological Instruction." *Neotestamentica* 42.2 (2008) 269–87.

———. "Why Have We Stopped Reading the Catholic Epistles Together? A Reception History of an Early Collection." In *Christian Origins and the Establishment of the Early Jesus Movement*, edited by Stanley E. Porter and Andrew W. Pitts. Early Christianity in its Hellenistic Context 4. Leiden: Brill, forthcoming.

Maynard-Reid, Pedrito U. *Poverty and Wealth in James*. Maryknoll, NY: Orbis, 1987.

McKnight, Scot. *Letter of James*. NICNT. Grand Rapids: Eerdmans, 2011.

Moo, Douglas J. *The Letter of James*. PNTC. Grand Rapids: Eerdmans, 2000.

Niebuhr, Karl-Wilhelm. "Der Jakobusbrief im Licht frühjüdischer Diasporabriefe." *New Testament Studies* 44 (1998) 420–43.

———. *Gesetz und Paränese. Katechismusartige Weisungsreihen in der frühjüdischen Literatur*. WUNT 2.28. Tübingen: Mohr Siebeck, 1987.

Nienhuis, David R. and Robert W. Wall. *Reading The Epistles of James, Peter, John, and Jude as Scripture: The Shaping and Shape of a Canonical Collection*. Grand Rapids: Eerdmans, 2013.

Osborn, Grant. *The Hermeneutical Spiral: A Comprehensive Introduction to Biblical Interpretation*. 2nd ed. Downers Grove, IL: InterVarsity, 2006.

Painter, John, and David A. deSilva. *James and Jude*. Paideia Commentary Series on the New Testament; Grand Rapids: Baker, 2012.

Painter, John. "The Johannine Epistles as Catholic Epistles." In *The Catholic Epistles and Apostolic Tradition*, edited by Karl-Wilhelm Niebuhr and Robert W. Wall, 239–305. Waco, TX: Baylor University Press, 2009.

Penner, Todd. *James and Eschatology: Re-reading an Ancient Christian Letter*. JSNTSup 121. Sheffield: Sheffield Academic Press, 1996.

Perdue, Leo. "The Social Character of Paraenesis and Paraenetic Literature." *Semeia* 50 (1990) 5–39.

Poirier, John C. "'Theological Interpretation' and its Contradistinctions." *Tyndale Bulletin* 61 (2010) 105–18.

Poythress, Vern S. "Dispensing with Merely Human Meaning: Gains and Losses from Focusing on the Human Author, Illustrated by Zephaniah 1:2–3." *Journal of the Evangelical Theological Society* 57 (2014) 481–99.

Rae, Murray A. *History and Hermeneutics*. London: T. & T. Clark, 2005.

Stowers, Stanley K. *Letter Writing in Greco-Roman Antiquity*. Library of Early Christianity. Philadelphia: Westminster John Knox, 1986.

Treier, Daniel J. "Biblical Theology and/or Theological Interpretation of Scripture?" *Scottish Journal of Theology* 61 (2008) 16–31.

———. *Introducing Theological Interpretation of Scripture: Recovering a Christian Practice*. Grand Rapids: Baker, 2008.

Trimm, Charlie. "Evangelicals, Theology, and Biblical Interpretation: Reflections on the Theological Interpretation of Scripture." *Bulletin of Biblical Research* 20 (2010) 379–98.

Toom, Tarmo. "Was Augustine and Intentionalist? Authorial Intentions in Augustine's Hermeneutics." *Studia Patristica* 54 (2012) 1–9.

Vanhoozer, Kevin. *Is There a Meaning in This Text?: the Bible, the Reader, and the Literary Morality of Literary Knowledge*. Grand Rapids: Zondervan, 1998.

Voss, Hank. "From 'Grammatical-historical Exegesis' to 'Theological Exegesis': Five Essential Practices." *Evangelical Review of Theology* 37 (2013) 140–52.

Wachob, Wesley Hiram. *The Voice of Jesus in the Social Rhetoric of James*. SNTSMS 106; Cambridge: Cambridge University Press, 2000.

Wall, Robert W. *Community of the Wise: The Letter of James*. New Testament in Context; Valley Forge, PA.: Trinity, 1997.

Webster, John. *The Domain of the Word: Scripture and Theological Reason*. London: T. & T. Clark, 2012.

———. *Holy Scripture: A Dogmatic Sketch*. Cambridge: Cambridge University Press, 2003.

Witherington, Benjamin. *Letters and Homilies for Jewish Christians*. Downers Grove, IL: InterVarsity, 2007.

5

Against Historicism

The Rule of Faith, Scripture, and Baptismal Historiography in Second-Century Lyons

D. Jeffrey Bingham

This is a study of different historiographies, different hermeneutical perspectives: one ancient and ecclesiological, one modern and secular. I present it as a means of clarifying the difference between two paradigms in order to encourage discussion about methodological origins and presuppositions among readers of Scripture.

Not too long ago, a former student asked me the following question: "If you were to write a contemporary *Adversus haereses*, what would you put in the place of *haereses*?" We were in a taxi and just getting ready to exit, so I thought quickly and said, "Well, I guess it would have to be historicism." My answer at that point was quick and not well thought through. The question and response were quickly forgotten as we went on to enjoy our sushi dinner. But, I have come back to it in my own mind repeatedly, and I think my first instinct was right. I'm against historicism. So, where Irenaeus had his heresies that bubbled forth from the fount of Valentinus, Marcus, Cerinthus, and the "gnostics," I have my historicism, my Ranke, and my Meinecke. I say this, of course, somewhat tongue in cheek. But my point is still quite serious. The historiography of historicism and its hermeneutic have resulted in an approach to history, Scripture, and early Christianity that is disconnected from ecclesiology. The idea of the community of the Spirit, as a unique, privileged group of readers of Scripture, has been disavowed by historicism.

I present the approach of Irenaeus of Lyons as a contrast to historicism and as a thoroughly ecclesiological model of historiography and hermeneutics.

Historicism: A Modern Model

Ranke's Historicism

Ranke was the sometime theorist of nineteenth-century historicism. In his 1830s essay, "On the Character of Historical Science," we find him expressing his thoughts on the differences between philosophy and history. His aim is to establish that history, in contrast to philosophy, is a science and to justify it "against the claims of philosophy."[1] On the one hand, the philosopher, incorrectly, begins with a truth, external to the epoch or epochs under consideration. By means of this presupposed concept, the philosopher constructs all of history in a manner that is peculiarly related to the preconception. The philosopher, therefore, "subordinates the very events" to the untested, but organizing idea.[2] Only through such subordination does the philosopher recognize the veracity of history. The result, however, is "a mere construct of history."[3] With the philosopher's approach, Ranke says, "It would never be possible to reach certainty about the course of universal history through the study of history."[4] The problem of the philosopher, for Ranke, is also the problem of the early theologians, at least the earlier ones. In their case, a few revealed propositions controlled their attempt to interpret the fullness of phenomena. Either procedure, philosophical or theological, in his thinking, prevents us from arriving at a comprehensive account of history in which we might have confidence. Either procedure causes history to lose "an inherent interest of its own" and erases the value of studying history, "since it would already be implicit in the philosophic concept."[5] If either way were retained in historiography, "history would lose all scientific footing and character."[6]

The historian, on the other hand, puts aside the "speculative concept," "the supreme idea."[7] In their place the historian takes up "deducing the diversity of phenomena," "the conditions of existence," "particular interest,"

1. Ranke, "On the Character of Historical Science," 9.
2. Ibid., 10.
3. Ibid.
4. Ibid.
5. Ibid.
6. Ibid.
7. Ibid., 10–11.

"the particular," and that which exists in the past.[8] He advocates an interest and value in each historical particular in place of a universal preconception. It is on this note that we hear him saying to Maximillian II of Bavaria, rather religiously, "Every epoch is immediate to God, and its worth is not based on what derives from it but rests in its own existence, in its own self."[9] Ranke puts history's focus upon the individual and the particular together this way:

> While the philosopher, viewing history from his vantage point, seeks infinity merely in progression, development, and totality, history recognizes something infinite in every existence: in every condition, in every being, something eternal, coming from God; and this is its vital principle.[10]

His religious language continues as he describes history's allegiance to contemplation over presupposition, an allegiance that betrays a hierarchy between phenomena, the concrete, and the abstract: "History elevates, gives significance to, and hallows the phenomenal world, in and by itself, because of what it contains."[11] It is not that Ranke lacks appreciation for universal connection or the causal nexus. He holds to the teleological education of humanity through history, having as he did, belief in both panentheism, and, in continuity with his Lutheran heritage, divine providence. He affirms connections between factors in particular, diverse phenomena. He wants to work toward the unreachable human goal of an account of universal history. Rather, even with his loyalty to the moral supremacy of his own form of Christianity, he seeks such interrelatedness, such totality, free from prejudice, or what he terms, "pure cognition undulled by preconceived notions."[12] He wishes to portray the richness of individual events with utter objectivity and impartiality. Against subjectivity and rhetorical flourish, Ranke, through exhaustive research into particulars, was on a quest for how "it had really been (*wie es eigentlich gewesen*)," for "naked truth without ornamentation."[13]

8. Ibid.

9. Ranke, "On the Progress of History," 21. Friedrich Meinecke will cite these words in the conclusion to his essay, "Values and Causalities in History," 288.

10. Ranke, "On the Character of Historical Science," 11.

11. Ibid., 12.

12. Ibid., 13.

13. Ranke, *Geschichten der romanischen und germanischen Völker von 1494 bis 1514*, vii; Ranke, "Preface to the First Edition of *Histories of the Latin and Germanic Peoples*," 86; Ranke, *Zur Kritik neuerer Geschichtschreiber*, 24.

Meinecke's Historicism

Meinecke defended and developed Ranke's theory, though he did not share Ranke's optimism in teleology. In his essay, "Values and Causalities in History (1928)," we find a formative expression of his thought in relation to Ranke's. His concern is to maintain the validity in historical method of searching for, comprehending, and expositing both causalities and values, both the sphere of natural, earthly agencies and the sphere of divinity, spiritual life, morals, ideals, however one conceives them. Against the temptation to ignore the necessary balance between the two he writes, "no causalities without values, no values without causalities."[14] In his mind, though Wilhelm von Humboldt inaugurated the notion of history moving toward spiritual values founded upon the inquiry of causes, it was Ranke who achieved the perfect balance, for Ranke "sought God in history."

The methodological direction that Meinecke wished to take the discipline was one that gravitated toward ideal values through "delight in concrete reality," and "contact with the soil."[15] The ideal, spiritual values were to be discovered by savoring the individual phenomenon, the "inherent value of historical individualities."[16] In this way, it is "history's own value which becomes valuable to us."[17] Historians are to practice "the pure appreciation of historical individualities."[18] Ranke's approach of "indefinable finesse" and "artistic intuition" in interpreting individual phenomena was to remain unstained by the philosopher's dubious "logical-abstract procedures" or "transcendental solution" or subjectivism.[19]

Ranke and Meinecke propose, then, a historiography that grants insight into values and ideals, the spiritual, the moral, the divine. They are only glimpsed, however, through the pure investigation of historical individualities, the particular, earthly, natural and transitory phenomena, free from preconceptions.[20] The two basic ideas, which together characterize the approach of Ranke's historicism, are "individuality and individual development."[21] In this development, which is never straight or calculable,

14. Meinecke, "Values and Causalities in History," 276.

15. Ibid., 276–77.

16. Ibid., 280, 283.

17. Ibid., 284.

18. Ibid.

19. Ibid., 270, 276, 278, 282.

20. Hinrichs, "Introduction," l. "In history, we do not see God, we only sense his presence in the clouds that surround him" (Meinecke, *Werke*, vol. 1. *Die Idee der Staatsräson in der neueren Geschichte*, 510; trans. Anderson, *Historism*, L).

21. Meinecke, "Leopold von Ranke," 504.

there constantly appear new individualities, and thereby new values, that are temporal, natural, plastic, fluctuating and ever fresh, and therefore never absolute, but always "relative and conditioned."[22]

Historicism and Biblical Studies

Our investigation into historicism is not unrelated to biblical and early Christian studies.[23] Following Ranke's emphasis on discovery of the facts, how "it had actually been," biblical scholars, in addition to criticism of their linguistic sources sought to reconstruct the context out of which their sources arose. Here they were interested in discovering the "piety and *real* religious life" of the societies that would produce these documents.[24] In many cases the historical reliability of biblical texts was questioned in the search for what had actually happened. Fueled by Ranke's thirst for brute facts they attempted to penetrate behind what many saw as pre-modern, scientifically untrustworthy, non-historical sources.[25] Hermann Gunkel, for example, saying that the historian takes joy in reality and in describing "real life," quoted Ranke's formula, contrasted history and legend, and wrote, from the perspective of form criticism, of the "legends of Genesis."[26] David Friederich Strauss' confident composition, *The Life of Jesus*, is another case in point. Following Ranke's quest for what really happened through a commitment to objectivity, he criticized earlier studies for inadequate analysis of the documents and concluded that the Gospel narratives were largely myth.[27] In Göttingen, we may even speak of the Rankean "school." In the rationalist intellectual tradition of Ranke we may place H. G. A. Ewald with his belief that the Pentateuch preserves some historical memory while including imaginative components.[28]Ewald's student and successor, Julius Wellhausen, employed source criticism in order to determine the reliable bases for reconstructing Israel's history. Guided by Ranke's principle in his

22. Ibid., 504–5; Hinrichs, "Introduction," xlix–l; Meinecke, *Schaffender* Spiegel, 84–85.

23. Scholtz, "The Phenomenon of 'Historicism,'" 64–89. For Ranke's influence on historical method in the study of ancient history, see Finley, *Ancient History*, 47–66.

24. Scholtz, "The Phenomenon of 'Historicism,'" 85. Italics added.

25. Provan, "Hearing the Historical Books," 256.

26. Gunkel, "Geschichtsschreibung im AT," 2:1350 (4b); Gunkel, *The Legends of Genesis*, 3–4, 37.

27. Reventlow, *History of Biblical Interpretation, vol.* 4, 305–6; Davaney, *Historicism,* 49–51.

28. Miller II, "Quest of the Historical Israel," 830; Miller, "Reading the Bible Historically," 23.

procedure, he concluded that the Pentateuch and its sources were unreliable for understanding Israel's history prior to the monarchy.[29]

Furthermore, influenced by the prominence of the idea of universality in Ranke's concept of historical method, biblical studies took interest in a diversity of ancient cultures and their supposed influence on biblical texts.[30] The study of the religion of ancient Israel, by means of the biblical writings, now required comparison with other religions and this broadened the disciplines in which biblical scholars would need to have proficiency as they sought respectability within the scientific community. As historians of religion they required skills in disciplines both philological and historical. And as biblical studies drew nearer to the history of religions they departed more and more from the life of the Church to the degree that Gunkel, in 1903, would speak of a "deplorable alienation" between the two.[31] This same tendency of universality in historicism would also impact modern concepts of revelation by moving them away from the uniqueness of the forms attested in biblical record. Ernst Troeltsch argued that the historical method, employed both in biblical studies and in Church history, must recognize the interconnectedness of religions and cultures and "religious intuition or divine revelation" as the root of all religions.[32] For Troeltsch, developing out from Ranke, history cannot establish absolutes, so Christianity cannot thereby be established as the absolute religion. All that can be suggested is that a religion is of supreme value for a particular culture. For Ranke and others who held to the teleology of history, however, the unique value of Judaism or Christianity was more certain.[33] Historicism, in the ways it influenced biblical studies, led away from the reliability of the biblical texts and the unique, supernatural identity of Christianity. The religion is seen as purely mundane and must be interpreted only within the context of other mundane religions. So, too, its texts are made merely mundane and "what really happened" is accessible only outside of them.

29. "What *must* have happened [according to Nöldeke] is of less consequence to know than what actually took place." Wellhausen, *Prologomena to the History of Israel*, 46. Italics original. Cf. Ska, "The History of Israel," 338–39. We could mention here also Abraham Kuenen, Bernhard Stade, and Martin Noth (Sasson, "On Choosing Models," 8–9).

30. Scholtz, "The Phenomenon of 'Historicism,'" 86.

31. *Israel and Babylonien*, 3.

32. Troeltsch, "Historical and Dogmatic Method in Theology," 20.

33. Scholtz, "The Phenomenon of 'Historicism,'" 86–87.

Historicism and Early Christian Studies

In regard to early Christian studies the effect of historicism is just as dramatic. Rather than Ranke, however, our attention now turns to Meinecke. Kurt Rudolph argues that there is

> no support for the notion that there was a "pure and unadulterated" Christianity in a historical sense even in its beginnings. This indeed could not have been the case, since the canonical writings of the New Testament, including the Gospels, and even Jesus himself did not propagate a message that was "pure" and isolated from the surrounding world. For the history of religions, there has never been a "pure religion"; this would be an ahistorical construct. . . . It makes no historical sense to speak of an "essence" of Christianity, except to say that the "essence" of Christianity is its history.[34]

Rudolph, here, is advocating a historiography closest to that of classical historicism linked to Meinecke. In his Haskell Lectures, he contrasts his preferred historiography to the Hegelian concept of development.[35] Hegel, in his *Lectures on the History of Philosophy* (1892), had argued for a particular conception of "development" which finds its most helpful analogy in the field of horticulture.[36] For him, "the germ cannot remain merely implicit, but is impelled towards development," so that it "will produce itself alone and manifest what is contained in it."[37] In development there is both continuity and discontinuity. Although the fruit is different from the original seed, they are also the same. Development, then, has a doubling effect.[38] It is when something implicit becomes explicit, when something is unfolded, unrolled, unwrapped.[39] No novel content has been produced, yet difference exists, and this difference is the result of development.

Rudolph, in his history-of-religions approach, thinks this notion of development is untenable. To his aid he calls Meinecke with whom he offers an alternative understanding of development. As he points out in his analysis of Meinecke, the notion of development within historicism differs from that of the idealism of Hegel; it is not purely organistic, natural, or

34. Rudolph, "Early Christianity as A Religious-Historical Phenomenon," 17 and 17 n. 40.

35. Rudolph, *Historical Fundamentals and the Study of Religions*, 87–92.

36. Hegel, *Hegel's Lectures on the History of Philosophy*, 20–22.

37. Ibid., 22.

38. Ibid.

39. Ibid., 21; Rudolph, *Historical Fundamentals and the Study of Religions*, 88.

necessary.[40] Instead, Meinecke sees development as "an uninterrupted continuity of activity" resulting primarily from the creative, ineffable power of the individual within the dynamic drama of particular historical circumstances.[41] In Meinecke's, as in Ranke's historicism, "Individual historical development is no mere evolution of tendencies already present in the germ cell. Rather does it possess a large measure of plasticity, of capacity to change and be regenerated as it is worked upon by the ever-changing forces of time."[42] To a concept of biological development, historicism adds individuality and plasticity. Specific historical factors can bring change to forms.[43] The development of early Christianity, then, for Rudolph must be understood within the parameters of classical historicism as a pattern of individualized interpretations of Jesus effected by the freedom and necessity within dynamic historical situatedness.[44] It is important to note, in order to bring the ramifications of historicism up to date, that its values also inform the theses of Walter Bauer and Bart Ehrman.[45] Ehrman reveals his hand when he recounts the historiography that led to Bauer's claims.[46] He employs Albert Schweitzer to speak in a positive way of Hermann Reimarus' Rankean-like quest to "establish what really happened." Also, he introduces a basis for the "widely recognized" assumption that the historical accuracy of Acts is questionable by relating F. C. Bauer's belief that Acts is not an account of "what actually happened" due to its late and catholic composition.

The Baptismal Rule of Lyons: An Ancient Model

Ranke, according to Meinecke, was attempting to address the ancient problem of how to account for the ideal and the real.[47] He was investigating how the mundane, in its particulars, could manifest the celestial. If we put it in terms of eternal and temporal, heavenly and earthly, Creator and creature, spirit and flesh, it is the same problem that Irenaeus of Lyons and his opponents were attempting to address in the second century. Both, however, began their different accounts with dominant, unchanging metanarratives. The metanarratives may be different from sect to sect, community to com-

40. Rudolph, *Historical Fundamentals and the Study of Religions*, 90–91.

41. Meinecke, "Ein Wort über geschichtliche Entwicklung," 96–97.

42. Meinecke, *Historism*, 504.

43. Ibid., 3.

44. Rudolph, "Early Christianity as a Religious-Historical Phenomenon," 18–19.

45. Bauer, *Orthodoxy and Heresy in Earliest Christianity*, xxii–xxiv.

46. Ehrman, *Lost Christianities*, 169, 172.

47. Meinecke, "Leopold von Ranke," 508-10.

munity, between Valentinian, Sethian, and Thomasine, but they held the necessity of received interpretive metanarratives in common.

Historicism's way of dealing with the problem was to proceed as if the spiritual was to be discovered within concrete, earthly, historical individualities studied without prejudice. This is a way of solving the problem from below with full confidence in the method and the potential of the phenomena to manifest the ideal. As we have seen, this approach frequently ended up discounting certain data, in particular the biblical, as being historically reliable. Irenaeus's opponents, on the other hand, solve the problem through appeal to myths that disparage the earthly, the creature, and the flesh while exalting the heavenly and pleromatic. The myths serve to explain how the historical particularities are properly comprehended only when the drama of the heavenlies is known. This approach solves the problem from above by means of a received cosmogony. This first model is, in many ways, the opposite of the second. Historicism's satisfaction with what is below and its confidence in a method free from preconception reverses the role of the interpretive myth of the heavenlies in the second. Irenaeus's own model goes a third way.

Irenaeus's Theology of History

Contrary to historicism and the condition lamented by Gunkel, Irenaeus conceived of a historiography that was prejudicially Christian and ecclesiological. The way in which mundane particularities should be read is in light of the Church's one theological Rule, "hypothesis," "preaching," "faith," "Body of Truth," frequently referred to as "the Rule of Truth," that the believer receives through baptism.[48] One begins with the received Rule and from it interprets the historical individualities. The heavenlies are certainly manifested in the mundane. The Father through his Son and Spirit created the mundane, the Son of God has become mundane in history, and the Spirit sanctifies the mundane progressively within history. In Irenaeus's mind the "*datum* of all Christian theology" is redemptive history as presented

48. *Haer.*1.9.4–10.2; 1.22.1; 2.27.1; 3.11.1; 3.12.6; 3.15.1; 4.25.1; *Dem* 1, 3. Cf. Hefner, "Theological Methodology and St. Irenaeus," 298. The critical edition of *Adversus haereses* used throughout this study is: *Irénée de Lyon: Contre les hérésies, Livres 1–5* (hereafter SC), nos. 263, 264 (book 1), 293, 295 (book 2), 210, 211 (book 3), 100.1, 2 (book 4), 152, 153 (book 5). A convenient, yet dated, English translation is available: *Against Heresies, Books 1–5 and Fragments* (referenced below as ANF 1). The critical edition of *Demonstratio (Epideixis)* used is: *The Proof of the Apostolic Preaching, with Seven Fragments*. Cf. *Irénée de Lyon Démonstration de la predication apostolique*, SC 406; *Irénée de Lyon Démonstration de la Prédication apostolique*, SC 62.

in the Scriptures.[49] For Irenaeus, the Scriptures treat selected events in the course of universal history from creation to consummation as they portray God as Creator-Redeemer. They may, within that tapestry of redemptive history, be interested in providing the baptized with an interpretation of only a relatively few number of events. Those few events nonetheless, account for redemption, occur within and as part of the mundane order, and constitute the critical datum. The failure of his opponents, in his opinion, is based on their disparagement of that datum. So with Irenaeus there is no disparagement of the mundane. "The gnostics had seen their salvation as *by* nature, *from* history: Irenaeus sees salvation as *by* history, *in* nature."[50] His theology of history centers on two notions: First, there is the harmony of the disparate components within history that reveals the one, true Creator and Redeemer. Christianity accounts for the Old and the New by demonstrating how there is one divine plan that unites Abraham and Apostles, promise and fulfillment, beginning, middle, and end.[51] Second, there is the anthropological utility of history that reveals the utter difference between Creator and creature and perfects humanity to the glory of God. Through the various economies of history God gradually educates and sanctifies humanity.[52] The unity and utility of the mundane cannot be properly understood or be read as pointing reliably to the ideals it reveals and anticipates without the means of the Church's one Rule. Against his opponents, who, he says, follow neither Scripture nor the apostolic tradition, he posits the Church's singular, trustworthily preserved and received system of truth, the faith, the Gospel.[53]

The Composition of the Rule

Irenaeus's Rule or Body of Truth is composed of different members, different elements of the Church's one faith.[54] He usually only presents selected features of the Rule at any one time and it can be set forth in different types of literature. In an earlier treatment of this question I contrasted didactic literature with narratival, saying that in "one place the Rule can be mainly

49. Markus, "Pleroma and Fulfillment," 219.

50. Ibid.

51. Daniélou, "Saint Irénée et les origeines," 230; Cf. Markus, "Pleroma and Fulfillment," 216–23.

52. Daniélou, "Saint Irénée et les origeines," 229; Markus, "Pleroma and Fulfillment," 212–16; Hitchcock, *Irenaeus of Lugdunum*, 52-64; *Haer.* 4.11.2; 4.37.7; 4.14.3–16.4; 5.1.1; 3.20.1, 2; 5.3.1; 4.38.4; 4.39.1, 2; 5.2.3.

53. *Haer.* 3. Pref. 3.4.2.

54. *Haer.* 1.8.1: "members of the truth."

didactic, while in another, didactic and narrative seem to join, with the narrative providing warrant for the didactic element."[55] I am no longer comfortable with such language or classifications. What I am still comfortable with however, is my earlier assessment that a Trinitarian structure characterizes the Rule, and, that in more polemical contexts, like *Adversus haereses*, Irenaeus prefers "Rule of Truth," while in contexts more catechetical, like the *Demonstration*, he seems to prefer the term "Rule of faith."[56]

This Rule is expressed in different summaries in both *Adversus haereses* 1.10.1 and 1.22.1. In the first summary it is simply called the Church's "faith," and in the second it is named "the Rule of Truth." I will treat the second first.

The Rule in *Adversus haereses* 1.22.1

In the second summary, a rule concerning God is expressed: "The Rule of Truth which we hold, is, that there is one God Almighty, who made all things by His Word, and fashioned and formed, out of that which had no existence, all things which exist." This statement of faith, it appears, Irenaeus inherited from Hermas, *Mandate* 1.1. Immediately, he substantiates this Rule by citing two biblical passages which together testify to the Rule, Psalm 33 [32]: 6 and John 1:3, and then alludes to several others.[57] I reproduce the entire passage for our consideration:

> The Rule of Truth, which we hold, is, that there is one God Almighty, who made all things by His Word, and fashioned and formed, out of that which had no existence, all things that exist (*Mandate* 1.1). The Scripture says, to that effect, "By the Word of the Lord were the heavens established, and all the might of them, by the spirit of His mouth." (Ps 33 [32]: 6) And again, "All things were made by Him, and without Him was nothing made." (John 1:3) There is no exception or deduction stated; but the Father made all things by Him, whether visible or invisible (Col 1:16), objects of sense or of intelligence, temporal, on account of a certain character given them, or eternal; and these eternal things (2 Cor 4:18) He did not make by angels, or by

55. Bingham, "Evangelicals and the Rule of Faith," 161, 161 n. 6: "*Haer.* 1.10.1; 3.3.3; *Dem.* 6."

56. Bingham, "Evangelicals and the Rule of Truth," 161, 161, n. 7: "*Haer.* 1.10.1; 1.22.1 (God and his Word); *Dem.* 6." *Haer.* 1.9.4; *Dem.* 3; Cf. J. Fantino, *La théologie d'Irénée*, 15–22.

57. See *Hermas, Man.* 1; cf. 2 Mac 7:28; Wis 1:14. Other biblical texts contributing to the network through allusion: Col. 1:16; 2 Cor 4:18; Gen 2:7; Matt 22:29; Exod 3:6.

> any powers separated from His Ennœa. For God needs none of all these things, but is He who, by His Word and Spirit Ps 33 [32]: 6; John 1:3), makes, and disposes, and governs all things, and commands all things into existence,—He who formed the world (for the world is of all),—He who fashioned humanity (Gen 2:7),—He [who] is the God of Abraham, and the God of Isaac, and the God of Jacob (Exod 3:6), above whom there is no other God, nor initial principle, nor power, nor pleroma,—He is the Father of our Lord Jesus Christ, as we shall prove. Holding, therefore, this Rule, we shall easily show, not withstanding the great variety and multitude of their opinions that these men have deviated from the truth.

Here we see that in this case, for Irenaeus, the Rule of Truth is a one sentence summary statement of the Church's faith in the one God who creates all things *ex nihilo* by his Word. Following the summary statement, however, he expands its meaning by introducing two quotations of Scripture introduced with "Scripture says." Psalm 33 is from the Old Covenant, the "prophets," while John 1 is from the New Covenant, the "apostles." Psalm 33 echoes the statement's language concerning the unique, omnipotent Lord's creation of all things by his word and introduces the spirit as a second means of creation. John 1:3, building off of the reference to the word in John 1:1, declares the Word of the Father as the means of the creation of all things. These texts support the Church's faith in the one God by naming him "Lord" and by using singular, masculine pronouns. They testify to the belief that he is Almighty by noting that he is the source of the might of the heavens and the author of all things. Their language proves the conviction that he creates by the agency of his Word (and Spirit).

Following these two biblical quotations, our bishop then theologically extrapolates out from them with the aid of additional biblical texts present in allusion. He develops three theological theses. First, he establishes the plenary character of the Lord's creation through his word thereby establishing the Creator's unique omnipotence. All things, with no exceptions, whether visible or invisible, whether temporal or eternal, were created through the agency of his Word. He calls upon Col 1:16 and 2 Cor 4:18 to prove this. Second, he establishes the all-sufficiency of the creative means of the Lord's Word and Spirit and thereby argues for divine aseity. He needs no angels or other powers. To prove this he again employs Col 1:16 and 2 Cor 4:18, but he also harks back to the language of agency in Psalm 33 and John 1. Third, he establishes that the Lord of creation is the one God of both covenants. He is the God of the patriarchs and the Father of Jesus Christ. Here Gen 2:7, Exod 3:6, and several New Testament passages (2 Cor 1:3; Eph 1:3; Col 1:3;

1 Pet 1:3). He then concludes that the Rule of faith just stated and elaborated upon is the standard by which the theological deviation of his opponents will be proven.

The second theological point derived from the expansion of the summary statement deserves a bit more development. Irenaeus must confront a thesis of his opponents. They believe that spiritual forces, spoken of as angels, principalities, dominions, powers, authorities, creators, or gods, formed the world. He connects the belief to Simon the Samaritan, the father of all kinds of heresies, Menander, Saturninus, Basilides, Carpocrates, the Ophites and Sethians.[58] But his opponents, Irenaeus is convinced, have it wrong.[59] God stands in need of nothing. He requires no intermediary powers in order to create. The Father along with his Word, through whom he creates, are alone the incomparable God and Lord.[60] The Father, his Word (and his Spirit) are totally self-sufficient, they are free from need. John 1:3 and Psalm 33 (32): 6 demonstrate that conclusion.[61]

Furthermore, another point, in relation to the brief summary statement and the second theological thesis he extrapolates from it, needs to be made. Recall, if you will, that the brief summary statement comes from *Mandate* 1.1. This text must be theologically interpreted. That is, it must be interpreted in a Christological, Trinitarian manner for it, to the untrained eye appears to be merely monotheistic and monarchian. *Hermas*, in order to provide a statement of the Church's faith, must be supplemented by biblical texts with Christological, Trinitarian content.

Take for instance, its appearance in book 4 of *Adversus haereses*. Here we will review the entire passage where Irenaeus cites Hermas, *Mandate* 1.1:[62]

58. See, e.g., *Haer.* 1.30.5. For the particular representatives see *Haer.* 1.23.2,3, 5 (SC 264:314.42, 48; 318.71; 320.98); 1.24.1–5 (SC 264:320.6, 7; 324.29, 36;326.46, 53, 56; 330.98, 101); 1.25.1, 4 (SC 264:332.2; 338.70, 80). See Epiphanius on the Sethians in *Haer.* 39.1.4 and cf. *Apoc. Jn.* 12.33–13.12; 15.1–19.13. See Valentinus, *Frag. 1*, 57–58, translated as "Fragment C" in Layton, *The Gnostic Scripture*, 235, and cf. Pétrement, *A Separate God*, 365–66. For my earlier discussion of Irenaeus's presentation of this matter, cf. Bingham, "Christianizing Divine Aseity: Irenaeus Reads John," 53–67.

59. For the exegesis of Irenaeus's opponents see *Haer.* 1.8.5 (SC 264:132.152–54); 3.11.1 (SC 211:140.18–142.38); cf. Tri. Trac. 96.17–24; 114.7–10; Clem. Alex. *Exc. Ex Theod.* 6.1–4. For the variety in Gnostic exegesis see E. H. Pagels, *The Johannine Gospel in Gnostic Exegesis*, 20–35.

60. Haer. 2.2.5 (SC 294:40.70–73); cf. Rousseau, SC 293:212; 3.8.2–3 (SC 211:94.45– 96.77).

61 *Haer.* 1.22.1 (SC 264:308.6–7, 14–15); 2.2.4–5 (SC 294:38.52–57, 65–40.73); 3.8.3 (SC 211:94.53–54, 73–74); 4.20.1 (SC 100.2:626.17–19); 4.32.1 (SC 100.2:798.20–21; *Cfr.* 4.32.2 [SC 100.2:800.40]).

62. *Haer.* 4.20.2 (SC 100.2: 628.24-33; Fr. Gr. 8.1-3).

> Rightly, then, [do we learn from] the Scripture (γραφή; *scriptura*) which said, 'First, above all, believe that there is only one God, who has created (κτίζω; *constituo*) and completed (καταρτίζω; *consummo*) all things, who has made (*facio*) all things to exist from nothing so that they might exist, who contains all things, and yet is contained by nothing.'[63] Rightly, also, from among the prophets, Malachi said: 'Is there not only one God who has created us? Do we not all have only one Father?'[64] Also, in accordance with these witnesses, the apostle rightly said, 'There is one God, the Father, who is above all, and in us all.'[65] In like manner, the Lord also said: 'All things have been handed over to me by my Father.'[66]

Irenaeus introduces his citation of Hermas's teaching on the unique Creator by identifying it as "Scripture," (γραφή; *scriptura*). Immediately following the words of Hermas are citations from Malachi, introduced as a prophet, Paul, introduced as an apostle, and Jesus, from Matthew, introduced as the Lord. The words of the Apostolic Father are joined to the words of a prophet, an apostle, and the Lord into a cento all of which contribute to the Church's faith that both Testaments proclaim that the Creator is the Father.[67] The texts of Mal 2:10, Eph 4:6, and Matt 11:27, and the preceding texts of Gen 1:26, 2:7 and John 1:1–3, are added to *Mandate* 1.1 because they make explicit that which is only implicit in *Hermas*: the one Creator of the Church's faith is the Father who creates by his Son and Spirit.[68] In addition to his emphasis on one Creator, Hermas's particular contribution comes in his three verbs that describe the Creator's act: create, make, complete. By means of the more explicit biblical witnesses, Irenaeus must interpret *Mandate* 1.1, to proclaim the common creative activity of the Three: the Father who creates, the Son who makes, and the Spirit who completes.[69] Three of

63. Hermas, *Mand.* 1.1. This translation takes account of Rousseau's later, corrective note in the 1979 critical edition and translation of *Haer.* 1 (SC 263, 264) that reflects back on the earlier 1965 edition and translation of *Haer.* 4 (SC 100.1, 100.2). For the corrective note (which takes into account the allusion to Wis 1:13, 14) concerning SC 264: 309, n.1 (*Haer.* 1.22.1) see SC 263: 276.

64. Mal 2:10.

65. Eph 4:6.

66. Matt 11:27.

67. A. Orbe, *Teología de San Ireneo IV*, 277.

68. In *Haer.* 4.20.1-3, before and after the cento, he will allude to John 1:3 and cite Gen 2:7; 1:26; Acts 10:42; Rev 3:7; Prov 3:19–20; 8:22–25 and 8:27–31 in support of his thesis, introducing the second Genesis text as the words of the Father to his Son and Spirit, and the Proverbs passage as the words of Solomon.

69. Fantino, *La théologie* d'Irénée, 284–85; 295–96.

the above biblical texts will be used in other occurrences of *Mandate* 1.1 for the same theological purpose.[70]

We find this same pattern repeated. Irenaeus, in two other places, freely reproduces the language of *Mandate* 1.1 while he introduces additional biblical and theological language into the material from *Hermas*.[71] In one, he adds specific mention of the Father. In the other, he adds, by means of Hebrews 1:3, the notion of the Father's Word as the Agent of creation ('by the Word of his power') and inserts as well the role of the Father's Wisdom in creation ('by his Wisdom'). Irenaeus must contribute, on his own, the concepts of the Father, Son, and Spirit (Wisdom) to Hermas's statement. The results are remarkable theological statements that, within the extended contexts, he expands into the Church's Trinitarian faith on God and creation. As he develops his thought out from his free, amended versions of *Mandate* 1.1, he makes allusions to an abundance of biblical material.[72] References to Psalm 32 [33]: 6; Eph 4:6; and Matt 11:27 are most useful.[73]

It is important for us to note that Irenaeus believes that the summative statement of the Rule of Truth derives from Scripture, although it is from Hermas, *Mandate* 1.1, and that he interprets it Christianly, by means of Scripture. In effect, he says, we confess such and such about God because Scripture says such and such. Indeed, to use his words, the prophetic and apostolic Scriptures furnish "proof" for the ecclesiological faith, tradition and practice, while the heretics have no such "proof" for theirs.[74] Furthermore, in the mind of our bishop, the "proofs contained in the Scriptures cannot be shown except from the Scriptures themselves."[75]

As we noted above, the historical particularities with which Irenaeus is peculiarly interested are those that are part of Scripture's collective presentation of redemptive history. Here his interest has been the event of creation and God's relationship to it. So his historiography involves employing summative statements of the Rule in conjunction with Scriptural material that further expounds the summative statement, in order to understand the

70. Ps 32 [33]: 6; Eph 4:6; Matt 11:27.

71. *Haer.* 2.30.9 (SC 294: 221–26); *Dem.* 4. Irenaeus, *The Proof of the Apostolic Preaching with Seven Fragments*, [10] 662–[11] 663). Cf. Rousseau's note (SC 293: 333–34).

72. See SC 294:321–23, nn. b–I; Irenaeus, *On the Apostolic Preaching*, 43, nn. a-d; and PO 12.5: pp. [11] 663, nn. 2–4, for a list of citations and allusions.

73. Psalm 32 [33]: 6 is found in *Haer.* 1.22.1; 4.20.2; and *Dem.* 4; Eph 4:6 is found in both *Haer.* 4.20.2 and *Dem.* 4; Matt 11:27 is found in both *Haer.* 4.20.2 and 2.30.9.

74. *Haer.* 2.32.5; 2.35.4; 3.Pref.1; 3.5.1; 3.11.7; 3.12.9; 3.21.1, 3; 4.24.1; 4.34.5; 5.Pref.; 5.14.4; 2.28.8; 2.30.5, 7; 5.18.1.

75. *Haer.* 3.12.9.

events that Scripture addresses. Before we proceed to examination of the second summary statement of the Church's faith, we need to better understand the function of summative statements within catechesis.

Summative Statements and Catechetical Hermeneutics

The Church has its own belief about God and God's relation to creation. It has its own faith concerning the origin of creation, its nature, its corruption, and redemption. It has its own tradition about revelation. This faith, this tradition has been preserved and handed down only within the Church, and it is substantiated and validated only by the Scriptures. Irenaeus may place before his readers short summary statements of the Church's Rule, in language that is particularly familiar to his community. But, he has in mind so much more than is explicitly stated. His explicit statement is pregnant with implicit beliefs. R. Rendall helps us understand the phenomena I am speaking about as he discusses the New Testament's usage of the Old. He alerts us to the reality that brief quotations within communities would have evoked the entire conceptual backgrounds of such texts and would have set off a chain reaction of related, complementary passages. He wrote,

> Quotations from the Old Testament in the New are commonly taken as isolated proof-texts only or as brief verbal prophecies that have found technical fulfillment. Occasionally too we may find it difficult to see their relevance to the later historical context. But this may only be because a superficial view is taken of the writer's purpose in using them, and sight lost of the essential richness of reference that they would have had for the original readers. These would for the most part have been Jews, or at least those who had some acquaintance with the Old Testament Scriptures and thus were able to recall from a single key-verse its historical and prophetical background. For this reason it is not so much the actual words of a quotation that matter (though these also have importance) but the wider passage of Scripture to which they are an index. Seen thus a whole perspective of reference opens out from a quotation enriching its illustrative value. . . . There is nothing fanciful about this mode of interpretation. Scripture is interlocked with Scripture, and in each a sort of chain-reaction takes place, triggering off a whole series of interrelated passages. These ramifications are not only verbal but reveal historical continuity, and so point to the grand unity of the divine purpose.[76]

76. Rendall, Quotation in "Scripture as an Index of Wider Reference," 221

C. H. Dodd had pointed out something similar. Early Christian biblical scholars selected whole portions of material from Isaiah, Jeremiah, the minor prophets and Psalms that were viewed as crucial to their polemic. However, although these selections were understood as a whole,

> particular verses or sections were quoted from them rather as pointers to the whole context than as constituting testimonies in and for themselves. At the same time detached sentences from other parts of the Old Testament could be adduced to illustrate or elucidate the meaning of the main section under consideration. But in the fundamental passages it is the total context that is in view, and is the basis of the argument.[77]

We see, then, of course, that we are operating in the sphere of allusions. We might define allusion in this way: "A literary device intentionally employed by an author to point a reader back to a single identifiable source, of which one or more components must be remembered and brought forward into the new context in order for the alluding text to be understood fully."[78] The success of allusions depends upon the audience. They must recognize the allusion and perceive that that author purposefully places it within a text. Then, they must recall elements of the original context, including interrelated passages.[79]

When it comes to the summative statement from *Mandate* 1.1, we must understand it as both an allusion and a quotation. It is a quotation of *Mandate* 1.1, yes, but it is much more than that in the understanding of Irenaeus. It is also an allusion to the Church's Rule of faith concerning God and creation. Irenaeus, in his theological exposition of the Hermas text, demonstrates as much. He makes explicit portions of the confessional Rule that the allusion of *Mandate* 1.1 is meant to evoke in the mind of the baptized reader. When the reader hears *Mandate* 1.1 Irenaeus means for it to evoke in her mind the apostolic teaching on the one Creator God. Therefore, he is comfortable labeling it the Rule of Truth, for it is an explicit, potentially explosive, component of the entire Rule. The implicit portions of the Rule, which include the Scriptures, he then goes forth to make explicit in part. So, we learn this about the Rule of Truth in Irenaeus. Although he may use short hand, sound bites, if you wish, of the Rule, he intends to evoke a more comprehensive expression of the Church's faith. He has so much more in mind than the allusion.

77. Dodd, *According to the Scriptures*, 126.

78. Beetham, *Echoes of Scripture*, 20.

79. Cf. Ibid., 19.

In Lyons, the Rule of Truth and its scriptural proofs would have been learned and received during a preparatory period for baptism with catechetical structure.[80] Because of the central place of baptism in learning the Rule, to deny the Church's baptism is to renounce the Church's entire faith.[81] What form might this catechesis have taken? Perhaps at this point we can say that catechesis in Lyons pivoted around learning particular biblical texts, or texts thought to be biblical, like *Mandate* 1.1, or John 1:3, or Psalm 32 [33]: 6. In the example just examined from *Haer.* 1.22.1, *Mandate* 1:1 is not being used so much in a proof-text fashion, that is as a text giving authoritative testimony to a claim within the catechism or Rule. Instead, Irenaeus is using it *as* the catechism or Rule. In the words of John Cavadini, "I think it would be fair to style this as *scriptural catechesis*, a catechesis carried out not simply with the support of the words Scripture, but *in* the words of Scripture."[82] It is a catechesis "that relies on the words of Scripture to speak its main points, so that it almost becomes a kind of glossed scriptural proclamation rather than a scripturally corroborated dogmatic statement."[83] The reception of the Rule of faith in baptism prepared the faithful believer to distinguish between an illegitimate collection of biblical texts that supported a corrupt and heretical system of faith and an ecclesiological network of biblical texts that proved an orthodox system.[84]

The Rule in *Adversus haereses* 1.10.1

The other expression of the Rule we will briefly examine in *Adversus haereses* 1.10.1, evidences similar features to those just mentioned. There the Rule is described as the Church's faith, its preaching. Irenaeus writes that:

> The Church, though dispersed through out the whole world, even to the ends of the earth, has received from the apostles and their disciples this faith: [She believes] in one God, the Father Almighty, Maker of heaven, and earth, and the sea, and all things that are in them (Exod 20:11; Ps 145 [146]: 6; Acts 4:24; 14:15) and in one Christ Jesus, the Son of God, who became incarnate for our salvation [John 1:14]; and in the Holy Spirit, who proclaimed through the prophets the dispensations of God, and the advents, and the birth from a virgin, and the passion, and

80. Cf. Fantino, *La théologie d'Irénée*, 20, n. 24.

81. *Haer.* 1.21.1.

82. Cavadini, "The Use of Scripture," 46.

83. Ibid.

84. *Haer.* 1.8.4.

> the resurrection from the dead, and the ascension into heaven in the flesh of the beloved Christ Jesus, our Lord, and His [future] manifestation from heaven in the glory of the Father "to gather all things in one," (Eph 1:10) and to raise up anew all flesh of the whole human race, in order that to Christ Jesus, our Lord, and God, and Savior, and King, according to the will of the invisible Father [Col 1:15], "every knee should bow, of things in heaven, and things in earth, and things under the earth, and that every tongue should confess" (Phil 2:10-11) to Him, and that He should execute just judgment [Rom 2:5] towards all; that He may send "spiritual wickednesses," (Eph 6:12) and the angels who transgressed and became apostates, together with the ungodly, and unrighteous, and wicked, and profane among humanity, into everlasting fire [Matt 18:18; 25:41]; but may, in the exercise of His grace, confer immortality on the righteous, and holy, and those who have kept His commandments [John 14:15], and have persevered in His love [John 15:10], some from the beginning, and others from their repentance, and may surround them with everlasting glory.

Here we note that his main concern is to display the Trinitarian nature of the Church's faith. The confession breaks into three parts: (1) the Church believes in one Creator-God, (2) the Church believes in one incarnate Son of God, and (3) the Church believes in the Holy Spirit, who proclaimed, through the prophets, the various economies and acts of Jesus Christ within redemptive history. These prophesied acts of Christ are given extensive treatment in the statement of faith, indicating a unity between promise and fulfillment, Old and New. They include both advents of Christ. First, Irenaeus mentions his virginal birth, his passion, his resurrection, and his fleshly ascension into heaven. Second, he mentions Christ's revelation from heaven in the Father's glory. Several things will take place in his second advent. He will recapitulate all things and will raise all humans in the flesh so that, in keeping with the Father's will, all creatures will be subordinate to him. He will also judge with justice wicked angels, wicked humans and righteous humans. The wicked he will consign to everlasting fire, the righteous to everlasting glory. Shortly after the confession, he highlights two of the three components which the heretics pervert and from which no one should drift: first, no one should conceive of a God other than the Creator, and second, no one should conceive of another Christ other than the incarnate one whose various acts were revealed by the Spirit (*Haer.* 1.10.3). However, further down, other components are also highlighted, but in an interesting manner. They are set forth as ecclesiological theological assumptions, foundational theological principles, to which all speculation about the parables, those ambiguous, obscure, enigmatic terms and portions within Scripture (*Haer.* 2.27.2), must conform. Where the reader finds enigma in Scripture, it must be read in concurrence, in consonance, in harmony with the Church's faith and preaching.[85] We find the principle expressed succinctly in book two (*Haer.* 2.28.3):

> If, therefore, according to the Rule which I have stated, we leave some questions in the hands of God, we shall both preserve our faith uninjured, and shall continue without danger; and all Scripture, which has been given to us by God, shall be found by us perfectly consonant (*consananans*); and the parables shall harmonize with those passages which are perfectly plain; and those statements the meaning of which is clear, shall serve to explain the parables; and through the many diversified utterances [of Scripture] there shall be heard one harmonious melody in us, praising in hymns that God who created all things.

The components of the Rule he mentions further down, those additional governing theological principles, which govern all Scripture reading, are twelve in number. In particular, he contrasts them to his opponents' theses concerning the Demiurge and the Pleroma. Here is his list: (1) the salvific economy of God; (2) God's longsuffering in the face of the evil of both angels and humans; (3) the diversity of the kinds of creatures within the creation of the one God (Eph 3:6); (4) the diverse means of God's self-revelation; (5) the multiplicity of God's covenants; (6) the particular character of each covenant; (7) God's consignment of all to unbelief and mercy (Rom 11:32); (8) the incarnation (John 1:14) and suffering of the Word of God; (9) the advent of the Son of God in the last times; (10) the Scripture's witness to eschatology; (11) God's inclusion of innumerable Gentiles (Hos 2:23/Rom 9:25; Isa 54:1/Gal 4:27); (12) the transformation of the mortal, corruptible body into that which is immortal and incorruptible (1 Cor 15:54). One may ask several questions in attempting to comprehend these revealed truths, but they themselves are beyond question. In attempting to understand the why and the how of the divine arrangement, one must never conclude a Demiurge or Pleroma or deny One Creator-God and one Christ and only-begotten.

85. Cf. Osborn, *Irenaeus*, 159–61, on *consonantia* in Irenaeus.

Components of the Rule: *Haer.* 1.10.1 and 1.22.1 Together

This extensive list of revealed realities, that can be examined and inquired after by the interpreter, demonstrates the multiple elements contained in the Rule of Faith and its diverse nature. One may, after our examination of *Adversus haereses* 1.22.1 and the beginning of 1.10.1, think that the Rule of Faith is essentially a Trinitarian formula, the triune faith, with a strong Christological center highlighting Christ's redemptive acts. Such an idea would fall short of Irenaeus's. The Rule of Truth is certainly triune. There can be no mistake. And it is certainly Christological. But it is more. It proclaims One Creator but many kinds of creatures. It proclaims one divine economy authored by one God within which he has instituted different covenants with different characteristics and within which he has employed different means of revelation. It declares the judgment of both humanity and the fallen angels, but also holds the longsuffering of God toward both. It proclaims that one God both consigns to unbelief and mercy. It proclaims a particular unfolding of things to come, the transformation of mortal, and the generous inclusion of the Gentiles.

All of these elements join together to form the boundaries within which harmonious interpretation must take place. We can say that in 1.10.1 the foundation of the Rule is the confession of Father as Creator of all things, Christ, the Son, as incarnate Savior, and Spirit as revealer, through the prophets, of the advents and acts of Christ. To these, however, must be added the dozen other beliefs. In 1.22.1, the components share similarities, but also differences. The Father as creator of all things is repeated, but the Son and Spirit are highlighted as the agents of creation and the Father's aseity is emphasized. The Father as the God of both covenants occurs both places. The discussion in 1.22.1 does not develop the advents or economical acts of Christ or the revelatory ministry of the Spirit. *Adversus haereses* 1.10.1–3 is more interested, it seems, in the economical ministry of the three, Father, Son, and Holy Spirit, in redemptive history after creation. *Adversus haereses* 1.22.1, on the other hand, seems more interested in the divine nature, the divine being, the Father, who exists and creates without need for mediators, for he has his Son and Spirit. Whereas 1.10.1–3 emphasizes the economical activities of the three in creation, redemption, revelation and judgment, with a concentration on Christ, 1.22.1 emphasizes the all-sufficiency of the Creator in himself with his Son and Spirit. The difference is between divine activity and divine sufficiency. Both are components of the Rule.

Scripture in Expressions of the Rule

Scripture also appears somewhat differently in each. In *Adversus haereses* 1.10.1–3, portions of Scripture are woven into the language of the Church's faith. In particular, in the statement itself, we find partial quotations of Eph 1:10; Phil 2:10–12; and Eph 6:12. In the statement of the twelve related components that follows we find additional partial quotations from Exod 20:11, Psalm 145 [146]: 6, Acts 4:24, or Acts 14:15; Eph 3:6; Rom 11:32; Hosea 2:23/Rom 9:25; Isa 54:1/Gal 4:27; and 1 Cor 15:54. Allusions or echoes appear from John 1:14; Col 1:15; Rom 2:15; Matt 18:18; 25:41; John 14:15; and 15:10. It is important to note that most of the biblical quotations come from the New Testament, more pointedly, from Paul, or from Old Testament quotations cited in the New Testament by Paul. In 1.10.1-3 we are not dealing with a confession simply derived from Christian readings of the Prophets. None of these seem to function quite in the same way as *Mandate* 1.1 in 1.22.1. Whereas in 1.22.1 *Mandate* 1.1 functioned both as scriptural catechesis, a statement of the faith in the words of Scripture, and as an allusion to a particular thesis within the Rule, the quotations we find in 1.10.1–3 serve basically as scriptural catechesis. Both expressions of the Rule, however, are meant to provide boundaries for the proper fit of Scripture in the Church's reading.

The Genre of the Rule

We are now at a point where we can discuss the nature of the Rule of Truth. Other studies have aided our thought. First, we briefly mention that of Paul Blowers. He writes,

> My premise here is that at bottom, the Rule of Faith (which was always associated with Scripture itself) served the primitive Christian hope of articulating and authenticating a world-encompassing story or metanarrative of creation, incarnation, redemption, and consummation. I will argue that in the crucial "proto-canonical" era in the history of Christianity, the Rule, being a narrative construction, set forth the basic "dramatic" structure of a Christian vision of the world, posing as an hermeneutical frame of reference for the interpretation of Christian Scripture and Christian experience, and educing the first principles of Christian theological discourse and of a doctrinal substantiation of Christian faith.[86]

86. Blowers, "The Regula Fidei," 202.

He further argues that:

> The Rule of Faith epitomized that metanarrative as authored by God the Father, as climaxing in the work of his Son Jesus Christ, and (according to its trinitarian renditions) as reaching full fruition through the Holy Spirit. . . . The Rule did not, any more than Scripture itself, purely and simply atomize "the faith once delivered" into propositions, since "the oneness or identity of the Christian faith, the way things hang together in the Christian scheme of things, has more in common with the oneness of a story with a single plot than with the oneness of a catalogue or list of objects of belief." The Rule projected a shared Christian vision, out of which a universal discipline of Christian self- understanding could be authorized and sustained.[87]

Our analysis of *Adversus haereses* 1.10.1–3 and 1.22.1 has presented a picture different from that of Blowers. Whereas he argues for a non-propositional, dramatic, narratival or meta-narratival character to the Rule, we have seen that it is indeed propositional though it does attest to the economical acts of the Father, Son, and Spirit. Others have recently taken issue with Blowers' claim. Nathan McDonald, for instance, argued that "Contra Blowers, we do not find 'a drama gradually unfolded with a coherent plot, climaxing in the coming of Jesus.' Rather, for Irenaeus, as for the later creeds, we find a confession that the Father is the Creator God juxtaposed with a confession about Christ Jesus."[88] Concerned basically with Irenaeus's *Demonstration*, he goes on to say that

> Irenaeus's intent is misconstrued when his work is read as an elaboration of the Rule of Faith understood as a scriptural narrative running from creation to consummation. The apostolic preaching is the triune faith that is, the Rule of Faith (*Epid*. 7.6) and the proof of it is derived from the OT Scriptures, just as the OT Scriptures only receive their true unity when read in the light of the Rule of Faith.[89]

Furthermore, he believes that,

> the Rule of Faith is not identical with Scripture, nor does it trace Scripture's narrative plot. Rather, the Rule of Faith provides Scripture's *hypothesis*. This hypothesis concerns the unified

87. Ibid., 225.

88. McDonald, "Israel and the Old Testament Story," 286; cf. L. G. Finn, "Reflections on the Rule of Faith," 221–42.

89. Ibid., 293.

> actions of Father, Son, and Holy Spirit, most especially the salvific events of the Son . . . .[90]

This emphasis on the Rule as a hypothesis derived from the Old Testament, a confession of the triune faith with the acts of Christ highlighted, and not as a rehearsal of the Old Testament's historical narrative finds additional support from Christopher Seitz. For him, the Rule of Faith

> is the scripturally grounded articulation, based upon a proper perception of the hypothesis of Scripture, that Jesus Christ is one with the God who sent him and who is active in the Scriptures inherited, the Holy Spirit being the means of testifying to his active, if hidden, life in the "Old Testament" and our apprehension of that."[91] Because Scripture's unity is to be found ultimately in Christ the Rule "takes the form, not chiefly of a kind of economic retelling, where the *magnalia dei* in the OT serve chiefly to describe crucial or merely preliminary episodes prior to Christ's advent."[92]

I think these corrections to Blowers are a move in the right direction. The Rule of Faith, as we have analyzed it, is a confession of the triune faith and is certainly Christocentric in its reading of the Spirit's revelation in the Old Testament. But our analysis has found additional elements. These demonstrate the breadth of the Rule and include: the self-sufficiency of the Creator; the diversity within creation; the multiple covenants with their idiosyncrasies; the destinies of the wicked and the just; the inclusion of the Gentiles and the transformation of the corporeal from mortality and corruption to immortality and incorruption. And finally, we must add that the Rule is not merely derived from a Christological reading of the Old Testament in the sense that its only subject is Christ. It is derived from an intertextual reading of the Prophets, Apostles or more particularly, an intertextual reading of the Law, Prophets, Apostles, Evangelists, and the words of the Lord and its subject matter is broad.

As to the genre of the Rule of Faith, our analysis has demonstrated that although there is a narrative element, for the Rule recounts the act of creation and provides a chronological account of the acts of Christ, it is not basically narratival in the sense that it recounts the biblical story or stories. Its prime character is didactic or propagandistic. Whether making propositions or recounting a story, the Rule of Faith intends "to persuade people

90. Ibid., 290.

91. Christopher Seitz, *The Character of Christian Scripture*, 298.

92. Ibid.

to support a particular religious or political cause. Propagandist writing is thus a kind of didactic literature directed toward changing or confirming readers' and audiences' allegiances."[93]

Conclusion

The Rule and a Christian Historiography

As we noted above, the historical particularities with which Irenaeus is peculiarly interested are those that are part of Scripture's collective presentation of redemptive history. In *Adversus haereses* 1.22.1 his interest was the event of creation and God's relationship to it. So his historiography involves employing summative statements of the Rule in conjunction with Scriptural material that further expounds the summative statement, in order to understand the beginning as Scripture addresses that event. The community of Lyons, in light of its baptismal catechesis, comprehends the event of creation as a revelation of the uniqueness, omnipotence, and self-sufficiency of God. In *Adversus haereses* 1.10.1, Irenaeus delineates the economical ministry of the Father, Son, and Spirit, mentioning the creation and the incarnation, but describing most thoroughly the prophetic ministry of the Spirit concerning the activity of the Son.

Contrary to historicism, in the historiography of Lyons, the biblical material reliably attests to what really happened, a prejudice is required to investigate the data, a comparison with a universe of options is unnecessary, and the entire historiographical-hermeneutical enterprise is ecclesiological. Events within history do indeed manifest spiritual truths. Ranke was right. But, for the Christians in Lyons, the historical particularity most worthy of investigation is part of Scripture's record and only the baptized may successfully interpret it.

The Rule of Faith, Scripture, and Exegesis

As we draw our study to a close, we should reflect upon the relationship between Scripture and the Rule. We have seen that Scripture is used as a summary of the Rule itself. We have seen that Scripture as the Rule functions to evoke other biblical texts that in turn are used to fill out or to interpret the Rule. We have seen that Scripture appears within the Rule of Faith as

93. Baldick, *The Oxford Dictionary of Literary Terms*, s.v. "Propogandism."

scriptural catechesis; Scripture itself becomes the language of the Rule, both in quotation and allusion or echo.

Irenaeus, then, demonstrates consonance and correspondence between the two. At times the Rule of Faith *is* Scripture. They are identical. Yet Scripture expounds and explicates the Rule of Faith while the Rule of Faith interprets the datum of history recorded in Scripture. They are complementary. What is foundational to the relationship is that the Old Testament has always contained the Rule of Faith, and at least some of its material can be identified with the Rule (e.g., *Mandate* 1.1), for it, through the Spirit's ministry, records the datum regarding creation, the incarnation, and the salvific and judgmental activity of the Son. Other Scripture, from both the Old and New Testament, by forming intertextual networks, can be called upon to demonstrate the Rule present in the Old Testament.

So, the purpose of the exegete, according to Irenaeus, is to demonstrate the Church's faith, the Rule, within the Old Testament Scriptures by means of intertextual, inter-canonical networks. The exegete is to give the Scripture, both the Old and New Testament, its proper fit, its proper connection in continuity with the Rule received in baptism.

Being against historicism, then, may I briefly outline for your consideration an Irenaean approach to the reading of Scripture with attention to reader, text, and sources? First, I would identify the properly equipped reader as one who is catechized and baptized. Training of such readers will require three things: (1) that the Church universal remain faithful to or recover as a constituent part of its theory of spiritual formation, a devotion to baptismal catechesis in conformity to historic Christian orthodoxy, (2) that the Church and not the academy be reconceived as the primary context for training in biblical studies, and (3) that theological, confessional presupposition be restored as a prime prerequisite for Christian exegesis. Second, I would clarify the reader's necessary satisfaction with the truthfulness and reliability of witness of the biblical text. The text's account is in harmony with "what actually happened" and there is no need to imagine that a more reliable account is available in the "brute facts" accessed through the methods of historical criticism. Third, I would note that there are only two requisite sources for biblical studies and they are uniquely ecclesiological: (1) the Scriptures, both Old and New Testaments, and, (2) the Rule of Faith received in baptism. Correlating the biblical texts with non-ecclesiological texts is unnecessary. There is contentment with the library of the ecclesia.

Bibliography

Baldick, Chris. *The Oxford Dictionary of Literary Terms*. Oxford: Oxford University Press, 2009.

Bauer, Walter. *Orthodoxy and Heresy in Earliest Christianity*. Translated by the Philadelphia Seminar on Christian Origins. Edited by R. A. Kraft and G. Krodel. Philadelphia: Fortress, 1971.

Beetham, Christopher. A. *Echoes of Scripture in the Letter of Paul to the Colossians*. Leiden: Brill, 2008.

Bingham, D. Jeffrey. "Christianizing Divine Aseity: Irenaeus Reads John." In *The Gospel of John and Christian Theology*. Edited by R. Bauckham and C. Mosser. Grand Rapids: Eerdmans, 2008.

———. "Evangelicals and the Rule of Faith: Irenaeus on Rome and Reading Christianly." In *Evangelicals and the Early Church: Recovery, Reform, Renewal*, edited by G. Kalantzis and A. Tooley, 159–86. Eugene, OR: Cascade, 2012.

Blowers, Paul M. "The Regula Fidei and the Narrative Character of Early Christian Faith." *Pro Ecclessia* 6 (1997) 199–228.

Cavadini. John C. "The Use of Scripture in the Catechism of the Roman Catholic Church." *Letter and Spirit* 2 (2006) 43–54.

Daniélou, Jean. "Saint Irénée et les origeines de la théologie de l'histoire." Recherches de *Science Religieuse* 34 (1947) 227–31.

Davaney, Sheila Greeve. *Historicism: The Once and Future Challenge for Theology*. Minneapolis: Fortress, 2006.

Dodd, Charles. H. *According to the Scriptures*. New York: Charles Scribner's Sons, 1953.

Ehrman, Bart D. *Lost Christianities*. Oxford: Oxford University Press, 2003.

Fantino, Jacques. *La théologie d'Irénée: Lectures des Écritures en réponse à l'exégèse gnostique, Une approche trinitaire*. Paris: Cerf, 1994.

Finley, Moses. I. *Ancient History: Evidence and Models*. New York: Viking, 1987.

Finn, Leonard G. "Reflections on the Rule of Faith." In *The Bible as Christian Scripture: The Work of Brevard S. Childs*, edited by C. R. Seitz and K. H. Richards, 221–42. Atlanta: Society of Biblical Literature, 2013.

Gunkel, Hermann. "Geschichtsschreibung im A.T." in *Religion in Geschichte und Gegenwart*. Edited by H. Gunkel, 2:1348–54. Tübingen: Mohr, 1909–1913.

———. *Israel and Babylonien: Der Einfluss Babyloniens auf die israelitische Religion*. Göttingen: Vandenhoeck and Ruprecht, 1903.

———. *The Legends of Genesis*. Translated by W. H. Carruth. Chicago: The Open Court, 1901.

Hefner, Philip. "Theological Methodology and St. Irenaeus." *The Journal of Religion* 44 (1964) 294–309.

Hegel, G. W. F. *Hegel's Lectures on the History of Philosophy*. Translated by E. S. Haldane and F. H. Simson. Atlantic Highlands, NJ: Humanities, 1996.

Hinrichs, Carl. "Introduction." In *Historism: The Rise of a New Historical Outlook*, trans. J. E. Anderson. New York: Herder and Herder, 1972.

Hitchcock, Francis R. M. *Irenaeus of Lugdunum*. Cambridge: Cambridge University Press, 1914.

Irenaeus of Lyons. *Against Heresies, Books 1–5 and Fragments*. In *The Ante-Nicene Fathers, vol. 1, The Apostolic Fathers with Justin Martyr*. Revised and translated by A. Roberts and W. H. Rambaut, 315–578. Peabody: Hendrickson, 1994.

———. *On the Apostolic Preaching.* Translated by J. Behr. Crestwood, NY: St Vladimir's Seminary, 1997.

———. *The Proof of the Apostolic Preaching, with Seven Fragments.* Armenian version edited and translated by Karapet ter Mekerttshian and S. G. Wilson with the cooperation of H.R.H. Prince Maxe of Saxony [Patrologia Orientalis 12.5]. Tournhout: Brepols, 1989.

———. *The Proof of the Apostolic Preaching with Seven Fragments.* Edited and translated by K. Ter-Mĕkĕrttschian and S. G. Wilson. *Patrologia Orientalis*, 12.5. Paris: Firmin-Didot et Cie, 1919.

Irénée de Lyon. *Contre les hérésies, Livres 1–5*. Edited, translated, and annotated by A. Rousseau, L. Doutreleau, B Hemmerdinger, and C. Mercier, 10 vols. Paris: Cerf, 1965– 2002.

———. *Démonstration de la predication apostolique*. Edited by A. Rousseau, SC 406. Paris: Cerf, 1995.

———. *Démonstration de la Prédication apostolique.* Edited by L.M. Froidevaux, SC 62. Paris: Cerf, 1959.

Markus, Robert A. "Pleroma and Fulfillment: The Significance of History in St. Irenaeus' Opposition to Gnosticism." *Vigiliae Christianae* 8 (1954) 193–224.

McDonald, Nathan. "Israel and the Old Testament Story in Irenaeus's Presentation of the Rule of Faith." *Journal of Theological Interpretation* 3 (2009) 267–84.

Meinecke, Friederich. "Leopold von Ranke (Memorial Address Given on 23 January 1936 in Preussische Akademie der Wissenschaften)." In *Historism: The Rise of a New Historical Outlook*. Translated by J. E. Anderson. New York: Herder and Herder, 1972.

———. *Schaffender Spiegel: Studien zur deutschen Geschichtsschreibung und Geschichtsauffassung*. Stuttgart: Koehler, 1948.

———. "Values and Causalities in History." In *The Varieties of History: From Voltaire to the Present*. Edited by Fritz Stern and translated by Julian H. Franklin. New York: Vintage, 1973.

———. *Werke, vol. 1. Die Idee der Staatsräson in der neueren Geschichte*. Edited by Walther Hofer. Munich: R. Oldenbourge, 1957.

———. "Ein Wort über geschichtliche Entwicklung," in *Aphorismen und Skizzen zur Geschichte*. Leipzig: Koehler & Amelang, 1942.

Miller II, R. D. "Quest of the Historical Israel." In *Dictionary of the Old Testament: Historical Books*, edited by B. T. Arnold and H. G. M. Williamson, 830–37. Downers Grove, IL: InterVarsity, 2005.

Miller, J. Maxwell. "Reading the Bible Historically: The Historian's Approach." In *To Each Its Own Meaning*, revised and edited by S. L. McKenzie and S. R. Haynes, 17–34. Louisville: Westminster John Knox, 1999.

Orbe, Antonio. *Teología de San Ireneo IV: Traducción y Comentario del Libro IV del 'Adversus haereses*. Madrid: Biblioteca de Autores Cristianos, 1996.

Osborn, Eric. *Irenaeus of Lyons*. Cambridge: Cambridge University Press, 2004.

Pagels, Elaine H. *The Johannine Gospel in Gnostic Exegesis*. Atlanta: Scholars, 1989.

Pétrement, Simone. *A Separate God*. Translated by C. Harrison. New York: Harper Collins, 1990.

Provan, Iain. "Hearing the Historical Books." In *Hearing the Old Testament: Listening for God's Address*, edited by C. G. Bartholomew and D. J. H. Beldman, 254–76. Grand Rapids: Eerdmans, 2012.

Ranke, Leopold von. *Geschichten der romanischen und germanischen Völker von 1494 bis 1514*, 3rd ed. Leipzig: Duncker & Humblot, 1885.

———. "On the Character of Historical Science." In *The Theory and Practice of History*, edited by G. G. Iggers and translated by W. A. Iggers, 8–16. New York: Routledge, 2011.

———. "On the Progress of History (From the First Lecture to King Maximillian II of Bavaria, 'On the Epochs of Modern History.'" In *The Theory and Practice of History*, edited by G. G. Iggers and translated W. A. Iggers, 20–23. London: Routledge, 2011.

———. "Preface to the First Edition of Histories of the Latin and Germanic Peoples." In *The Theory and Practice of History*, edited by G. G. Iggers and translated W. A. Iggers, 85–88. New York: Routledge, 2011.

———. *Zur Kritik neuerer Geschichtschreiber*. 3rd ed. Leipzig: Duncker & Humblot, 1884.

Rendall, Robert. "Quotation in Scripture as an Index of Wider Reference." *Evangelical Quarterly* 36 (1964) 214–21.

Reventlow, Henning G. *History of Biblical Interpretation: From the Enlightenment to the Twentieth Century.* Translated by L. G. Perdue. Vol. 4. Atlanta: Society of Biblical Literature, 2010.

Rudolph, Kurt. "Early Christianity as a Religious-Historical Phenomenon." In *The Future of Early Christianity: Essays in Honor of Helmut Koester*, edited by B. A. Pearson, 16–34. Minneapolis: Fortress, 1991.

———. *Historical Fundamentals and the Study of Religions*. New York: Collier Macmillan, 1985.

Sasson, Jack M. "On Choosing Models for Recreating Israelite Pre-Monarchic History: To Michael C. Astuor on His 65th Birthday." *Journal for the Study of the Old Testament* 21 (1981) 3–24.

Scholtz, Gunter. "The Phenomenon of 'Historicism' as A Backcloth of Biblical Scholarship." In *Hebrew Bible/Old Testament: The History of Its Interpretation, From Modernism to Post-Modernism: The Nineteenth and Twentieth Centuries*, edited by Magne Sæbø, volume 3.2, 64–89. Göttingen: Vandenhoeck and Ruprecht, 2013.

Seitz, Christopher. *The Character of Christian Scripture: The Significance of a Two-Testament Bible*. Grand Rapids: Baker, 2011.

Ska, Jean Louis. "The 'History of Israel': Its Emergence as an Independent Discipline." In *Hebrew Bible/Old Testament: The History of Its Interpretation, From Modernism to Post-Modernism: The Nineteenth and Twentieth Centuries*, edited by Magne Sæbø, volume 3.2, 307–45. Göttingen: Vandenhoeck and Ruprecht, 2013.

Troeltsch, Ernst. "Historical and Dogmatic Method in Theology." In *Religion in History*, translated by J. L. Adams and W. F. Bense, 11–32. Minneapolis: Fortress, 1991.

Valentinus. "Fragment 1." In *Quellen zur Geschichte der christlichen Gnosis*, edited by W. Völker, 57–58. Tübingen: J. C. B. Mohr, 1932.

———. "Fragment C." In *The Gnostic Scripture*, edited by B. Layton, 232–33. Garden City: Doubleday, 1987.

Wellhausen, Julius. *Prologomena to the History of Israel.* Translated by J. S. Black and A. Menzies. Edinburgh: Adam and Charles Black, 1885.

6

From Catechesis to Exegesis

The Hermeneutical Shaping of Catechetical Formation in Irenaeus of Lyons

Stephen O. Presley

Introduction

The development of hermeneutical theory in the early church is intimately connected with the rise of catechetical formation. No doubt the seedbed of catechetical instruction is already evident within the writings of the New Testament, but as the church expanded rapidly throughout the ancient world the formal practice of catechumenate began to take shape in the post-apostolic age. One of the earliest Christian catechetical manuals available is a short work composed by Irenaeus of Lyons entitled the *Epideixis* (*Epid*) or *Demonstration of Apostolic Preaching*.[1] This is one of only two extant works attributed to him and it is relatively short in comparison to his immense five-volume refutation against Gnosticism.[2]

1. English translations of Irenaeus's *Epideixis* are based upon Behr's work, *On the Apostolic Preaching*, though certain renderings were altered based upon comparisons with Rousseau's critical edition: Irénée de Lyon, *Démonstration*. Translations and references to Irenaeus' work *Adversus Haereses* are based upon Rousseau's critical editions: Rousseau et al., *Contre les hérésies, Livre 1–V* (hereafter *Haer*).

2. Eusebius records this text among Irenaeus' non-polemical works. Eusebius, *Ecclesiastical History*, 5.36. It was lost until 1904 when it was discovered in the library of the church of the Holy Mother of God in Erivan, Armenia. Rousseau's critical study of the manuscript revealed that the text was translated from a Greek manuscript, between the fifth and seventh centuries and the Armenian translator followed the Greek text

At the same time, despite its brevity this highly organized treatise boasts an impressive collection of Scriptural quotations and allusions. The work is composed for a disciple named Marcianus, who was most likely a catechist commissioned to use this short manual to prepare young catechumen for baptism. In contrast to other early catechetical works such as the *Didache* or *Epistle of Barnabas*, the *Epideixis* offers a detailed and coherent summary of the apostolic teaching with special attention given to Scriptural interpretation.

Not all scholars, however, believe the purpose of Irenaeus' *Epideixis* is *primarily* catechetical. Some suggest it is apologetic or even polemical. The careful internal analysis of the manuscript began with Harnack's early translation and arrangement. As a whole he considered the treatise refreshing and even "catechetically uplifting" in contrast to the complex polemical discourse of *Adversus Haereses*.[3] For Harnack, the text is a straightforward non-polemical summary of the preaching of the apostles. More recently, MacKenzie also observes Irenaeus' limited concern with heresy in the text and suggests that his purpose is to set out the "positive substance of the faith."[4] Minns argues this same point saying, "[a]lthough it was written after *Adversus Haereses*, to which it refers, and is meant to assist in the fight against false teaching, it has almost none of the polemical tone of the larger work and often suggests a more primitive theology, unrefined by the conflict with heresy (Dem 1; 99)."[5] Behr agrees with these descriptions when he characterizes the *Epideixis* as a "clear, coherent, and concise exposition of the apostolic teaching" and the "earliest summary of Christian teaching, presented in a non-polemical or apologetic manner, that we now have."[6] Behr notes that Irenaeus relies heavily on the exegesis of the Old Testament and has only minimal use of the New Testament writings.

On the other hand, the French translation by Tixeront in 1916 suggests the work is principally apologetic rather than catechetical, since Irenaeus omits any discussion of ecclesiastical or liturgical matters.[7] Tixeront acknowledges Irenaeus' discussion of baptism in several paragraphs, but he regards these as theological references and not formal descriptions of the practice. In other words, Irenaeus does not describe the particular ceremonial practice of the early Christian baptism, but instead simply describes the

closely. Rousseau, *Irénée de Lyon, Démonstration*, 19–21.

3. Harnack, *Des heiligen Irenaüs Schrift*, 65–66.

4. MacKenzie, *Irenaeus's Demonstration*, 31.

5. Minns, *Irenaeus*, 6.

6. Behr, *Irenaeus of Lyons*, 132.

7. Saint Irénée, "Démonstration," 361–432.

faith of the church that is received by the catechumen at baptism. Smith's English translation also follows Tixeront's line of reasoning. He remarks that any attempt to classify the *Epideixis* as catechetical must be "accepted with reserve" because the real aim is "apologetic rather than catechetical."[8] Smith notes that Irenaeus focuses his treatment on key theological points that the heretics denied in order to defend the reliability and integrity of the apostolic testimony. He recognizes Irenaeus' debt to a stream of apologetic writings, but distinguishes this style from that of the other second century apologists including Justin, Athenagoras, and Theophilus that defended the faith against their Jewish and pagan interlocutors. Irenaeus' apologetic is a more positive attempt to establish the "credentials of the orthodox Church."[9] The strongest evidence is Irenaeus' concluding reference to his fierce debates with the various Gnostic sects and his warning about the deception of their arguments.[10]

More recent studies, including the works of Torrance, Drews, Ferguson, and Graham have advanced the debate by comparing the *Epideixis* with other ancient catechetical, apologetic, and philosophical treatises. Torrence situates the book within the pastoral context of ancient Christian preaching, and argues for a kerygmatic intention to the work. The true purpose of the text, according to Torrance, is "to offer a summary account of the structure of Christian belief through bringing to light the inner connection of the saving truths it embodies . . . "[11] The content, therefore, is an outline of the *kerygma* of the apostles that is put to work in either a polemical, apologetic, or catechetical context. Torrence argues that the general sketch of the work follows the Trinitarian scheme of the rule of faith described in *Epideixis* 6 and works through the economic relationships of the Father, Son, and Spirit as they are revealed in scripture and the history of salvation. But the scheme of Torrence's Trinitarian summary is too rigid and the integration of the work of each person of the Trinity is much more complex. Ferguson also provides some structural and rhetorical analysis, but suggests the *Epideixis* does not strictly follow the common order for forensic speech.[12] Instead, Ferguson proposes that the scheme of the work is a "history of salvation" that begins with the preexistence of the Father with the Son, and moves through the ordered events of the history of salvation culminating in the

8. Smith, *St. Irenaeus*, 19.

9. Ibid., 21. Even the translation of Επίδειξις in the title as either "demonstration" or "proof," reflects this debate over the purpose of the work.

10. *Epid* 99.

11. Torrance, "Kerygmatic Proclamation," 108.

12. Ferguson, "Irenaeus' Proof," 126.

work of Christ, the church, and the general resurrection. The *narratio* and *confirmatio* of rhetorical speech are evident, as well as a general Trinitarian scheme, but they are secondary, in the words of Ferguson, "to the arrangement according to Biblical history."[13] Finally, the recent studies of Drews and Graham compare the relationship between the *Epideixis* and other ancient catechetical and philosophical handbooks. Drews makes some interesting observations concerning the catechetical nature of Irenaeus' work and the general correspondence to other texts such as the *Apostolic Constitutions*, but nothing concrete enough to confirm its catechetical purpose.[14] Graham, on the other hand, argues that Irenaeus adopts the form of the ancient Hellenistic handbook, or εἰσαγωγαί, which originated in Stoic circles, and offers introductory treatises to various disciplines in a bipartite form. This type of introductory treatise was well-attested by the second century and if Irenaeus' work is in fact bipartite than Graham's case is certainly plausible. Irenaeus is no doubt aware of these handbooks and could have easily adopted their structure for his own theological and doctrinal purpose. But like the rhetorical, dogmatic, and kerygmatic analysis mentioned above, the parallels between the *Epideixis* and the handbooks are only convincing in the macrostructure of the work as a bipartite summary. As Ferguson and Torrance observe, Irenaeus is thinking in terms of a history of salvation, so the general thrust of the work as a whole is narratival or chronological, not necessarily bipartite. Thus, the internal and external analysis has not fully settled the debate concerning the nature and purpose of Irenaeus's *Epideixis*.

At the same time, the opening chapters of the work also illustrate Irenaeus's concern for the spiritual lives of his readers, which corresponds more closely with other ancient Christian catechetical works. He begins with a description of the "Two Ways" moral path of the divine life, which is characteristic of catechetical training and prominent in both the *Didache* and the *Epistle of Barnabas*.[15] Both of these texts, in contrast to the *Epideixis*, emphasize the *ethical* dimension of Christianity spirituality. They draw on the first and second commandment and implore the faithful to flee evil, avoid sin and immorality, and pursue righteousness.[16] Irenaeus, on the other hand, is not merely content with ethical formation, but balances

13. Ibid., 129.

14. Drews, "Der literarische Charakter," 226–33.

15. His reading of the "Two ways" is, like the rest of his work, rooted in scripture. He conflates the "two ways" imagery of Ps 1:1–3 and Matt 7:13 with the revelation of the divine name in Exod 3:14. For a further discussion of the "Two Ways" tradition see Stewart-Sykes, *On the Two Ways*.

16. *Didache*, 1–6, *Epistle of Barnabas* 18–20. Translations of the Apostolic Fathers are from *The Apostolic Fathers, Volume 1*.

both aspects of the spiritual life. He argues that it is possible to deviate from the righteous path if the faithful are not pure in *both* body and soul. For Irenaeus, catechetical training is not merely ethical formation, but also doctrinal or hermeneutical formation. Irenaeus rejects the anthropological dualism and argues that the catechumen needs both the ethical purity of the "holiness of the body" and the doctrinal purity of the "holiness of the soul."[17] Again he returns to this same anthropology in the concluding chapters where he writes that the faithful must exhibit both "good works and sound mind."[18] No doubt Irenaeus could, like the *Didache* and *Barnabas*, provide a more detailed treatment of the ethical dimension, but he recognizes the importance of hermeneutical formation within the catechetical setting. He aims to strengthen the faith of the catechumen and prepare them to read the Scriptures faithfully in any context.

Building upon these studies, I want to argue that the more general purpose of Irenaeus's little work is as much hermeneutical as it is catechetical. Irenaeus aims to offer a demonstration of the apostolic preaching in order to guide young catechumen in a distinctively Christian way of reading Scripture that could be applied in any context. Irenaeus never intended his little work to be the end unto itself, but to be used as a hermeneutical instruction manual that exemplifies the way the faithful should read the Scriptures in light of the revelation of the person and work of Christ. To put this in modern terms, this work is a required textbook for a course on the introduction to biblical hermeneutics in the late second century catechetical curriculum. Irenaeus is known for emphasizing hermeneutics in his polemic against the Gnostics, but this demonstration is a much more constructive attempt to equip the catechist with the hermeneutical means to communicate a distinctively Christian reading of the Scriptures.

The argument of this paper will proceed along two lines. First, several statements in the work communicate Irenaeus's hermeneutical intention and the assumption that the reader should apply the teaching in this short work to the understanding of *all* the Scriptures. This particular-to-general logic is reiterated in the introduction and conclusion. This same general hermeneutical intention is also restated directly and indirectly throughout the work as a whole. Second, the basic assumption guiding the general structure of his Scripture hermeneutic is a theological perspective described in *Epideixis* 5. Irenaeus argues that under the economic administration of the Father, the Spirit-inspired prophets announce the coming of the Son and the coming of the Son interprets the prophets. This Trinitarian view of inspiration creates

17. *Epid* 2.

18. Ibid., 99.

a theological principle of coherence among the written revelation that is often defined simply as Scripture interprets Scripture (*scriptura scripturam interpreter*). This same hermeneutical principle is also applied throughout his work and serves as an extension of his doctrine of God and creation, as well as his economic understanding of the Trinitarian activity recorded in both the Old and New Testaments. This hermeneutical assumption guides both the general aspects that connect the larger structural patterns of his work and the particular aspects that are applied to specific Scripture passages. The general aspects of his hermeneutical framework demonstrate how Irenaeus navigates between the various biblical genres and unites common sections of Scripture. These general aspects include narratival summaries of biblical history including the Old Testament and the apostolic accounts, covenantal fulfillment (including the Abrahamic, Mosaic, Davidic, and New covenants), and Christological catalogs of prophecy. At the same time, these general sections are constructed by particular intertextual readings of Scripture that exhibit an assortment of exegetical reading strategies including: verbal associations, quotations, centos, prophecy-fulfillment, narrative summaries, chronological inversion of texts, supportive texts, typology, prosopological interpretation, illustrative interpretation, allegorical interpretation, and intentional connections between the words of a prophet and apostle. This list is by no means exhaustive and Irenaeus is not beholden to any particular set of exegetical methods of biblical interpretation or textual correspondence. Instead he is beholden to a particular faith of the work of God in Christ and the Spirit that informs any applied method(s) of exegesis.

Together these aspects suggest that Irenaeus' *Epideixis* is not merely a summary of Christian doctrine (Torrance), a catechetical manual (Drews and Ferguson), or an introductory theological or philosophical handbook (Graham), but an introduction to Christian hermeneutics that exemplifies for any catechumen how to interpret the Scriptures faithfully in light of the person and work of Christ. The style of exegesis depicted in his work could be put to use in any polemical or apologetic context—after all that precisely what Irenaeus does in his larger work *Adversus Haereses*—but the true purpose is to foster hermeneutical formation within a catechetical setting.

The Hermeneutical Purpose of Irenaeus's *Epideixis*

First of all, Irenaeus' hermeneutical purpose is expressed in his own rhetorical descriptions of his work. These descriptions form an *inclusio* that frame his summary as a whole. Beginning in the opening paragraph Irenaeus writes:

> But, since at this present time, we are separated from each other in body, we have not hesitated to speak a little with you, as far as possible, by writing, and to demonstrate, by means of a summary, the preaching of the truth, so as to strengthen your faith. We are sending you, as it were, a summary memorandum, so that you may find much in a little, and by means of this small [work] understand all the members of the body of the truth, and through a summary receive the exposition of the things of God so that, in this way, it will bear your own salvation like fruit, and that you may confound all those who hold false opinions and to everyone who desires to know you may deliver our sound and irreproachable word in all boldness.[19]

Irenaeus uses several parallel rhetorical statements that explain how his work is intended to be a brief treatment that should guide the reader toward a greater understanding of all the Scriptures. Irenaeus terms the *Epideixis* a "summary" (*compendiosa*), "summary memorandum" (*summarium commentarium*) a "little [work]" (*pauca*), a "small [work] (*modica*)," and, again, a "summary" (*compendiosa*).[20] For Irenaeus, this work is not an exhaustive treatment of Scriptural interpretation, but a brief treatment that "demonstrates" (*ostendere*, ἐπιδείκνυμι) the basic contours under which Scriptural interpretation should proceed. Certainly Irenaeus has the theological and exegetical acumen to produce a more developed treatment, which only reinforces the point that he feels a basic summary is all that is necessary to introduce his readers to the practice of Christian hermeneutics.

The purpose of the summary, however, is not simply to demonstrate the apostolic preaching, but to provide a means to understand the entire breadth of divine revelation. Irenaeus states that he is writing "to demonstrate the preaching of the truth" (*veritatis ostendere praedicationem*), to "understand *all* the members of the body of the truth" (*omnia membra corporis veritatis . . . intellegens*), and to receive a demonstration of the "things of God" (*rerum (quae) a Deo*).[21] The implication is that his brief presentation of biblical exegesis should equip his disciple to understand the rest of divine revelation. In each statement there is a clear particular-to-general rhetorical argument. From Irenaeus' *little* treatment the catechumen can understand *much*, from a *small* work the catechumen can understand *all* the members of the body of truth, and through a *summary* treatment the catechumen can

19. *Epid* 1.
20. Ibid.
21. Ibid.

receive things of God.[22] He does mention that this work should contribute to the spiritual edification of the reader, the refutation of the heretic, and the bold proclamation of the apostolic testimony. These statements, however, describe the *application* of Irenaeus' hermeneutical presentation not necessarily its essential purpose within catechetical formation. The true purpose, then, is to understand the "preaching of the truth," "body of truth," or the "things of God." These phrases are common Irenaean terminology for the revelation of the Scriptures. Similar phrases are found elsewhere in the *Epideixis* and in other hermeneutical discussions in *Adversus Haereses.*[23]

Like the opening paragraphs, the closing paragraphs of the *Epideixis* also return to this general-to-particular summary, which forms an *inclusio* emphasizing the hermeneutical purpose of the work. In *Epideixis* 98–99 he writes:

> This, beloved, is the preaching of the truth, and this is the character of our salvation, and this is the way of life, which the prophets announced and Christ confirmed and the apostles handed over and the Church, in the whole world, hands down to her children. . . . And others, again, despise the advent of the Son of God and the economy of His Incarnation, which the apostles handed over and the prophets foretold would be the recapitulation of mankind, as we have briefly demonstrated to you.

Irenaeus' parting words reveal his pastoral concern for his catechist and his desire to instruct the neophytes in the basic teaching of the Scriptures. What Irenaeus expresses in his text is the "preaching of the truth" that locates the continuity between the prophets and the work of Christ. However, Irenaeus remarks that he has only "briefly demonstrated" (*pauca ostendimus*) the teaching of the prophets and apostles, which implies, once again, that this work is an abridgment of this kind of biblical interpretation that should characterize Christian hermeneutics communicated within the church.[24]

Similar statements evidencing Irenaeus' hermeneutical purpose also surface in other chapters throughout the course of his work. For example, he emphasizes the hermeneutical application of the work amid the sequence of his Christological catalogue of prophetic texts in the second part. Having just summarized a series of Old Testament texts communicating Son of God's preexistence and divinity, he writes:

22. Ibid.

23. Irenaeus seems to relate *a veritate corpus* and *regula veritatis* in *Haer* 2.27.1. See Rousseau, *Contre les hérésies, Livre II*, 294. *cf. Haer* 1.14.3 and *Haer* 1.18.1.

24. *Epid* 99.

> So, that Christ, being the Son of God before the whole world, is with the Father and with men, and King of all, since the father has subjected all things to Him and he is the Savior of those who believe in Him—these are demonstrated by such [passages of] Scripture. Since it is not possible to draw up an ordered account of all the Scriptures, from these [passages] you can also understand others, which speak in a similar manner, believing Christ and seeking wisdom and understanding from God, in order to understand what was said by the prophets.[25]

Irenaeus recognizes that this brief survey does not address all passages related to the preexistence of the Son and the Son's personal activity in the Old Testament. He recognizes that it is not possible in this little work "to draw up an ordered account of all the Scriptures" (*non enim est fas-et-possibile omnem Scripturam incomputationem-ordinatim-mittere*) He assumes that his reader will apply the hermeneutical perspective in order to "understand others" (*ex his autem et reliqua intelleges [quae] similiter his dicta [sunt]*). He views his work as exemplifying a distinctively Christian way of reading Scripture that should be applied to any number of other passages. Considering the broader structure of Irenaeus's work, this suggestion is strategically placed in order to emphasize the importance of locating the pre-incarnate activity of the second person of the Trinity within the Old Testament accounts. As he also mentions in the closing lines above, Irenaeus reiterates that his general purpose is to understand what was spoken in the prophets. He expects that the catechumen will receive this catechetical hermeneutic and apply it to other passages not explicitly discussed in his treatment.

In another example amid his narrative summary of the Old Testament, Irenaeus summarizes the book of Deuteronomy and its place within the context of the Mosaic Covenant in *Epideixis* 28 saying:

> Moses recapitulated everything, recounting the great deeds of God up to that day, preparing and forming [those who] had grown up in the desert, to fear God and to keep His commandments, and laying down for them, as it were, a new legislation, adding to what was before—and this was called Deuteronomy, in which also are written many prophecies about our Lord Jesus Christ, and about the people and about the calling of the Gentiles, and about the kingdom.[26]

Irenaeus implies that his interpretation of Deuteronomy could be much more developed and he explains the way that the legal material contained

25. *Epid* 52.
26. *Epid* 28.

within Deuteronomy supplements the commandments given in the other books of the Law. However, he also mentions that Deuteronomy contains "many prophecies" (*multae prophetiae*) about Christ, the people of God, the calling of the Gentiles, and the Kingdom of God.[27] This statement is particularly interesting since Irenaeus only explicitly alludes to Deuteronomy in two other paragraphs that contain a total of three prophetic passages.[28] More importantly, these three references to Deuteronomy include only one prophecy about Christ's crucifixion (Deut 28:66) and two about the Gentile inclusion into the people of God (Deut 28:44 and Deut 32:21). There is no reference to any prophecy about the kingdom of God in Deuteronomy mentioned elsewhere in the *Epideixis*. These three explicit prophecies from Deuteronomy could hardly account for the "many prophecies" (*multae prophetiae*) about Christ, the church, and the kingdom of God that Irenaeus mentions in *Epideixis* 28.[29] Instead, the bishop of Lyons only makes a passing reference to Deuteronomy and expects the young catechumen to apply the hermeneutic of prophecy and fulfillment to other parts of Deuteronomy not discussed in his work.

Finally, in the same general context, after summarizing the work of God from creation to the Deuteronomy in twenty paragraphs (*Epid* 8–28), Irenaeus condenses all of Deuteronomistic history (Joshua—2 Kings) and all the prophets into only two paragraphs (*Epid* 29–30). This abrupt conclusion leaves little doubt that Irenaeus could extend this summary, but evidently he feels confident that his demonstration is sufficient. His synopsis of the Old Testament is intended to be brief and provisional and he must expect that those who are trained up in the faith will continue working through these events in more detail. Therefore, like the statement in Deuteronomy, Irenaeus expects his ready to apply the same hermeneutical practices to understand the sacred text.

In order to visualize the how Irenaeus imagines this hermeneutical work to be applied to the faith of the catechumen, it might be helpful to consider the famous Irenaean image of the mosaic that he uses to discredit the Gnostic exegesis of Scripture.[30] Irenaeus compares Gnostic exegesis to the practice of removing the tiles of a mosaic that depicts the image of a king

27. *Epid* 28.

28. These allusions include: Deut 28:66 in *Epid* 79, and Deut 28:44 and Deut 32:21 in *Epid* 95. There are a few other possible echoes and allusions including: Deut 9:10 in *Epid* 26, Deut 1:22–23 and Deut 1:26–28, *Epid* 27, and Deut 21:23 in *Epid* 56. However, most of these are difficult to verify and most are related to similar language in other passages.

29. *Epid* 28.

30. *AH* 1.8.1. See also the similar image of the Homeric cento in *AH* 1.9.1.

and rearranging them to form the image of a fox or a dog. True interpreters will, no doubt, recognize the faulty image and promptly rearrange the same tiles to depict the true kingly image once again. Pressing this analogy even further, what Irenaeus gives his catechist in this little work is a rudimentary outline of the true mosaic of Scripture that is yet to be completed by the faithful who apply this hermeneutic to the reading of Scripture. Irenaeus sets the boundaries of the image and provides many of the essential tiles through his short treatment. The faithful catechumen that receives this instruction must continue to place the Scriptural tiles within the mosaic in order to illuminate an even fuller portrait of the king.

The *Epideixis*, therefore, is a basic hermeneutical guide for young converts to the faith. Irenaeus explains the essential contours of the apostolic faith for the early Christians who are at the beginning the catechetical formation and instruction. He expects these new converts to receive this faith at baptism and then view this faith as a hermeneutical guide for the right reading of Scripture. For Irenaeus catechetical formation is hermeneutical formation. The faithful are not merely schooled in the basic ethical commands of the faith, but a distinctively Christian way of reading Scripture in light of the work of God in Christ.

The Basic Framework of an Irenaean Hermeneutic

The previous examples explain the prevailing hermeneutical purpose behind the *Epideixis* and how Irenaeus expects his readers to model this brief work in the formal process of interpretation. Irenaeus delivers to his reader a basic introduction to biblical interpretation and expects his catechist to follow his example as he trains others in the faith. In the process of explaining the hermeneutical purpose of this work, he also explains the features of his hermeneutical approach. This approach begins with general theology of inspiration expressed in a principle of coherence described in *Epideixis* 5 that is an extension of his Trinitarian theology.

Catechetical hermeneutics, for Irenaeus, must assume an essential conviction about the nature of God, Christ, and the Spirit. He describes the Trinitarian confession of faith received at baptism in *Epideixis* 7. This confession also assumes a particular theology of creation along with the economic administration of the divine persons over all things. Citing a conflation of Ps 32:6, Eph 4:6, Rom 8:15, and Rom 8:28 he describes the foundational aspect of his catechetical hermeneutic in *Epideixis* 5 saying:

> In this way, then, it is demonstrated [that there is] One God [the] Father, uncreated, invisible, Creator of all, above whom

> there is no other God, and after whom there is no other God. And as God is verbal, therefore He made created things by the Word; and God is Spirit, so that He adorned all things by the Spirit, as the prophet also says, "By the Word of the Lord were the heavens established, and all their power by His Spirit" [Ps 32:6]. Thus, since the Word "establishes," that is, works bodily and confers existence, while the Spirit arranges and forms the various "powers," so rightly is the Son called the Word and the Spirit the Wisdom of God. Hence, His apostle Paul also well says, "One God, the Father, who is above all, and through all and in us all" [Eph 4:6]—because "above all" is the Spirit, who cries, "Abba, Father" [Rom 8:15] and forms man to the likeness of God [Rom 8:28, cf. Gen 1:26]. Thus, the Spirit demonstrates the Word, and, because of this, the prophets announced the Son of God, while the Word articulates the Spirit, and therefore it is He himself who interprets the prophets and brings man to the Father.[31]

It is evident that Irenaeus' catechetical hermeneutic beings with his doctrine of creation and more general understanding of revelation. Both allusions to Ps 32:6 and Eph 4:6 teach that God is the Creator and Sustainer of all things. The later passage is most attentive to God's work in creation. In Irenaeus's reading the Psalmist depicts the way the Word of God confers existence upon all things, and the Spirit of God orders and arranges that which is made. The mutual interaction of the Father, Son, and Spirit brings order and harmony to all that God has created. Within creation, the Father, Son, and Spirit also attend to the formation and salvation of humanity. Citing Eph 4:6, he describes how the Son and the Spirit work together to conform the faithful to the image of God and restore them back to the Father. Thus, these two passages circumscribe that Trinitarian activity amid God's work in creation and salvation. The final lines apply this divine activity specifically to the inspiration and interpretation of the prophets of the Old Testament, which includes all key biblical figures beginning with Moses.[32] The Spirit of God, working through the prophets "demonstrates" (*ostendit*) the Word, which is a reference to the sacred oracles of the prophets.[33] This synopsis explains Irenaeus' Christocentric understanding of the prophetic literature, because their message, in general, is to anticipate the person and work of the incarnate Son of God.[34] Reciprocally, the Spirit also inspires the prophets,

31. *Epid* 5.

32. He begins with the account of Moses in *Epid* 11.

33. *Epid* 5.

34. Irenaeus sees no disparity between the spoken Word of God and the inscribed Word of God. He cites the Old Testament liberally and never questions the

while the Son "articulates the Spirit" (*articulate Spiritum*) and subsequently interprets the prophets.[35]

As a result, this summary communicates the essential aspects of Irenaeus' hermeneutic, and sets the backdrop for his reading of Scripture. Through the mediation of the Son, the Spirit inspires the prophets to proclaim the coming of the Son and likewise the incarnation of the Word illuminates the meaning of the prophets. This establishes a theology of coherence for the Scriptural material and is reminiscent of the interpretive principle "Scripture interprets Scripture" (*scriptura scripturae interpres*) that precipitates through the rest of the history of biblical interpretation.[36] The coherence of scripture, both Old and New Testaments, establishes the basic hermeneutical premise that Irenaeus wishes to communicate to the catechumen. Scriptural interpretation is rooted in the confession of the existence of only one true God who created all things by means of the Son, and to believe that the Spirit inspired the prophets to announce the coming Son. At the same time, the coming of the Son also interprets the prophet.

Therefore, having established this key feature of Irenaeus' Scriptural interpretation, the rest of the *Epideixis* illustrates the application of this hermeneutic to both general and particular aspects of the Scriptures. The general patterns of Irenaeus' biblical interpretation are evident in the broader structural features of this short catechetical work.[37] These general aspects apply a more expansive view of Scriptural coherence between the disparate biblical epochs and genres, especially as they relate to the work of Christ. These general strategies include narratival summaries of biblical history including: both the Old and New Testaments, covenantal fulfillment, or typology, and catalogs of Christological prophecies. Each of these general aspects is also strategically arranged in the following manner: narrative summary (*Epid* 8–30), covenantal or typological fulfillment (*Epid* 30–39), recapitulation and transition (*Epid* 40–42a), catalog of Christological prophecies (*Epid* 42a–85), catalog of prophecies of the New Covenant (*Epid* 86–97).

These general reading strategies explain how the young catechumen should approach the Scriptures as a whole and unite the general portions of Scripture as they relate to Christ. The narrative summaries of the Old Testament history, the covenantal fulfillment, and typological correspondence, the proof from prophecy, and description of the New Covenant demonstrate

correspondence between the text and its historical referent.

35. *Epid* 5. For a more developed discussion of Irenaeus' hermeneutical strategies see: Presley, "The Demonstration of Intertextuality."

36. For example see: Holder, *John Calvin*, 108.

37. For a more detailed discussion of these reading strategies see: Presley, "The Demonstration of Intertextuality."

for his disciple how to work through the major genres of Scripture and how each portion relates to the larger Christological themes. Irenaeus' hermeneutical theory rooted in the theological principle of Scripture interpreting Scripture brings unity to these sections and the general aspect of the work of redemption in Christ.

Within the general contours of Irenaeus' catechetical hermeneutic, and these general reading strategies, he also interprets particular passages through an assortment of exegetical reading strategies. These reading strategies delineate the specific ways that Ireaneus applies his hermeneutical principle *scriptura scripturae interpres*. The particular reading strategies include: verbal association, quotations of Scripture, Scriptural centos, prophecy-fulfillment, typology, narrative summaries, chronological inversion of texts, supportive texts, prosopological interpretation, illustrative texts, allegorical interpretation, and intentional connections between the words of a prophet and apostle.

These analytical descriptions of Irenaeus' reading strategies circumscribe the particular nature of his applied exegesis within the structure of his catechetical hermeneutic and his emphasis on Scripture interpreting Scripture. Each of these particular reading strategies functions in various ways depending upon the particular passage or the location of the text with in the flow of Irenaeus' summary of the work of God in the economy of salvation. Irenaeus does not defend any particular method of exegesis, but instead demonstrates for the catechumen a variety of methods of reading Scripture that could be applied to any number of other passages and contexts. All of these methods are shaped by his concern for the theological coherence of Scripture that derives from the Trinitarian activity of God.

Conclusion: The Hermeneutical Purpose of Irenaeus' *Epideixis*

In conclusion, Irenaeus' *Epideixis* is a basic introduction to early Christian hermeneutics that was intended to be used and taught in catechetical contexts. It is not a summary of Christian doctrine, nor a simple catechetical manual stressing particular doctrinal or moral formation, nor was it a theological or philosophical handbook. Instead, Irenaeus' purpose in the *Epideixis* is hermeneutical formation within a catechetical setting. He provides the catechumen with an introduction to hermeneutics that exemplifies a distinctively Christian way of reading Scripture. Irenaeus' hermeneutical intention forms an *incluiso* as it is expressed in the opening and closing portions of the text and also reiterated at several points throughout the course of his summary. The basis of his catechetical hermeneutic begins with the theological assumption that Spirit-inspired prophets announce the coming of the Son, and coming of the Son interprets the prophets, which is more commonly described as Scripture interprets Scripture (*scriptura scripturam interpreter*). This basic hermeneutical premise sets forth a principle of coherence that also guides the general and specific aspects of Irenaeus' applied exegesis in a variety of contexts. From these examples, the bishop of Lyons fully expects that the young catechumen who receives this hermeneutical instruction will apply it in any liturgical, polemical, or apologetic context. For Irenaeus, his use of Scripture communicates the role of hermeneutics in the catechetical formation of early church. Perhaps the hermeneutical purpose also explains why the *Epideixis* was eventually lost. Introductory textbooks are often set aside as students advance in learning. It is possible that the ancient catechist and catechumen mastered the basics of Irenaeus' catechetical hermeneutic and moved on to apply the general and particular aspects of scriptural interpretation to other passages and contexts. If so, it seems that was Irenaeus' intention all along.

Bibliography

Andresen, Carl. "Zur Entstehung und Geschichte des trinitarischen Personbegriffes." *Zeitschrift für die Neutestamentliche Wissenschaft* 52 (1961) 1–39.

Bacq, Philippe. *De l'ancienne à la nouvelle Alliance selon S. Irénée: unite du livre IV de l'adversus haereses*. Paris: Lethielleux, 1978.

Bates, Matthew W. *The Hermeneutics of the Apostolic Proclamation: The Center of Paul's Method of Scriptural Interpretation*. Waco: Baylor University Press, 2012.

Behr, John. *Irenaeus of Lyons: Identifying Christianity*. Oxford: Oxford University Press, 2014.

———. *St Irenaeus of Lyons, On the Apostolic Preaching*. Crestwood, NY: St Vladimir's Seminary Press, 1997.

Drews, Paul. "Der literarische Charakter der neuentdeckten Schrift des Irenäus Zum Erweise der apostolischen Veründigung." *Zeitschrift für die Neutestamentliche Wissenschaft* 8.1 (1907) 226–33.

Eusebius of Caesarea. *The Ecclesiastical History*. Translation by Kirsopp Lake. Loeb Classical Library. London: W. Heinemann, 1926.

Ferguson, Everett. "Irenaeus' Proof of Apostolic Preaching and Early Catechetical Instruction." *Studia Patristica* 18.3 (1989) 119–40.

Des heiligen Irenäus Schrift zum Erweise der Apostolischen Verkündigung. EIS EPIDEICIN TOU APOSTOLIKOU KHRUGMATOS. In "Armenischer Version entdeckt, herausgegeben und ins Deutsche übersetzt von Karapet Ter-Mĕkĕrttschian und Erwand Ter-Minassiantz. Mit einem Nachwort und Anmerkungen von Adolf von Harnack." TU 31,1. Leipzig, 1907.

Holder, R. Ward. *John Calvin and the Grounding of Interpretation: Calvin's First Commentaries*. Leiden: Brill, 2006.

Lake, Kirsopp, trans. *The Apostolic Fathers, Volume 1: I Clement, II Clement, Ignatius, Polycarp, Didache, Barnabas.* Loeb Classical Library. Harvard: Harvard University Press, 1998.

MacKenzie, Iain M. *Irenaeus's Demonstration of the Apostolic Preaching: A Theological Commentary and Translation.* Burlington, VA: Ashgate, 2002.

Minns, Denis. *Irenaeus: An Introduction.* New York: T. & T. Clark, 2010.

Presley, Stephen O. "The Demonstration of Intertextuality in Irenaeus of Lyons." in *Intertextuality in the Second Century*, edited by D.J. Binghaur and C. Jefford, 195–213. Leiden: Brill, 2016.

———. "Irenaeus and the Exegetical Roots of Trinitarian Theology." in *Irenaeus: Life, Scripture, Legacy*, edited by P. Foster and S. Parvis, 165–72. Minneapolis: Fortress, 2012.

Rondeau, Marie-Josèphe. *Les commentateurs patristiques du Psautier (IIIe-Ve siècls)*, 2 vols. Rome: Pont. Institutum Studiorum Orientalium, 1982, 1985.

Rousseau, Adelin, et al. *Contre les hérésies, Livre 1–V.* Sources Chrétiennes vols. 100, 152, 153, 210, 211, 263, 264, 293, 294. Paris: Éditions du Cerf, 1965–82.

———. *Irénée de Lyon, Démonstration de la Prédication Apostolique*, introduction, traduction, et notes par Adelin Rousseau, Sources Chrétiennes vol. 406. Paris: Les Éditions du Cerf, 2011.

Saint Irénée. *Démonstration de la prédication apostolique.* Translation and Introduction by Joseph Barthoulout and Joseph Tixeront. *Recherches de Science Religieuse* 6 (1916) 361–432.

Slusser, Michael. "The Exegetical Roots of Trinitarian Theology." *Theological Studies* 49 (1988) 461–76.

Smith, J. P. *St. Irenaeus Proof of the Apostolic Preaching, Ancient Christian Writers.* Westminister, MD: Newman, 1952.

Stewart-Sykes, Alistair. *On the Two Ways: Life or Death, Light or Darkness: Foundational Texts in the Tradition.* New York: St Vladimir's Seminary Press, 2011.

Torrance, T. F. "Kerygmatic Proclamation of the Gospel: The Demonstration of Apostolic Preaching of Irenaeus of Lyons." *Greek Orthodox Theological Review* 37 (1992) 105–21.

7

Land Entry and Possession in Origen's Homilies on Joshua

Deep Reading for the Christian Life

LISSA M. WRAY BEAL

Introduction

IN THE LAST YEARS of his life, Origen (AD 185–250)—confessor, churchman, scholar—delivered twenty-six homilies on the book of Joshua. The homilies reveal a pastor exhorting his flock, and a passionate apologist. In them, Origen wrestles with a difficult text within the context of his conviction that the Scriptures of the Old and New Testaments witness to Jesus Christ and serve to edify the church.

Access to the full homilies is through Rufinus' Latin translations. In his Preface, Rufinus notes that Origen delivered them "extemporaneously in church from beginning to end."[1] The extant homilies are a treasure, for extensive patristic treatments of Joshua are rare.

Modern interpretation of Joshua wrestles with several interpretive and theological challenges such as Israel's possession of the land, the dispossession of the resident population, warfare conducted at God's direction, and the ban—the utter destruction of the population. While the contemporary post-colonial context may heighten awareness of these challenges, the pre-modern era was likewise attentive to them.[2] Origen was cognizant

1. White, *Homilies*, 24.

2. For use of the book of Joshua in colonial enterprises, see Comaroff and Comaroff,

of these difficulties, acknowledging them at many of the same points as do modern interpreters. However, Origen's hermeneutical method that sought to resolve these difficulties was unlike the historical-critical, literary, and historical approaches of modern interpreters. Moving beyond a literal reading, Origen applied a sophisticated hermeneutic of figural readings toward theological understanding.

Origen's homilies on Joshua reveal this hermeneutic and the first portion of this chapter explores its explicit statement, and the many places it is demonstrable throughout the homilies. Then, this chapter explores Origen's interpretative work through the lenses of Christology, Soteriology, and Christian praxis. Finally, attention is given to Origen's treatment of problematic texts regarding warfare and the ban. A concluding discussion reflects on the possibility of reclaiming Origen's readings for today, particularly in light of renewed interest in theological reading in the academy and the church. This concluding discussion critiques Origen's christological hermeneutic as valuable but inadequate to engage the text's own discrete witness. Rather, a trinitarian hermeneutic is forwarded as providing a better reading of Joshua as Christian Scripture, and one that is better situated to address the troubling interpretive issues in Joshua noted above.

An Inductive Reading of Origen's Hermeneutic in *Homilies of Joshua*

Origen's homilies do not present a systematic account of his hermeneutic; one turns to the fourth book of *De Principiis* for that.[3] But in the homilies Origen does make some explicit statements of his hermeneutical motives and methods. These are then wholly demonstrable elsewhere in the homilies.

Origen expounds Joshua to edify his audience, saying, "Let us see, therefore, what is indicated by all this and what the present reading may add to our edification."[4] That same homily argues that correctly reading the Old Testament opens the mind and understanding of Jesus to the reader. Like the Emmaus-road disciples, the hearts and minds of Origen's hearers should burn as the Law and Prophets reveal all that was written concerning

Of Revelation and Revolution; Prior, *The Bible and Colonialism*.

3 Daniélou, *Origen*, 140. Daniélou discusses the scriptural, theological, and philosophical aspects of Origen's hermeneutic. Further exposition of Origen's hermeneutic can be found in Crouzel, *Origen*.

4. *Hom Josh* 9.1. Translations of Origen's Homilies on Joshua are from Cynthia White, *Origen*, 2002. Homilies are cited by number and section.

Jesus.[5] Origen's first homily asserts that Joshua "does not so much indicate to us the deeds of the son of Nun, as it represents for us the mysteries of Jesus my Lord."[6] In Joshua, these mysteries are revealed in Christian catechesis, baptism, and victory over sin. Throughout the homilies, the focus on edificatory reading is everywhere upheld.

Origen's passion to edify his audience is informed by his own experience. The text "deeply moves [him]," for in it he sees the "people blessed" and the "world . . . overcome."[7] His joy at the book's ability to edify believers overflows at the close of each homily in a doxological statement that responds to the edifying power of the Word. Each doxology draws upon Gal 1:5 or (alone or in combination) 1 Peter 4:11 and Rev 5:13.

Origen finds hermeneutical motivation for edificatory reading in Prov 22:20. Of the counsel ascribed to Solomon, Origen comments that "we 'read to be transcribed in the heart in a threefold manner.'"[8] Edification is the transcription upon the heart and it notably occurs in a threefold manner. For Origen, this provides warrant by which Scripture speaks at three levels of meaning: literal, moral, and spiritual.[9]

The primary means by which Origen expounds Joshua is spiritual reading, which moves beyond the literal sense to that which reveals the "mysteries of Jesus my Lord."[10] Such reading ascends from "the letter to the spirit, from the figures to the truth" and enables the Christian to ascend to maturity.[11] Thus, in reference to Josh 1:9 ("Every place, wherever you will ascend with the soles of your feet, I shall give to you"), Origen interprets:

> What are the places we ascend with the soles of our feet? The letter of the Law is placed on the ground and lies down below. On no occasion, then, does the one who follows the letter of the Law ascend. But if you are able to rise from the letter to the spirit and also ascend from history to a higher understanding, then truly you have ascended the lofty and high place that you will receive from God as your inheritance. For if in these things that are written you perceive types and observe figures of heavenly

5. *Hom Josh* 9.8.

6. *Hom Josh* 1.3.

7. *Hom Josh* 7. 2, 3.

8. *Hom Josh* 21.2. Origen here works with the LXX reading in which one is admonished to record the sayings "three times [or in a threefold manner] on the table of your heart." MT reads "I have written for you thirty sayings."

9. See the discussion of Origen's threefold method in Barbara J. Bruce's introduction to Origen's homilies in White, *Homilies*, 6-9.

10. *Hom Josh* 1.3.

11. *Hom Josh* 3.1.

> things, and with reflection and intuitive feeling "you seek those things that are above, where Christ is sitting at the right hand of God," then you will receive this place as your inheritance.[12]

At its worst, literal reading is of the "letter that kills," a comparison explicitly made in the homily on the covenant renewal of Josh 8:34:

> An explanation of the history is indeed easy, how the son of Nun read "all the words of the Law that Moses wrote in the presence of the whole church of the sons of Israel." But to point out how our Lord Jesus may do this to his own people, does not seem useless to me. . . . Jesus himself is the one who recites these things in the ears of all the people, admonishing us that we do not follow "the letter that kills" but that we hold fast 'the life-giving spirit.'[13]

Origen does not, however, wholly dismiss a literal reading.[14] He acknowledges its value in his homily on Josh 10:1–16, in which the heavenly bodies fight on behalf of Israel. While acknowledging a literal reading, Origen moves quickly to the greater value of spiritual reading:

> Certainly these deeds, according to history, proclaim the wonders of the divine power to all ages, and since their light flashes from within, they do not need interpretation from without. But, nevertheless, let us inquire what the spiritual interpretation finds within these things.[15]

Elsewhere, Origen remarks on the inadequacy of a literal reading because it is insufficient to explain the text. For instance, the phrase "unto this day" describes Rahab's ongoing habitation amongst the Israelites (Josh

12. *Hom Josh* 2.3.

13. *Hom Josh* 9.8.

14. Helpful discussion of the "literal meaning" in Origen's exegesis can be found in Crouzel, *Origen*, 61–84; Daniélou, *Origen*, 131–99. Origen is a critical exegete, as witnessed by his attention to critical textual work in the *Hexapla* and it is on this careful work that Origen bases his interpretation. After critical textual work, the literal meaning (also referred to as the historical or corporeal meaning; Crouzel, *Origen*, 61) is, for Origen, found in the "raw matter of what is said, before, if it were possible, any attempt at interpretation is made" (Ibid., 62). The literal meaning relates events of history, and may speak prophetically of a messianic figure. Origen does not dismiss the literal meaning but as it does not find its *telos* in Christ, he finds it inadequate for an authentic Christian reading of the Old Testament. Seeking the spiritual meaning arising out of the literal meaning is authentic Christian reading. In it, the Old Testament "in its entirety is a prophecy of Christ, who is the key to it" (Ibid., 64).

15. *Hom Josh* 11.1.

6:25), and the ongoing presence of the Jebusites within Israel (Josh 15:63). Origen comments regarding Rahab:

> But the woman Rahab, how is she said to be joined to the house of Israel up to this very day? Is a succession of posterity on her mother's side ascribed so that she is considered to be preserved in a renewal of offspring? Or rather must it be understood that she has really been bound and united to Israel up to this very day?[16]

And regarding the Jebusites:

> Therefore, let them [those who rely on a literal interpretation] explain to me how the Jebusites dwell with the people of Judah as long as the age remains when, obviously, not even the sons of Judah themselves dwell in Jerusalem. Since not even the Jews themselves dwell in it, it cannot be true that the Jebusites dwell with the Jews in Jerusalem.[17]

Origen's puzzlement is apparent. The literal reading is unable to explain the text and thus no edification can occur. For this reason, Origen moves beyond the literal reading to spiritual reading.

In other instances, Origen's objection is that a literal reading renders the text's action questionable on moral or exemplary grounds. Regarding the casting of lots to allocate the land (Joshua 17–19) Origen writes, "Several times I have asked myself if the holy fathers would ever have committed to the casting of lots a judgment about something so great and important."[18] Origen concedes some value in a literal reading, for "When a lot is drawn out of a sound faith and after prayer, it clearly declares to the people that which the will of God preserves in secret."[19] But such a reading does not suffice. He therefore pursues a spiritual reading by which "through the ineffable providence and foreknowledge of God, a model of the future inheritance in heaven is dimly sketched."[20]

Spiritual reading is the hermeneutic of choice in instances where the text appears contradictory, patently obvious, or distasteful. To resolve the conundrum of whether the land was taken or not taken (Josh 11:23 compared to 13:1), Origen turns to spiritual reading: "Do you think the Scripture would contain things contrary to itself? This must not be lightly regarded. Let us return to the spiritual understanding, and you will find that

16. *Hom Josh* 7.5.
17. *Hom Josh* 21.1.
18. *Hom Josh* 23.1.
19. *Hom Josh* 23.2.
20. *Hom Josh* 23.4.

there is nothing conflicting in it."[21] Likewise, when confronted by the comment on Joshua's old age (Josh 13:1) which Origen says would be patently obvious to all, a spiritual reading provides meaning. Notably, his reading is both christological and moral so that the believer is edified:

> I don't know if we can understand in this passage that the Lord was telling Jesus[22] what all saw and all knew concerning his old age. Indeed, are any of those divine oracles that are reported by people so great that they tell an old man what all saw and all knew: "You are old"? On the contrary, it seems to me that some great testimony is being given here by the Lord to the son of Nun, when it is said to him, "You are advanced of days." And, indeed, as much as it is permitted us to share or disclose of the divine mysteries, I think that just as the sun makes the days of this world, so also the "sun of righteousness" [Mal 3:20] makes those spiritual days that are illumined by the splendor of truth and the lamp of wisdom. Therefore, if in accordance with the commandments of God, anyone passes through this present life—which, just as Jacob said, is "of few and evil days" [Gen 47:9]—and keeps himself unstained from this world and subdues every spiritual adversary and enemy, that person is carried from these "few and evil days" and moved forward to those eternal and good days adorned by the light of the eternal sun. Thus, in the same kind of way, we must also understand Jesus to be proclaimed "advanced of days" by the divine oracles.[23]

Likewise, where the text is distasteful, spiritual reading is utilized. The destruction of Ai (Joshua 8) Origen finds disgusting and distasteful. Thus, a literal reading is inadequate for:

> [People say], "What is this to me? What does it contribute to me if I know that those who were living in Ai were conquered, as if similar or even mightier wars either have not been waged or are being waged? Was this the concern of the Holy Spirit that with so many great and noble cities deserted and demolished, the battle of the city of Ai might be ordered written in the sacred scrolls?"[24]

21. *Hom Josh* 16.3. This particular interpretive question is readdressed later in this paper.

22. Origen uses the name Jesus here, but refers to Joshua as a type of Jesus. The basis of much of Origen's treatment of the person Joshua relies on the fact that in Greek, his name is the same as that given Jesus. More on this follows below in the treatment of Origen's Christology.

23. *Hom Josh* 16.1.

24. *Hom Josh* 8.2.

Lest the hearer be left only with antiquarian information or puzzlement, Origen applies a spiritual reading, for "in order to explain them we need the grace of the Holy Spirit"[25] so that "we are able to find, even in this problem, something worthy of the utterances of the Holy Spirit."[26]

Finally, when mounting an apologetic against Jewish or "heretical" interlocutors, a spiritual reading strategy is used.[27] The Jewish reader, Origen asserts, reads only with "the exterior circumcision in the flesh."[28] In consequence, "they understand nothing in them except wars and the shedding of blood, from which their spirits, too, were incited to excessive savageries and were always fed by wars and strife."[29] By contrast, the Christian reads with a circumcised heart and thus "understands that all these things are mysteries of the kingdom of heaven."[30] The heretic also reads literally. Origen charges that from the warfare texts they "[teach] cruelty"[31] and thus "make malicious charges against our Lord and Savior, 'who commands the kingdom of heaven,' which he had promised to those who believe in him, 'to be seized through violence.'"[32] By employing only a literal reading strategy, the heretics introduce "perverse doctrines . . . [that] . . . introduce into the churches sects not fitting to us, and to pollute all the Church of the Lord."[33] Here, Origen returns to his concern that the church be edified in the faith for,

> If the soul less instructed in the divine Scriptures hears these things, it can in consequence be enfeebled and endangered, so that it may shun the catholic faith; for they do not understand their [the heretics'] deceptions.[34]

These examples reveal Origen employs a spiritual reading strategy for many reasons: where the text is opaque, seemingly immoral, contradictory,

25. *Hom Josh* 8.1.

26. *Hom Josh* 8.4.

27. See an extended discussion of Origen as apologist in Daniélou, *Origen*, 99–127. Within the *Homilies* Origen often refers generically to "heretics," but does twice name three heretics of note: Marcion, Valentinus, and Basilides (*Hom Josh* 7.7, 12.3). These individuals introduced gnostic teachings into the church (White, *Homilies*, 83, n.51). Further polemic against gnostic teaching may be found in *Hom Josh* 10.2, 11.6, 12.3, 14.2, 18.3).

28. *Hom Josh* 13.1.

29. *Hom Josh* 14.1.

30. *Hom Josh* 13.1.

31. *Hom Josh* 11.6.

32. *Hom Josh* 12.2.

33. *Hom Josh* 7.7.

34. *Hom Josh* 10.2.

obvious, distasteful, or where the church must be defended against heresy. While the *Homilies* do not contain a systematic exposition of Origen's hermeneutic, it is everywhere apparent, and at times explicitly enumerated. With this investigation of Origen's hermeneutic, the more specific homily themes of Christology, Soteriology, and Christian living can be encountered with greater understanding.

Origen on Christology, Soteriology, and Christian Living

In the *Homilies*, Origen expounds the Christian life from baptism to resurrection and the eschaton by way of extended typological readings, and allegory. Utilizing the events of the book of Joshua, the Christian enters the Promised Land (life in Christ) through baptism (crossing the Jordan) by the ministry of Jesus (of whom Joshua is a type). In the land, the Christian wages war against the enemies of the soul and of the church. This deep reading is traced below through the themes of Joshua as Jesus, salvation through the Red Sea and Jordan, and Christian discipleship as warfare against enemies.

Joshua Son of Nun: Christ in the *Homilies on Joshua*

Origen takes as his starting point the fact that in the Greek Old Testament, the name given Joshua is identical to that given Jesus. As no other Old Testament luminary has this name, Joshua holds a unique role in a Christian reading. The book recounts not so much "the deeds of the son of Nun" as "the mysteries of Jesus my Lord."[35]

Joshua (hereafter "Jesus," following Origen's practice) is granted primacy of leadership as Moses relinquishes it to one greater.[36] Origen equates Moses with the Old Testament Law, yet the death of Moses does not relegate the Law to the realm of unspiritual uselessness. Citing the *Assumption of Moses,* Origen notes a dual reality of Moses: one "alive in the spirit, another dead in the body."[37] Thus, when the Law is considered only according to the letter, it is Moses dead in the body; when considered as spiritual (achieved through Origen's christological reading), it is Moses alive in the spirit. To this living Moses Jesus is the assistant, bringing the people into the land of promise.

35. *Hom Josh* 1.3.
36. *Hom Josh* 1.1.
37. *Hom Josh* 2.1.

In addition to seeing Joshua as Jesus, Origen sees in the Transjordanian and Cisjordanian tribes a figure of the Trinity and the relationship between the Old Testament saints and the church. In this reading the Transjordanian tribes are a figure of the Old Testament saints, the Cisjordanian tribes are the church, and the half tribe of Manasseh on either side of the Jordan figures the knowledge and reception of the Trinity and the Spirit of God:

> Because of this divided tribe, neither is the third number here made complete [ie., the two and a half tribes as the Old Testament saints], nor the tenth there perfectly and entirely consummated [i.e., the nine and a half tribes as the church]. In these things, I see an indication that those prior ones who used to be led by the Law did indeed touch upon the knowledge of the Trinity, yet not entirely and perfectly but "in part." Concerning the Trinity, they lacked the knowledge of the incarnation of the only begotten one. . . . Therefore those tribes are neither two, lest the fathers [the Old Testament saints] be outside the faith and salvation of the Trinity, nor three entire and perfect, lest the mystery of the blessed Trinity seem already fulfilled among them.[38]

Notably, Origen does not discount a literal reading of the tribes' geographic location, or God's work in the Old Testament saints. They are within the family of salvation yet have not experienced the fullness of God's Person and Work in Christ and the Spirit. Origen does go beyond the literal reading to take up christological realities. Turning to that reality as expressed in the nine and a half tribes (the church), he continues:

> I think that probably not even in the coming of Jesus or in his incarnation do we learn what is perfect and complete. . . . We still have need of another who uncovers and reveals everything to us. Hear the Lord himself in the Gospels saying, "I still have many things that I would tell you, but you are not able to hear them yet. The Spirit of truth who proceeds from the Father will come, and he will take from what is mine, and he will make all things known to you" [John 16:12-14]. . . . None of these things will be considered perfect in anyone for whom is lacking the Holy Spirit, through whom the mystery of the blessed Trinity is fulfilled.[39]

For the people of God on either side of the Jordan there is necessity for something to be added to their faith. The Old Testament saints need the

38. *Hom Josh* 3.2.

39. *Hom Josh* 3.2.

Incarnation and the full revelation of the Trinity; the church needs the full revelation of the Trinity in the Spirit. Without the Spirit, the church remains incomplete and unable to grasp the true interpretation of the mysteries of Christ.

Not only does Origen's spiritual reading find in Joshua a figure of the Trinity, but the Incarnation as well. Working with the etymology of Rahab's name (from the Hebrew root *rhb* with connotations of "broad, wide"), Origen cites Rahab as a type of the church, a communion drawn broadly from "sinners as if from prostitution."[40] Using a common allegorical trope, the church:

> puts the scarlet-colored sign in her house, through which she is bound to be saved from the destruction of the city. No other sign would have been accepted, except the scarlet-colored one that carried the sign of blood. For she knew that there was no salvation for anyone except in the blood of Christ.[41]

In this trope, those who enter the house—the church—are saved; those who remain outside cannot be purified. But Origen then takes the imagery in a new direction so as to figure the Incarnation. He notes the cord is hung in a window which illumines the house, giving light to those within:

> not wholly but enough, enough to suffice for the eye and for our vision. Even the incarnation of the Savior did not give us pure wine and the whole aspect of divinity, but through his incarnation, just as through the window, he makes us behold the splendor of the divinity. For that reason, so it seems to me, the sign of salvation was given through a window.[42]

Although in this passage Origen notes the Incarnation does not give the "whole aspect of divinity," the lack is remedied in the exaltation of Joshua at the Jordan crossing (Josh 4:14). Here Origen sees the revelation of the full splendour of Christ's divinity. This exaltation is, in Origen's reading, intimately connected to the initiation of baptism, figured in the Jordan crossing, and to which we now turn.

40. *Hom Josh* 3.4.

41. *Hom Josh* 3.5.

42. *Hom Josh* 3.5.

Red Sea; River Jordan: Salvation in the *Homilies on Joshua*

Origen utilizes both the crossing of the Red Sea and the River Jordan as figures of Christian initiation, an interpretive strategy not uncommon in his day.[43] Most frequently, the Jordan figures baptism, while the Red Sea figures entry to the Catechumenate. Less frequently, it is the Red Sea that figures baptism.[44]

In the more frequent figure (the Jordan as baptism), the Red Sea crossing signifies entry to the Catechumenate. The catechumen has "followed Moses by observing the precepts and commandments of the Law"[45] and been "baptized into Moses in the cloud and in the sea."[46] During this initiatory period the catechumen learns of Christian faith and tests the desire to join the church. The catechumen has "undertaken to submit to the precepts of the church, [has] parted the Red Sea and, placed in the stations of the desert, [is daily devoted] to hearing the Law of God and looking upon the face of Moses, through which the glory of the Lord is revealed."[47]

In the initiation into Moses the catechumen is witness to great things: manna from heaven, springs in the wilderness, and the Law of Moses given on Sinai. But only when the Catechumenate leads to baptism and full initiation into the church does one experience the glories of Christ. At the "mystic font of baptism" and "with the Jordan parted, you will enter the land of promise by the services of the priests."[48] In the baptism of the Jordan one sees Jesus exalted, for "Jesus is not exalted before the mystery of baptism."[49] Thus, expounding Josh 4:14 in which Joshua at the Jordan is exalted in the sight of all Israel, Origen reflects that:

> I myself think that he was always exalted and elevated in the presence of the Father. But it is necessary that God exalt him in *our* sight. He is exalted in my sight when the sublimity and loftiness of his divinity is disclosed to me. When, therefore, is his lofty divinity revealed to me? At that time, assuredly, when

43. Daniélou, *Origen*, 58.
44. This less frequent image is taken up later in this section.
45. *Hom Josh* 1.7.
46. *Hom Josh* 5.1. See 1 Cor 10:2.
47. *Hom Josh* 4.1.
48. Ibid.
49. *Hom Josh* 4.2.

> I crossed over the Jordan and was equipped with the various defenses of the sacraments for the future battle.[50]

Once over the Jordan, one has fully entered the church, figuratively represented by the prostitute Rahab.[51] As a prostitute, Rahab was under the wrath of the king of Jericho. Jericho is a figure of the world out of which Rahab is saved.[52]

Reflecting further on the Jordan crossing as an image of baptism, Origen recalls the people crossed the Jordan in haste (Josh 4:10) and finds here a spiritual truth: the reception of baptism and the sacraments should not be undertaken idly or negligently but hastily—that is, with an attitude of concentrated attention. In this way the baptized "should hurriedly press on all the way until we cross over everything"[53] and thus "accomplish all the things that are commanded."[54]

This posture of haste is to continue after the baptism of the Jordan crossing, particularly in the face of persecution. The believer should receive persecution humbly and hasten through its burden (that is, pass through with concentrated attention). By this, the believer demonstrates the virtue of patience. More, the believer is to seek "earnestly and swiftly—not slowly and languidly—those individual things that pertain to the glory of virtue."[55]

Elsewhere, Origen uses a different figure for the stages of Christian initiation. Rather than entry to the Catechumenate understood as passing through the Red Sea, Origen uses the figure of a "first circumcision." By this circumcision the catechumen casts off idolatry, superstition, and the worship of images.[56] In this figure, the "second circumcision" is baptism so that, if one:

> comes from the Law and the Prophets to the gospel faith, then he also receives the second circumcision through "the rock, who is Christ" . . . so that if anyone has not been cleansed through the gospel by a second circumcision, he is not able to put aside the reproach of Egypt, that is, the allurement of fleshly vices.[57]

50. *Hom Josh* 5.3.
51. *Hom Josh* 1.4; 3.4; 6.4.
52. *Hom Josh* 7.
53. *Hom Josh* 5.1.
54. Ibid.
55. Ibid.
56. *Hom Josh* 5.5.
57. *Hom Josh* 5.5-6. See also *Hom Josh* 1.7.

Origen is not entirely consistent in figuring the Red Sea as entry into the Catechumenate, and the Jordan crossing as baptism. In his final homily on Joshua, and amidst a discussion of the rock knives by which Jesus circumcised the Israelites (citing Josh 21:42 in the LXX), he equates baptism with the Red Sea. After baptism, one must be circumcised by Jesus who applies the word of God to remove all impurities and vices. The necessity of this circumcision is apparent:

> For what good is it for us to have gone forth from Egypt and yet carry around with us the reproaches of Egypt? What good is it to travel through the wilderness, that is, what does it help us to have renounced this age in baptism but to retain the former filth of our behavior and the impurities of our carnal vices? Thus it is fitting, after the parting of the Red Sea, that is, after the grace of baptism, for the carnal vices of our old habits to be removed from us by means of our Lord Jesus, so that we can be free from the Egyptian reproaches.[58]

In addition to exploring the means of initiation into salvation, Origen considers salvation's consummation. He sees in the book of Joshua the final salvation and inheritance of heaven. This inheritance is figured by the casting of lots.[59] Origen is troubled by the inclusion of chance (i.e., lot casting) in the pages of Scripture but by his spiritual hermeneutic the lot is interpreted to indicate the rich inheritance distributed amongst the saints according to their warrants.

For Origen the book of Joshua and the events of escape from Egypt and entry to the land are figures of Christian initiation, baptism, Christian life, and future salvation. All of these are construed in relation to Jesus, the one who takes up Moses' leadership, perfecting and completing its deficiencies.

Fighting and Conquering: Christian Living in the *Homilies on Joshua*

Origen repeatedly uses the Jordan crossing as a figure for baptism. He also uses it as a figure for the believer's entry to eternal life. In this formulation, it is the Passover that figures baptism. The Passover is the "mystery of the lamb . . . in Egypt"[60] through which the believer "has escaped the errors of

58. *Hom Josh* 26.2.

59. For the land in Joshua 17–19 see *Hom Josh* 23 and for the portion granted the levitical tribes see *Hom Josh* 17, 25.

60. *Hom Josh* 4.4.

the world [Egypt]."[61] The Jordan crossing, then, becomes the day in which one "enter[s] the land of promise, that is, the blessedness of perfection."[62]

Origen notes that baptism (the Passover) and entry to eternal rest (the Jordan crossing) occur on the same day (the tenth day of the first month; see Exod 12:3; Josh 4:19). This one day figures the entirety of the believer's life in Christ, "this day in which we live in this age."[63] In this one "day" the believer is urged to the perfecting work of discipleship:

> [We are] instructed through that mystery [i.e., the Passover/baptism] to not put off our acts and works of righteousness until tomorrow, but rather "today"—that is, while we are living, while we are lingering in this world—to make haste to accomplish all things that pertain to perfection.[64]

In Origen's more common image of the Jordan crossing as baptism, it is the life in the land that depicts Christian living. Thus, warfare in the land is the Christian struggle against sin and the battle is led by Christ who:

> wars against opposing powers and casts out of their cities, that is, out of our souls, those who used to occupy them. And he destroys the kings who were ruling in our souls "that sin may no longer reign in us," [citing Rom 6:12] so that, after he abolishes the king of sin from the city of our soul, our soul may become the city of God and God may reign in it, and it may be proclaimed to us, 'Behold, the kingdom of God is within you.'[65]

In this battle, the Christian takes up spiritual weapons: prayer, the Word of God, good deeds, and good thoughts, all while invoking the help of Jesus Christ. Only in this way does the Christian withstand the works of the Devil.[66]

The book of Joshua provides Origen with many figures for Christian warfare. For instance, in a literal reading the Canaanites who dwell amongst the tribes (Josh 16.10) are to be defeated, enslaved, or driven out. Origen interprets this as a figure of our flesh—initially ungovernable, but over time brought into submission and finally exterminated. In the extermination of

61. Ibid.

62. Ibid.

63. Ibid.

64. Ibid.

65. *Hom Josh* 13.1. The passage cites Luke 17:21.

66. *Hom Josh* 16.5.

the flesh, the believer comes to the perfection of those who belong to Christ and have "crucified the flesh with its vices and lusts."[67]

Elsewhere, Origen interprets the five kings of Josh 10:5 as the believer's assailant. The kings are identified as the five corporeal senses of sight, hearing, taste, touch, and smell "for it must be through one of these that each person falls away into sin."[68] Origen interprets the five kings hiding themselves in earthly caves as revealing the insidious nature of the five senses for, "after being placed in the body . . . [they] immerse themselves in earthly impulses and do nothing for the work of God but all for the service of the body."[69] Victory over these senses comes as Jesus conquers the five kings and takes over their kingdoms. Once subdued by Jesus, the senses become servants working the righteousness of God.

The Canaanite kings of Joshua 11 likewise provide a figure for the Christian battle against sin and the flesh. In *Homily* 14 Origen employs complex etymology and word association. By this method, the names of kings and places in Joshua 11 are accorded spiritual meaning.[70] For instance, the etymology of King Jabin's name (Josh 11:1) is rendered as "thought" or "prudence." Origen links this idea with the kingly pride noted in Isa 10:12–13 and concludes that "Jabin" represents "proud thought." Further reflection connects this to the serpent which was more prudent than all the animals (Gen 3:1) and thus Jabin is a figure for the Devil. Jabin attacks the Christian by sending for kings in the Arabah (Josh 11:2), a place name Origen interprets as meaning "ambushes." Thus the Devil summons "the powers of waylayers, which entrap human souls not by strength nor by open battles, but by unforeseen and cunning ambushes."[71] To complete the figure, Hazor (King Jabin's city) means "court" and thus the Devil "holds the supremacy of the whole earth as though of one court."[72]

Through such figures, Origen sees "the entire army of invisible foes who are assembled by King Jabin in order to fight against us who follow

67. *Hom Josh* 22.1–2. The passage cites Gal 5:24; see similar figures in *Hom Josh* 21 and 24.

68. *Hom Josh* 11.4.

69. Ibid.

70. Hanson, "Interpretation of Hebrew Names," 103–23. Hanson investigates Origen's etymological method, concluding that he starts either with the Greek word, dividing it into syllables, translating the syllables into Hebrew and then attempting to derive an interpretation, or by starting with the Hebrew word, making sense of it either as it stands or through syllabification.

71. *Hom Josh* 14.2.

72. Ibid. See similar comment in *Hom Josh* 15.3.

Jesus, our leader and Savior."[73] Origen concludes this homily by exhorting his listeners not to fear or shrink back from such battles, stating that their enemies' doom is sealed at the consummation of the age. Then, all such powers will be pulled down and those who have faithfully followed Jesus in the battle will have conquered and taken full possession of the land.

In the Christian battle, Origen urges his listeners to be like Caleb, whose name is read to mean "as a heart." Caleb's heart is "devoted to divine understandings" and "conducts all things wisely and reasonably."[74] In battle Caleb attacks the difficult high places (the "doctrines of the ungodly and the syllogisms of the philosophers . . . and the heretics" by proclaiming the truth of Christ.[75] For his victory, he is granted Hebron (Josh 14:6–15). All of this stands as a figure to edify the believer:

> But you, too, if you are willing to give attention to studies and wisely to contemplate the Law of God and to be made a "heart" in the Law of God, you can overthrow these great and fortified towns, that is, the assertions of falsehood. Then you also may deserve to be blessed by Jesus and to receive Hebron from him.[76]

Warfare and Land: The "Joshua Problem" in the *Homilies on Joshua*

Origen, like many modern interpreters, is deeply troubled by interpretive issues in Joshua such as the apparent contradiction of the land being both taken and not taken (compare, for instance, Josh 11:23 to 13:1), the presence of warfare in Scripture, and the destruction of the inhabitants (Josh 6:21; 8:22, 26; 10:40; 11:20; see also Deut 7:2; 20:16). Origen does not wholly dismiss a literal reading and therefore he is faced with these challenges. But as noted earlier it is precisely the text's contradictions and distastefulness that signal the necessity of spiritual reading so as to enable edification. Often this is accomplished through a christological lens by which Origen asserts the true sense of the text is revealed.

In regard to the claim that all the land is taken (Josh 11:23), Origen acknowledges the limitation of a literal reading, for historical Joshua did not take all the earth or give it "rest from war" as the verse indicates. Of course, this difficulty is apparent to modern interpreters too. Origen's resolution

73. *Hom Josh* 14.2.

74. *Hom Josh* 18.2.

75. *Hom Josh* 18.3.

76. Ibid.

differs from those of modern interpreters who may (for instance) argue that hyperbole is here in effect. By spiritual reading Origen understands "total possession" to mean the multitude of believers from all over the earth who have flocked to Jesus. And, in the remission of sins through baptism,

> Your land [speaking to individual believers] has ceased from wars if you still "carry around the death of Jesus Christ in your body" so that, after all battles have ceased in you, you may be made "peaceable" and you may be called "a child of God."[77]

Further, in the contradiction of the land both taken and not taken, Origen discerns a figure of Christ's first and second coming.[78] At his first coming, he sowed the seed of his word; this is the land taken. Many, however, have not responded to the word for Christ's rule does not yet extend to all. This, then, is the land that remains to be taken at the second coming of Christ.

Origen is deeply perplexed by the presence of warfare and destruction in Scripture, as noted in the opening of *Homily* 15:

> Unless those physical wars bore the figure of spiritual wars, I do not think the books of Jewish history would ever have been handed down by the apostles to the disciples of Christ, who came to teach peace, so that they could be read in the churches.[79]

He charges those who read only at a literal level as reading with the Jews and heretics.[80] To ensure such texts are worthy of inclusion within Christian Scripture, Origen urges his audience to "understand the wars of the just by the method [spiritual reading] I set forth . . . that these wars are waged by them against sin."[81]

Finally, Origen spends little time addressing the problematic issue of the ban. His discomfort with a literal reading is apparent, for he characterizes his spiritual reading as "more devout and more merciful."[82] But, by understanding the ban as Jesus' destruction of all the enemies of the believer's soul, the troubling question of wholesale slaughter of real peoples while acknowledged, is diverted by a spiritual reading directed toward edification.

77. *Hom Josh* 15.7. This passage cites 2 Cor 4:10 and Matt 5:9.

78. *Hom Josh* 16.3.

79. *Hom Josh* 15.1.

80. Ibid.

81. *Hom Josh* 8.7.

82. *Hom Josh* 13.3.

Conclusion: Towards Present-Day "Deep Reading"

This chapter explored and demonstrated Origen's hermeneutic applied to the challenging book of Joshua. Origen's spiritual reading strategy often relieved his discomfort with the text's literal meaning. What can be said toward reclamation of Origen's methods as a reading strategy for this problematic text? Given recent exploration and adoption of theological reading strategies, can (or should) Origen's method be taken up to read Joshua? What follows are some preliminary reflections on the question.

One readily sees in Origen's homilies an interpreter working within the Rule of Faith. There is an interpretive "family resemblance" that is recognizable as he seeks to give a "faithful witness to Jesus Christ."[83] Much of his work still edifies, and his evident love for Christ and the church is stirring.[84] This attitude is apparent even toward those texts that most tax the interpreter. He acknowledges where the text is inscrutable but maintains clear respect for it. He remains committed to exegete the text for the benefit of the church. This is an attitude for emulation.

Further, Origen's stance is a corrective to approaches that seek meaning for the book of Joshua *only* in historical exploration, either antiquarian interest in "what actually happened" or the text's compositional history. Such investigation behind the text can add to an understanding of the message of Joshua and provide fruitful engagement; more, such work need not be devoid of theological concern.[85] It is when the meaning of Joshua is *tied* necessarily to historicizing concerns that the message of Scripture *qua* Scripture can be lost.[86] Thus, Christopher Seitz rightly argues that "Only when the literal sense is reencountered in our time, apart from a valorizing of 'proximity to the real,' in history or in tradition, will the way forward be found again for a Christian handling of Old and New Testaments as scripture for the church and world."[87]

83. Childs, *The Struggle to Understand Isaiah*, 322.

84. In a recent Old Testament Theology class at Providence Theological Seminary (an evangelical seminary), I shared some of Origen's homilies. Interestingly, students took encouragement from Origen's work and passion, even if discounting some of his interpretive methods.

85. One need only engage commentaries such as Hess, *Joshua* to see the value of historical inquiry toward hearing the message of scripture; the two pursuits need not be contradictory.

86. Douglas S. Earl warns of this in *Reading Joshua*, 35, when he comments that "Joshua has become 'tired', with its significance assumed to lie in historicizing terms." Christopher R. Seitz makes a similar appeal in *Figured Out*, 13–47.

87. Seitz, *Figured Out*, 47.

Besides this corrective, Origen engages the thorny challenge of the relationship of the two Testaments. He is instructive in his unabashed stance regarding the unity of Scripture, a stance that enables his exegetical method. Both Testaments speak of the one reality of Jesus Christ and the literal meaning (while instructive) is only the foundation of the fuller meaning revealed through the Spirit and which everywhere points to Christ.

It is this christological hermeneutic that drives Origen's figural readings. These might be typological or allegorical in nature and, at times, the strict division between these two types of figural readings are not as clear-cut as modern definitions suggest; nor does Origen himself use such labels.[88] It may be that "figural reading" is the better term, enabling a spectrum of "imaginative exploration of the significance of the symbolism in a new context as a *development* of the original act of discourse."[89] Such reading is "an effort to hear the two-testament witness to God in Christ, taking seriously its plain sense, in conjunction with apostolic teaching."[90] Origen's work is an important conversation–partner in the current consideration of the present-day definition, value, and limits of figural reading.

Origen's figural reading of the Jordan crossing as Christian initiation, and the possession of the land as Christian discipleship holds promise for integration into present-day theological readings. Such is the case with Richard Ounsworth in *Joshua Typology in the New Testament*.[91] Working primarily with the Letter to the Hebrews (chs. 3–4, 11), Ounsworth presents a sophisticated and largely compelling reading of Joshua typology in that letter.[92] He acknowledges his debt to Origen by beginning his discussion with Origen's own warrant for a Joshua-Jesus typology: that in the LXX, the name "Joshua" is the same as the name for Jesus.

Affirming a figural reading, however, is not the same as reclaiming all of Origen's methods for today's Joshua interpreters. Two main reasons for such hesitation are here considered. First, Origen works with a wholly christological hermeneutic. By this, he fails in reading the Old Testament

88. Ibid., 9. Part of the impetus of Seitz's work in this volume is to question the assertion of a sharp contrast between typology and allegory (vii).

89. Earl, *Reading Joshua*, 124. In Earl's larger discussion of the development of textual themes, he notes that "Calvin's comments on the text are not too far removed from Origen's" and concludes, "In a sense then, traditional readings manifest what it is in the original act of discourse that can be developed, in an imaginative existential manner, to find enduring significance in a Christian context."

90. Seitz, *Figured Out*, 10.

91. Ounsworth, *Joshua Typology*.

92. Ibid., 53; Ounsworth here summarizes the chapter by providing his typological reading strategy.

as a discrete witness within the context of ancient Israel. This witness is, on its own terms, able to speak within the Christian canon of God's work in and through the Israelites. There is a supersessionism in Origen that should not be reclaimed. The Christian canon can (and should) allow that God did reveal himself to the Israelites and that Christians can observe that for their spiritual benefit.

Rather than a christological hermeneutic, which (certainly as Origen applies it) limits or squashes the discrete witness of the Old Testament's revelation to the same saving God as revealed in the New Testament, a trinitarian hermeneutic appears more apt for reading the Old Testament. A trinitarian hermeneutic, likes Origen's christological hermeneutic, is Christocentric and Christotelic. But it holds the Testaments together through the affirmation that "the God and Father of our Lord Jesus Christ is the God of Israel."[93] It thus maintains the ontological connection between the two Testaments while allowing the Old Testament to speak on its own terms. In this way, it reveals God's work within Israel and prepares for the fuller revelation of God in Christ.[94]

With such a hermeneutic, historic Joshua's entry to the land remains a witness to God's work amongst and to the Israelites. Additionally, it allows the text to be couched in the culture and literary genres of its time, and study of such contexts sheds light on understanding the witness of the book. Here, for instance, one thinks of the value of reviewing the genre of ancient conquest accounts, or the study of the phenomenon of the ban, or the data on historical questions such as the nature of the walls' construction at Jericho. Attending to questions of ancient Near Eastern culture, language, genre, and so on goes a long way to lessen, explain, and perhaps remove many of the text's difficulties that spurred Origen's christological interpretation. Further, such study can preclude Origen's egregious use of etymology to find spiritual meaning.

Applying a trinitarian hermeneutic rather than a christological one allows the text's discrete witness to God's activity within the Old Testament to remain and speak to a Christian audience. But the fuller witness gained by its *telos* in Christ is not hindered. One still moves to its fuller message revealed in Christ and New Testament realities—whether through typological, thematic, or other means.

The second hesitation here forwarded for not affirming a full reclamation of Origen's christological hermeneutic in Joshua is that, by seeking the fuller, christological meaning, he is freed to bypass the difficulties of the

93. Bartholomew, "Listening," 8.

94. Ibid. See also Seitz, *Figured Out*, 4–6.

literal meaning. Origen need not answer the difficult questions of the literal text such as: *why* does God command the ban? *what* of the intended wholesale takeover of another peoples' land? *how* are these actions compatible with a God of love?

Given the real history of abuse using the Joshua texts—abuse against real people in real places—it seems less than theological to read these texts without addressing the questions of a literal and historical reading.[95] The employment of a trinitarian hermeneutic does not avoid these questions, but must face them. Should the church wish to speak theologically to itself and to the world it serves, this is a difficult task that must be undertaken. This is best done within a trinitarian reading that hears the Old Testament on its own terms while also attending to the text's *telos* in Christ.

Bibliography

Bartholomew, Craig. "Listening for God's Address: A *Mere* Trinitarian Hermeneutic for the Old Testament." In *Hearing the Old Testament: Listening for God's Address*, edited by Craig Bartholomew and David J. H. Beldman, 3–20. Grand Rapids: Eerdmans, 2012.

Childs, Brevard. *The Struggle to Understand Isaiah as Christian Scripture*. Grand Rapids: Eerdmans, 2004.

Comaroff, Jean, and John Comaroff. *Of Revelation and Revolution: Christianity, Colonialism, and Consciousness in South Africa*. Volume 1. Chicago: University of Chicago Press, 1991.

Crouzel, Henri. *Origen*. Translated by A. S. Worrall. San Francisco: Harper & Row, 1989.

Daniélou, Jean. *Origen*. Translated by Walter Mitchell. New York: Sheed and Ward, 1955.

Earl, Douglas S. *Reading Joshua as Christian Scripture*. Journal of Theological Interpretation Sup 2. Winona Lake: Eisenbrauns, 2010.

Hanson, Richard P. C. "Interpretations of Hebrew Names in Origen." *Vigiliae Christianae* 10 (1956) 103–23.

Hess, Richard S. *Joshua: An Introduction and Commentary*. The Tyndale Old Testament Commentaries. Downers Grove, IL: InterVarsity, 1996.

McConville, J. Gordon, and Stephen N. Williams. *Joshua*. Two Horizons Old Testament Commentary Series. Grand Rapids: Eerdmans, 2010.

Origen. *Homilies on Joshua*. Edited by C. White and translated by B. J. Bruce. The Fathers of the Church 105. Washington: The Catholic University of America Press, 2002.

Ounsworth, Richard. *Joshua Typology in the New Testament*. Wissenschaftliche Untersuchungen zum Neuen Testament 2. Reihe 328. Tübingen: Mohr Siebeck, 2012.

95. See a well-executed example of a reading that addresses literal and historical questions while reading theologically in McConville and Williams, *Joshua*.

Prior, Michael. *The Bible and Colonialism: A Moral Critique*. Sheffield: Sheffield Academic, 1997.

Seitz, Christopher R. *Figured Out: Typology and Providence in Christian Scripture*. Louisville: Westminster John Knox, 2001.

8

Integrating Systematic and Biblical Theology

Creation as a Test Case

Craig Blaising

At its initial meeting, the "Biblical Theology, Hermeneutics, and Theological Disciplines," section of the Institute for Biblical Research proposed the idea of discussing the integration of biblical and systematic theology. After some conversation around the table in which we introduced ourselves, our projects, and our interest in this dialogue, I agreed to help us launch the discussion with a proposal on Creation as a thematic area in which the possibilities of such integration might be tested. This essay is that proposal.

It is my hope in this exercise to demonstrate the benefit that may come by bringing the interests of these two fields to bear upon a common topic. In doing so, my hope is to encourage and perhaps stimulate further discussion on such integration generally as well as on the topic at hand. I certainly do not intend or claim to present any kind of thoroughgoing integration of the two fields in this essay. Rather, this proposal is more like a draft experiment or trial balloon intended to get us talking about integration issues in general, as well as the topic of Creation in particular.

Now a purist might object that it is more reasonable to begin with prolegomena, focusing on matters of field definition and methodology, before actually undertaking the task of integrating our two disciplines on a particular doctrinal theme. What is Biblical Theology? What is Systematic

Theology? What are the methodological approaches of these disciplines, and how might integration be attempted methodologically with due respect to the interests of both fields?

I am quite sympathetic to an objection of this sort. I certainly agree that field definition and methodology are important. However, there are a couple of problems with beginning in this way. First, the two fields are contested on method, approach, and even major aspects of content. Some have expressed doubts whether either of these fields, as traditionally conceived, are even possible methodologically. Books on Biblical Theology with titles containing words like "Crisis," "Collapse," or "Beyond" certainly give one pause.[1] And, in some traditions, the coherence of theological work is so contested that one is more likely to find histories, handbooks or dictionaries of theology than *systematic* theologies per se. Given the state of things, this IBR section could occupy itself entirely with methodological issues without ever attempting the actual integration of which we would be merely theorizing.

That prospect leads to the second problem, which is that even though we as academics can sustain ourselves at length in theoretical discussions of this nature, beyond the endurance of ordinary folks, even we have to admit that lengthy theoretical discussion tends to be boring. It is much more interesting to talk about theory when one has some live specimen on the table. Or, to change the metaphor, perhaps we can see ourselves as Alton Brown-like chefs in the kitchen discussing scientific aspects of a proposed recipe while throwing real food in pots and giving it a stir! Even if the experiment turns out to be a disaster (which it never does for Alton Brown), not to worry—we weren't planning to serve it today anyway. But, maybe we can learn something in the process.

So, with the reservations duly noted and throwing caution to the wind, let's put the doctrine of creation on the table and see what we have here. Keeping our culinary metaphor, we will put a measure of systematic theology and a measure of biblical theology in the bowl and see what we get when we combine them. Let's start by noting the two ingredients separately to see what we are facing in the integrative attempt.

Traditionally in systematic theology, Creation fits into the loci just after the doctrine of God. It's primary concern is with the nature or essence of things vis-à-vis God.[2] The chief point to be made is that all things were

1. Childs, *Biblical Theology in Crisis*; Perdue, *The Collapse of History*; Räisänen, *Beyond New Testament Theology*.

2. Note as a typical example, the treatment of creation in Hodge, *Systematic Theology*, 1:550–74.

created by God *ex nihilo*.[3] This is set forth in contrast to other religious, philosophical, or scientific views theologians have contended with from late antiquity to the modern era. Ideas of causation, design, and order are typically discussed, keeping in view the primary concern for the ontological status of all things with respect to God. The primary biblical basis for the doctrine is Genesis 1–2 with other texts from Psalms, Isaiah, or the New Testament brought in as well.

The creation of man, or humankind, is also discussed by the systematicians ontologically and teleologically. Attention is typically focused on the *imago dei*, with comparisons drawn between human moral, rational or spiritual qualities, and the divine attributes. Systematically, this presentation forms the necessary preunderstanding for hamartiology, including its doctrines of the Fall and original sin. This is further connected to considerations of Christological ontology and soteriology. However the theologians may construe their *system*, typically the doctrine of creation presents the ontological standing of all things, including the reflected image of God, in relation to God himself and in accordance with his plan and purpose.

Instead of ontology, biblical theologies of creation, typically highlight creation over against chaos.[4] Many acknowledge creation *ex nihilo* as a valid inference from Scripture—biblical texts do stress the radical contingency of creation by divine Word. However, it is the act of bringing an order into existence over against disorderliness that is the particular focus in the various biblical theologies. Typically, creation is discussed in comparison with and in contrast to religious views in the ancient Near East, especially the notion of a *Chaoskampf*. Although opinion is divided on the matter, most generally acknowledge that although the imagery of *Chaoskampf* is used in different ways in Scripture, the *Kampf* functions as a demythologized metaphor.[5]

Biblical theologies also tend to stress the connection of creation and history which in turn leads to the thematic link of creation and redemption. One can see therein a link between creation and eschatology with it expectation of a new creation. In biblical narrative, creation appears at the beginning of the history of Israel, a historical narrative in which types of creation imagery replay themselves (as for example in the Exodus). Israel in

3. Note the presentation of the classical theological formulation of the doctrine of creation by Hartt, "Creation and Providence," 142–52.

4. On the treatment of the theme of creation in Old Testament Theology, see Anderson, ed. *Creation in the Old Testament*. For an overview of the more recent focus on creation in Old Testament theology, see the section, "Creation Theology," in the chapter by Perdue, "Old Testament Theology Since Barth's *Epistle to the Romans*," 91–102.

5. See Anderson and Bishop, *Contours of Old Testament Theology*, 87–88. Note the recent publication by Tsumura, *Creation and Destruction*.

particular is the creation of God.[6] One might say that in biblical theology, redemption history is continuous creation—a different notion than what is usually expressed in traditional systematic theology. In the New Testament, the relation of Christ and creation is especially developed and the eschatological notion of new creation is reaffirmed along with the eschatological nature of the kingdom of God.

Biblical theologies may be structured thematically or textually, but they are typically informed by some construal of historical development, whether that be a critical history of religion, tradition history, or the narrative history presented by the canonical text. Each of the notions of history and historical development has a bearing on how the textual material is arranged for theological reflection. With respect to the theme of creation, this affects how one assesses the major textual sources, from early Genesis to latter Isaiah, the Psalms and Wisdom sources.

Since the work of Brevard Childs, a number of projects have focused on the canonical, or final form, text over against critical reconstructions of textual history.[7] Such focus privileges the narrative history presented by the text as that which is most important for theological study. This refocusing of biblical theology has been hailed by some as a recovery of the theological sense of Scripture. We may also see it as one which marks an opportunity for reconsidering the relationship between biblical theology and systematic theology.

My own interest in biblical theology lies at the level of the canonical text and the narrative history presented by the text. On the systematic theology side, I take a high view of the authority of Scripture, which means that Scripture functions for me as a textual form of verbal revelation. Methodologically, I see the interpretation of revelation as central to systematic theology. Consequently, the construal of Scripture as verbal revelation orients the hermeneutical work of theology to the canonical text of Scripture. This in turn accords well with a biblical theological approach which also focuses on the canonical text.

In what follows, I would like to propose a list of theological points which in my opinion arise from an integration of the concerns and interests of our two fields, given the common textual focus I have just noted. It is beyond the scope of this paper to offer extensive justification for these points. Some are arguably more obvious than others. My purpose is more

6. The relation between creation and history was acknowledged by Von Rad although he had earlier relegated the theology of creation to a late Wisdom tradition. See: von Rad, *Old Testament Theology*, 1:136, 138–39.

7. Childs, *Biblical Theology of the Old and New Testaments*; see also idem, *Old Testament Theology in a Canonical Context*.

provocative than demonstrative, given the purpose of this volume. However, I do believe that these points, while sometimes drawing more on the interests of one field than the other, nevertheless integrate to some degree the concerns of both. The final two points will be described more at length. They suggest, what I think is the promising direction for integrative thought on the theme of Creation.

I do need to note that for the purpose of this discussion, I am bracketing the question of the relationship of the language of Genesis 1–2 to scientific theories of origins for the simple reason that this can easily dominate a theological discussion of Creation. There is so much to be said about the theology of creation regardless of how one takes the "days" in Genesis 1 or relates them to scientific views on earthly or cosmic formation. Having said all that, I would suggest that an integrative (biblical and systematic) theology of Creation might include the following key points.

All things are radically contingent on the free will and purpose of God.

Here we find creation *ex nihilo* tied to the uniqueness of God which points to the ontological distinction of all things and radical dependence of all things on God. Some of biblical language that informs this view (but not taken as "proof texts") include:

1. In the beginning, God created the heavens and the earth (Gen 1:1).
2. I am the Lord, who made all things, who alone stretched out the heavens, who spread out the earth by myself (Isa 44:24).
3. It is he who made the earth by his power, who established the world by his wisdom and by his understanding stretched out the heavens (Jer 10:12).
4. He calls into existence things that do not exist (Rom 4:17).
5. By him all things were created, in heaven and on earth, visible and invisible (Col 1:15).

Creation and re-creation (redemption) takes place by the Word of God, which not only imparts and empowers existence but also brings order and beauty as opposed to disorder and sterility.

Some of the biblical language bearing on this point would include the set of speech-acts in Genesis 1. Also:

> By the word of the Lord, the heavens were made, and by the breath of his mouth, all their host . . . Let all the earth fear the Lord, let all the inhabitants of the world stand in awe of him, for he spoke and it came to be, he commanded and it stood firm. (Ps 33:6, 8–9)

But, we would also note the history of the Word as such in Scripture connecting the original creation by the Word to the history of humankind's relationship to the Word, in both reception and rejection, in both salvation and condemnation.

Creation is framed by Wisdom such that wisdom is suitable for life in creation even if wisdom fails to fully comprehend it.

The textual bases for reflection on this point come primarily from the wisdom material of Scripture, such as Proverbs 8 (within the context of Proverbs generally) as well as material from Job and Ecclesiastes.

The Creation and re-creation of humankind individually and corporately by the Word and with wisdom completes the divine design.

This in no way imperils the non-human creation but rather is intended to preserve and bless it. We would include here the position of and function imparted to *adam* in the creation sequence of Genesis 1. Also, by way of negative example the cause of judgment in the Flood narrative and reordered conditions afterwards. But even more, applicable here would be the intended relationship of Israel to the promised land as exemplifying the divine intent which is later promised in eschatological order of the new creation. There is a harmony of human and non-human creation that extends from original design to eschatological vision.

Israel is a constitutive feature of the anthropology of creation.

This observation comes from the narrative connection of original creation to the formation of Israel, a formation which is repeated in Isaiah as an act of creation and set in parallel to original creation: "I am the Lord, your Holy One, the Creator of Israel, your King" (Isa 43:15).

However, one also needs to note the anthropological development from the *adam* of Genesis 1 to Abraham, who becomes a nation and mediates a promise of blessing for all nations on earth (looking back to Genesis 10–11 and forward eschatologically to Isaiah 2). The important point is that human corporate particularity is a constituitive feature of biblical anthropology such that the redemption of Israel in its corporate particularity is part and parcel of the redemption of humankind generally in this sense (the sense of multiple corporate particularities).

Christ is the key to understanding Creation.

The patterns of creation and the revelation of creation power converge in the person of Jesus presented to us in New Testament Scripture. His birth from Mary and his resurrection from the dead are both brought about by divine power, mediated by the Spirit, in fulfillment of the Word of Promise. In his ministry, Jesus speaks the Word of power, pacifying a storm and raging waves, saving a boat of humans on the sea, healing, restoring, raising the dead, expelling demons, forgiving sins. He is the Word of God incarnate.

In the incarnation, two aspects of the creation account are brought together. The Word of God by which everything is created is united with man to whom everything created is given. In this is revealed the Son of God, *through whom* and *for whom* all things were created:

> He [the beloved Son] is the image of the invisible God, the firstborn of all creation, for by him all things were created, in heaven and on earth, visible and invisible, whether thrones, dominions, rulers, or authorities, all things were created through him and for him. (Col 1:16)

> In these last days, God has spoken to us by a Son, Whom he appointed the heir of all things, through whom he also created the world. (Heb 1:2)

The Word of God incarnate fulfills the Word of Promise and Command. He heals the guilt and repairs the breach caused by the human rejection of the Word. People now receive the Word by receiving him, a reception mediated by the Spirit of God so that he dwells in, sanctifies, and gives life to those who receive him. They become new creatures, anticipating a new creation, into which they are and will be raised from sin and death. He, the last Adam, becomes the first, the one to whom all dominion is given. In him, the fulfillment of messianic kingdom prophecy, the promises concerning Israel, and all peoples, takes place in the fulfillment of the purpose and plan for all creation—a plan which, as Paul says, all things in heaven and on earth will be united in Christ (Eph 1).

Creation is best understood theologically as an inter-trinitarian gift.

A key theme running throughout biblical theology is the theme of the gift.[8] In the first chapter of Genesis, God prepares a place of blessing and gives it to humankind as a place in which to live. Later, a promise is made to Abraham, Isaac, and Jacob, and repeated to Israel, of a land of blessings which God will give them. It is a gift and it comes promised in the covenant form of a grant. The grant form reappears in Scripture in the covenant given to David concerning a house and kingdom that God will give. This gift harkens back to the declaration in Genesis 1—Let them have dominion. That dominion is a gift which in its fulfillment is a world of lands, a kingdom of kingdoms, given to the Son of David. But when we come to understand that this Son of David is in fact the eternal Son of God, incarnate, the theme of creation as a gift rises to a higher level of significance.

Creation did not come about because of some necessity in itself or in God. It did not come about as a remedy to a divine deficit or defect, such as divine loneliness, or some such inadequacy. It is only in light of the Trinitarian existence of God that the meaning and significance of creation is revealed. We come to understand the true significance of creation when we see that it is a gift from the Father to the Son, prepared by the Holy Spirit.

Creation is grounded in inter-trinitarian relationality.[9] It is utterly contingent, but it is a special kind of contingency—it is gratuitous—a freely willed expression of love and honor from the Father to the Son. As such, it is both non-necessary, in its radical contingency, but stable and preserved

8. Note, for example, the study by Brueggemann, *The Land: Place as Gift, Promise, and Challenge in Biblical Faith.*

9. The grounding of creation in trinitarian reality was a particular emphasis in the work of Colin Gunton. See for example, Gunton, *The Triune Creator*; and Gunton, *The One, the Three, and the Many: God, Creation, and the Culture of Modernity.*

in keeping with *the intention of the gift*, an intention grounded in the eternal love of the Father for the Son. Herein also lies the value of creation, for a gift cannot function as a gift except that it be valued by giver and receiver. And this is also why creation had to be redeemed!

Redemption secures the value of creation and allows the purpose of the gift to be accomplished. Accordingly, the Lamb was slain from the *foundation of the world.* The love and honor of the Father given to the Son is mutual. The gratitude of the Son to the Father is expressed eschatologically in reciprocal love and honor when he hands over the kingdom to God the Father so that God is all in all (1 Cor 15). The gift, then, is a mutual gift between Father and Son, sanctified by the Holy Spirit of God.

This last point helps us to see how an integrationist approach addresses the concerns of both disciplines. From a systematic perspective, the doctrine of creation does not just follow the doctrine of God as the next topic in the theological loci. Rather, it is systematically connected to it, vital to the understanding of the Christian doctrine of God. From a biblical theology standpoint, the narrative redemption-history presented by Scripture remains essential for theological reflection. In the integrative work, the concerns of both disciplines are not only addressed but also affirmed, perhaps even advanced. Our "kitchen experiment" may not yet qualify for service as an entre at a formal banquet. But who knows? Maybe an entre will yet come of it, if we work on it a bit.

Bibliography

Anderson, Bernhard W., and Steven Bishop. *Contours of Old Testament Theology.* Minneapolis: Fortress, 1999.

Anderson, Bernhard W. *Biblical Theology of the Old and New Testaments: Theological Reflection on the Christian Bible.* 1st ed. Minneapolis: Fortress, 1992.

———. *From Creation to New Creation: Old Testament Perspectives, Overtures to Biblical Theology.* Minneapolis: Fortress, 1994.

———, ed. *Creation in the Old Testament, Issues in Religion and Theology* 6. Philadelphia: Fortress, 1984.

Brueggemann, Walter. *The Land: Place as Gift, Promise, and Challenge in Biblical Faith,* 2nd ed. Overtures to Biblical Theology. Minneapolis: Fortress, 2002.

Childs, Brevard S. *Biblical Theology in Crisis.* Philadelphia: Westminster, 1970.

———. *Biblical Theology of the Old and New Testaments: Theological Reflection on the Christian Bible.* Minneapolis: Fortress, 1992.

———. *Old Testament Theology in a Canonical Context.* Philadelphia: Fortress, 1985.

Gunton, Colin E. *The One, the Three, and the Many: God, Creation, and the Culture of Modernity, The 1992 Bampton Lectures.* Cambridge: Cambridge University Press, 1993.

———. *The Triune Creator: A Historical and Systematic Study, Edinburgh Studies in Constructive Theology*. Grand Rapids: Eerdmans, 1998.

Hodge, Charles. *Systematic Theology*. 2 vols. Grand Rapids: Eerdmans, 1952.

Hartt, Julian N. "Creation and Providence." In *Christian Theology: An Introduction to its Traditions and Tasks*, edited by Peter C. Hodgson and Robert H. King, 115–40. 2nd ed. Philadelphia: Fortress, 1985.

Perdue, Leo G. *The Collapse of History: Reconstructing Old Testament Theology, Overtures to Biblical Theology*. Minneapolis: Fortress, 1994.

———. "Old Testament Theology Since Barth's Epistle to the Romans." In *Biblical Theology: Introducing the Conversation, Library of Biblical Theology*, edited by Leo G. Perdue, Robert Morgan, and Benjamin D. Sommer, 91–102. Nashville: Abingdon, 2009.

Räisänen, Heikki. *Beyond New Testament Theology: A Story and a Programme*. 2nd ed. London: SCM, 2000.

Tsumura, David Toshio. *Creation and Destruction: A Reappraisal of the Chaoskampf Theory in the Old* Testament. Winona Lake, IN: Eisenbrauns, 2005.

von Rad, Gerhard. *Old Testament Theology*, 2 vols. New York: Harper and Row, 1962.

9

A Guiding Principle and a Question-based Strategy for Integrating Biblical, Systematic, and Practical Disciplines

SUSAN I. BUBBERS

Introduction

THE FIRST QUESTION WHEN we come to Scripture is not, "What does this have to do with me?" Instead it is, "What does this have to do with God?" Woven in, under, behind, and through Scripture is God's revelation of his own nature and character. All else flows forth from there. While this priority upon the principle of God's nature and character is broadly agreed upon, articulated in various ways, how adept are we at keeping it in view as a guide as we engage in interpretation? The interest is the dialogue between biblical, systematic, and practical disciplines. Therefore, the question becomes how adept are we at keeping this principle central as we engage in theology, in liturgy, in spiritual formation, and in mission? How might we practically integrate this principle into all of these endeavors? This essay is meant to be a contribution toward a methodology to help do this.

The basic thesis of this essay is that the nature of God serves as a guiding principle for biblical interpretation, theological reflection, and Christian formation. The meaning and ramifications of Scripture will ultimately be consistent with the God revealed therein. To discover scriptural meaning and impact, questions can be directed toward biblical topics (both general and special hermeneutics), systematic concerns (historical and doctrinal), and practical ramifications (individual and corporate). This essay will offer a practical strategy employing specific questions directed toward each area and then toward the integration of all the areas. Genesis 1 will help to illustrate how the guiding principle and probing questions serve to elucidate biblical, systematic, and practical insights.

After briefly describing the presuppositions, goal, and scope of this essay, I will discuss the nature of God as a guiding principle. Then, I will outline a question-based strategy for interpretation which seeks to keep this guiding principle central while also integrating biblical, systematic, and practical disciplines. This is a deliberate strategy which carefully maintains the integrity of each discipline while also bringing them into dialogue with one another. This strategy gives attention to the interpreter, to biblical and systematic studies, to liturgical and formational subjects, and finally to the integration of various combinations of these disciplines.

The Goal and Task of Integration

Basic assumptions for this essay are that Scripture is God's inspired self-revelation, in canonical cohesion within one unified book, and is to be understood in light of the rule of faith, Christian beliefs such as the Trinity, the divinity and resurrection of Christ, and the ongoing working of the Holy Spirit. Canon refers to the fourth century list of thirty-nine books, and those books are best understood in light of one another as a unified revelation from God. God refers to the trinitarian God, Father, Son, and Holy Spirit. This essay looks at several areas of interest and seeks to relate them to one another. This is a way to glimpse the big picture before moving on to discern and understand constituent parts.

This essay is not intended to be an exegetical study of Genesis 1, nor a theological commentary on it, nor an exposition of its significance. This essay is meant to be more of an expanded outline, an overview of how biblical, theological, and practical disciplines can be in dialogue. Genesis 1 will at times provide sound-bites of what such a dialogue would sound like.

The focus is on identifying questions and clarifying how to have a productive conversation between the disciplines. The focus is not on presenting definitive answers to the sample questions that are posed in regards to Genesis 1. For example, the goal is not to make a case for the creation account being a borrowed myth or an historical account or a literary construct. The goal is to identify questions which will help consider key dynamics: first, as much as possible of God's self-revelation through the text of Genesis 1; second, how this passage relates to the rest of Scripture; and third, how this guides a life lived in union with him. The essay is shaped as a discussion-starter, an overview involving our several areas of interest, rather than a study of one text or one discipline only.

Questions Are Key

The practice of asking questions as a way toward the truth is found in Scripture itself (consider Mark 8:29; 10:17, 18, 26; Matt 22:41). The final portion of this essay will provide specific example questions which are meant to be samples, not a comprehensive list. These questions will include well-known inquiries. *What was the human author's original intent? What is the position of this text in relationship to the rest of the canon? What is God revealing about his own character in this text? To what extent did the original audience grasp God's self-revelation in this case? How are pneumatology and ecclesiology to be related in light of this text? What personal virtue is the Christian called to pursue given these insights? How might the universal church become more mature if these insights were embraced?*

Such questions in dialogue can help to integrate biblical inquiry, theological reflection, and personal embodiment of the truth of Scripture. These questions maintain the integrity of each of the distinct disciplines. It is important to be clear about which discipline is primary at any point in the discussion. These questions also provide a way to relate the disciplines to one another, to integrate them in such a way that the sum is greater than the parts.

To keep the questions from drawing the reader toward diverging termini, as if the hermeneutical spiral has centrifugal force, there is a guiding principle which can exert the centripetal force necessary to keep our understanding rooted, reverent, and relevant. This principle is to always bring the discussion back to the nature of God. God's own character provides cohesion in the conversation between Bible, theology, worship, and discipleship.

Not every question offered in this essay will have relevance in every chapter of the Bible or every theological concern. Genesis 1 will serve to illustrate how several such questions may function.

A more particularized presupposition arises from the general assumptions stated above. Given that God is Trinity, this includes his being the Creator and Sustainer. The triune God is the origin and ruler of all things, and all things are for him. From this starting point, one can derive a guiding principle for integrative interpretation: the nature of God is the beginning, hub, and ultimate end of scriptural meaning and impact.

The nature of God can provide the weighty anchor which ensures that studies do not lose their moorings and practices of piety are not tossed-about. Seeking to understand the text, formulate theological systems, and form Christians, all questions are intended to ultimately return to the issue of God's own nature. What he said, what that means, and how we therefore live are inseparable issues, and they all are manifestations of God's own nature. Scripture is God's self-revelation. Scripture is firstly about God. All other questions are corollaries to *What is God revealing about himself?* Consideration of God's nature includes many other questions. *What is God revealing about himself through this actual historic event? Why did he inspire its inscripturation in this final form? What is he revealing about his relationships with his creation and his people? These questions validate the need for contributions from historic, literary, and canonical-creedal data. Establishing God's nature as the starting point for interpretation binds or directs the role of other disciplines with a unified and orderly 'raison d'être.'*[1]

I have written elsewhere in more detail about integrative interpretation, a synthesis of the best of literary-historical and canonical-creedal methodologies and tools, an approach I termed Scriptural Theology.[2] This blend of Biblical Theology and the Theological Interpretation of Scripture includes boundaries such as the rule of faith, a clear line of authority, and biblically justifiable trajectories of meaning. The underlying and overarching guiding principle holding all this together is the nature of God. This essay builds on my previous work and offers a question-based strategy for integrating biblical, systematic, and practical disciplines.

This Scriptural Theology approach to integrative interpretation seeks to answer not only the questions like: *What did the text originally mean? What was the "Sitz im Leben" of the text's writing and initial application? What is the divine author's intent for this text? What else does God reveal that provides further insight into this text? How then are we to live?* These questions probe not only the content of Scripture itself, but also issues of God's nature, God's use of history, and God's ongoing relationship with the community of faith.

The text reveals who God is; and, who God is guides how to interpret the text. It is important to discern what God is saying through the biblical text in a way that is consistent with whom that same text reveals God to be. And, this discernment manifests corporately over time in the shared

1. Bubbers, *Scriptural Theology*, 22.

2. Ibid., see chapter 1.

determinations of the universal community of faith. As this community experiences centuries of growth, it matures in its grasp of truth, recognizing both strengths and weaknesses of prior generations. This is the process of the maturing of the Bride of Christ, a progressive comprehension and *appropriation of truth*, as opposed to the concept of *progressive truth*. The Old and New Testaments provide the progressive revelation of God's character and purposes. The community of faith throughout history gradually grew in their understanding and embodiment of that truth. Although the canon is sealed, and God is no longer adding to that authoritative progressive revelation, God's people are still maturing in their grasp of it. Text, theology, and formation are integrally related. In summary, Scriptural Theology is an integrative interpretive approach where Scriptural meanings and effects are "grounded in historical *Sitz im Leben,* understood through a divinely designed canon *Sitz im Kanon*, and perceived amidst the maturing church *in der Mitte der reifenden Kirche*."[3] These meanings and effects will be consistent with God's own nature.

Once the nature of God is established as the guiding principle, one must consider how to practically include that guide in order to study, write, pray, worship, mature, and minister. I suggest the use of a question-based strategy. This strategy involves individually exegesis, theology, and practical disciplines; and, it also involves their integration.

So, having described the role of the nature of God as mooring and guide, and the dynamic of a maturing comprehension of the triune God, the next goal is to present questions and a process for asking them which is conducive to the overall goal of integrative interpretation. What follows is an outline of sample questions rather than a comprehensive list. These questions are intended to help to produce an interpretive process which integrates biblical studies, theological concerns, and also practical ramifications. It is not the claim here that any of these questions will be totally innovative. What is important is for interpreters to be self-aware about what they are doing and from what perspective, and to keep in view how the other disciplines may ultimately interact with the fruit of their labor.

The process is first, to ask these questions while always keeping the guiding principle of God's nature in view, then secondly, carefully to delineate specific areas of questions, and thirdly, to intentionally combine multiple areas through additional questions designed specifically for that purpose. This process will help to provide protection from the accidental, unaware, uninformed, and haphazard mixing of these various areas.

3. Ibid., 15.

The First Context to Consider is the Interpreter

The questions begin with the one doing the interpretation. Too often the reader looks immediately at what has been written, and does not take the time to learn about the writer. Example questions focused on the interpreter include: *From which discipline am I, or another interpreter, approaching the study?* It is important for the interpreter to be self-aware and to articulate for the reader which bag of tools is primarily in use, and which tools that interpreter is best prepared to employ. When studying Genesis 1, it is important to learn the backgrounds of, for example, commentators Reno, Ross, and Sarna, for they each have their own area of specialized training. Beyond training, it is also helpful to identify, if possible, the attitude with which the interpreter is approaching a study. For example, Reno admits an "exasperation with . . . antidogmatic . . . modern biblical scholarship."[4] It is important for the reader to know and remain aware of any polemical or responsive context for the writing.

It is important to ask: *What presuppositions does the interpreter have?* This is a significant step to take in interdisciplinary studies of all kinds. The presuppositions held by, for example, a Roman Catholic subscribing to the authority of the magisterium, a Protestant from a particular doctrinal heritage (which may at times function similarly to a magisterium), and a secular scholar who is an expert in the ANE, are each in essence guided by different rules. This would be akin to a baseball player, a football player, and a tennis player, all trying to agree on what constitutes the boundaries of a playing field. A common playing field and at least some common guidelines would need to be agreed upon before any meaningful game could occur involving all of them.

In addition, one should ask: *What other disciplines are shaping this interpreter?* Examples could be anthropology, sociology, or psychology. These can shape and even skew answers to other questions if presuppositions exist which prioritize these disciplines over biblical and theological ones. If, for example, a person prioritizes the view of secular psychology that there is no such phenomenon as a demon confusing one's thinking, then that interpreter's view of the changes between Genesis 1 and 3 will be quite different than an interpreter who subscribes to the existence of Satan and demons.

An illustration of the importance of identifying the interpreter's presuppositions is helpful. Consider an interdisciplinary discussion of the nature of existence in the heavens created by God in Genesis 1. How might a systematic theologian attempt to integrate 1 Cor 15:29, which mentions

4. Reno, *Genesis*, 44.

baptisms for the dead, with a discussion of an exegetical meaning of heaven and a heavenly-state for created beings? And, what happens when a liturgist with nineteenth-century psychology's presuppositions influences worship without proper dialogue with exegetes and theologians? This is clearly demonstrated by a single historical instance concerning the Book of Common Prayer.

In the Book of Common Prayer one finds the intercessory prayer, ". . . beseeching thee to grant them continual growth in thy love and service." This phrase is part of a prayer for the departed in The Prayers of the People.[5] This portion of the prayer for Christ's Church concerns the Church Expectant, that is, those Christians who have already died and are awaiting the Second Coming of Christ. This portion of the prayer has a different function than other portions which address the Church Militant, Christians who are still living. The selected text is a request for God to give growth in his love and service to those Christians who are now dead.

Since the time of Thomas Cranmer, the Book of Common Prayer had not included a petition for the dead. However, a major shift was introduced in the 1928 American edition of the Book of Common Prayer. The 1928 Prayer Book has the first appearance of the petition for the departed in its current shape. The 1979 Rite I wording differs from the 1928 version only in the addition of optional places to include names. The Chairman of the Joint Commission who proposed adding the prayer for the departed was the Rt. Rev. Charles L. Slattery, the Bishop-coadjutor of Massachusetts. In 1916, he published a book about life after death. In it he reveals his theology reflected in the addition made to the 1928 Prayer Book.

Slattery maintained that when a person believes in the afterlife, certain affects will be evident in that person's earthly life, since the "law which the psychologist clearly defines for this life must, if there is a life beyond this, be true also for that life." Slattery believed that one affect would be the aim to accomplish lofty goals, for work towards those goals continues after death. Another affect would be disciplined life, for the state in which you die is the state in which you experience the afterlife. "Death does not mean a huge leap, up or down. . . . If we die with a bad temper unconquered, we shall have to possess the ugly thing there; or else begin by the same painful discipline as is required here to rid ourselves of it there."[6]

Yet, paradoxically, Slattery held that persons are not responsible for their actions, for since God put us in this fallen creation, he will ultimately accept responsibility for our sins. Therefore, after death, Slattery believed

5. Book of Common Prayer, Rite I, 330.

6. Slattery, *Immortality*, 20, 22.

the dead would have the opportunity to be cleansed of their sins. These are the presuppositions behind " . . . beseeching thee to grant them continual growth in thy love and service."

Slattery's presuppositions were defined by the secular psychology of his day which shaped his interpretation of heaven. The biblical exegetes and theologians in the Episcopal Church at that time did not enter into a dialogue with this bishop, and the resulting liturgical practice has shaped millions of people for decades. Yes, this kind of inquiry into the interpreter may take time, and may seem tangential to interpretation projects, but it is essential for meaningful dialogue.

To conclude this particular interdisciplinary illustration, remember that there may be those who practice prayers for the dead based not upon textual exegesis, but upon historic precedent, or magisterial guidance, or apocryphal studies. It would be very helpful in interdisciplinary and ecumenical dialogues to be as clear as possible about the sources and methodologies used by interpreters as they reached their various conclusions.

There are more questions to pose regarding the interpreter. *With what personal piety is the interpreter approaching a study?* Given the presuppositions mentioned at the beginning of this essay, I believe the guidance of the Holy Spirit is a key ingredient in the integrative interpretation process. Therefore, the ability of the interpreter to discern what the Spirit is saying is key. This ability (Richard Hooker's actual meaning of the term "reason")[7] may be aided or impeded in many ways. It is worth asking: *Is an interpreter seeking to grow in Christlikeness?* And, depending on the answer: *How does that impact the interpretive process?*

Also consider: *At what stage in history and in what culture is the interpreter approaching a study?* As much as possible, it is important for the interpreter to be self-aware about modes of thinking, values, inherited background, and other factors which can influence interpretation. For example, a person who was raised in a culture and at a time in history which did not question the practice of slavery will read certain passages of Scripture with different expectations than someone raised in most parts of contemporary America.

7. Bubbers, *Scriptural Theology*, 19.

Methodology and Questions within Disciplines

Biblical Studies

In addition to the genre of questions dealing with the person of the interpreter, an integrative interpretation process will also include a genre of questions dealing with biblical studies. These are perhaps some of the most familiar hermeneutical questions, so this list includes only a few examples. *What segment of text will this study involve? What textual variants are involved? How might this text have developed into its final form? What are the meanings of specific terms and phrases based upon usage at the time? What are the grammatical and literary features of this text? What was the human author's original intent, the best that can be ascertained? What was the 'Sitz im Leben' of the text's writing and initial application?*

In Genesis 1, this genre of questions is illustrated for example by von Rad, Sarna, and Hamilton's studies of specific terms (e.g., beginning, create, make, hover, us, image, likeness)[8] and by Mathews' analysis of the orderly literary structure.[9]

The Integrative Work of Systematic Theology

For any system to function effectively, consistently, and predictably, the raw materials and the work done upon those ingredients must be subjected to careful quality control. It is crucial to carefully identify constituent parts before they are combined with other parts. And, it is crucial to know exactly what is being done to each part, and why. In an integrative interpretation system, this means clarity about insights derived primarily from biblical studies, clarity about belief systems derived from them, clarity about how those systems arose from those insights. This is largely dependent upon presuppositions and hermeneutical methods. Also, clarity about how those systems then re-engage in dialogue with the ongoing process of discovering more biblical insights.

For the purpose of offering some example questions whose aim is to provide such clarity, one should use the general categories of seven systematic areas of study: Theology proper, Christology, Pneumatology, Soteriology, Ecclesiology, Missiology, and Eschatology. Many questions would be relevant to all systematic areas and necessarily draw upon insights from biblical studies. Questions might include: *What is the divine author's intent*

8. von Rad, *Genesis*; Sarna, *Genesis*; Hamilton, *Genesis*.

9. Mathews, *Genesis*.

for this text? What might God's purpose have been in structuring or wording the text in such a way? Why might God have orchestrated history in such a way? What is God revealing about himself through this historic event? Why did God inspire the inscripturation of the event in this final form? What is the position of this text in relationship to the rest of the canon? What else does God reveal that provides further insight into this text? What is God revealing about himself through this divinely designed "Sitz im Kanon"? What OT antecedents provide insights to a NT text?[10] *What NT texts provide insights into an OT text? What other OT texts provide insight into an OT text? What other NT texts provide insight into a NT text? What is the text revealing about God, God's purposes, God's people? Did the first audience receive this revelation fully, in part, or at all? What impact did the perceived revelation have upon the first audience? What is God's intended impact for all audiences? How has God's intention for this text been received across time and cultures? What is the current perception amidst the maturing church 'in der Mitte der reifenden Kirche'?*

There are also questions to consider from particular disciplines.

Theology

Which of God's attributes are in view here? How can God's nature be articulated more clearly based upon this text? What does this text reveal about what God is not?

Christology

Does this text address (deal with) the second person of the Trinity? What does this text reveal about the eternal second person? What does this text reveal about the person and purpose of the Incarnate Christ? What does this text reveal about the resurrected, ascended Jesus?

Pneumatology

Does this text address directly or in some way consider the third person of the Trinity? What does this text reveal about the eternal third person? What does

10. See Richard Hays' extensive work on intertextual and figural reading, such as his *Reading Backwards*, which was published in 2014, the year following my initial writing of this essay.

this text reveal about the ongoing work of the Holy Spirit? What does this text reveal about concurrent workings of the God's Spirit and people?

Soteriology

Does this text address the concept of union with God? What does this text reveal about the condition of humanity? What does this text reveal about God's purpose to bring humanity into union with himself? What does this text reveal about atonement, repentance, or faith?

Ecclesiology

Does this text address or consider in some way the community of faith? What does this text reveal about God's intentions for the community of faith? What does this text reveal about God's design for the community of faith's purpose, health, structure, worship, or workings?

Missiology

Does this text address the involvement of the community of faith in the purposes of God? What does this text reveal about God's design for missional: preaching, activity, worship? What lessons, positive and negative, can the current community of faith learn from the community of faith shown in the text?

Eschatology

Does this text address the consummation of God's purposes? What does this text reveal about God's timing of that consummation? What does this text reveal about the role of the community of faith in that consummation? What does this text reveal about the experience of the community of faith at this consummation?

Illustrations of Integrating Disciplines

In Genesis 1, this genre of questions is illustrated for example by Ross' description of theological ideas, including his sub-questions such as: What *genre of literature is this?* Ross answers with a theological treatise and asks, *What are its main themes?* and Ross then elaborates on God's nature of sovereignty (theology proper), God's purpose for humans (soteriology), God's activity of separation (soteriology and eschatology) and asks, *Why did the new nation of Israel need to have this material and to have it written as it is?*[11]

Clarity concerning biblical insights and belief systems can come from examining what others have thought about them over time, and what kinds of modifications to these views have occurred throughout history. Example questions in the category of historical interpretation include: *How have other interpreters across centuries and cultures attempted to answer these questions? Which interpretations have withstood the tests of time and distance without much change? Which interpretations were significantly shaped by the culture of the interpreter? Which interpretations have been introduced in only the last century? From where did these more recent interpretations arise? Do they stem from biblically justifiable trajectories, from cultural expectations, or from secular interests?*

In Genesis 1, this genre of questions is illustrated, for example, by Westermann's analysis of nineteenth and twentieth century commentaries.[12] This genre of questions would also trace the church's progression from pre-modern, to modern, to post-modern approaches, and relate these to issues of creation. For example, questions such as: *How did the patristics, then the rationalists, then the Reformers, understand the time indicated by the seven days? What was the source and content of the influences which caused modifications in understanding?*

The impact of current polemic climates and contemporary cultural issues cannot be avoided in an integrative interpretation process. After a properly ordered investigation of Scripture,[13] these voices can then be heard and addressed. Questions in the category of contemporary voices include: *How does this text align with archeological discoveries, current scientific theories, or recent psychological studies? What does this text reveal about God's design for meaningful human relationships? What does this text reveal about the paradox of loving acceptance and uncompromising truth?* It is important to remember that all answers are to be rooted in the nature of God.

In Genesis 1, an example of this genre of questions would be questions that seek to engage contemporary studies in astrophysics in the area of dark matter and the primal role of hydrogen in an expanding universe theory. *How could there have been light and dark before the sun existed?* Remember, this is an interdisciplinary dialogue whose goal is an integration of exegesis,

11. Ross, *Creation & Blessing*, 102–3.

12. Westermann, *Genesis*, 164.

13. cf. section 1.1, Bubbers, *Scriptural Theology*.

theology, and practical disciplines. A question such as this is not attempting to exegete Genesis 1 to answer a question about dark matter. A question such as this is meant to bring the exegete and the astrophysicist into a conversation, and learn how their views may be consistent, with practical ramifications for apologetics and evangelism. Scientific studies of dark matter and primal hydrogen can serve to illustrate how light and dark could exist, and be separated, before the existence of earth and sun. This genre of questions could also probe insights which can be gained from God's various designs for participation in his works (e.g., Gen 1:11, 24, 22, 28),[14] and the current psychological theories which identify the core longings in every human to be love, belonging, purpose, significance, and security.

It is important to emphasize that the point of this category of questions is not the same as the point of the biblical studies category of questions. Neither is this category of questions to be elevated to that level, for that would not be interpretation in a proper order. This category of questions is not claiming that the text of Genesis 1 intends to address how light and dark could coexist. The text simply states it was so. Even if contemporary voices could not explain how, it would not change that the text says it was so. This category queries, *Given the truth revealed in Scripture, what is being discovered in contemporary science that aligns with that text?* Queries like this do not drive the bus, but may fill a seat and provide a fuller view of the truth. This kind of question does not ask, "Does the text address dark matter?" Rather, this category of question asks, "Given the text says light and dark existed and were separated before the existence of earth and sun, does contemporary astrophysics lend any insight into how this might have been possible?" If astrophysics has no answer, this would not change the biblical witness. In this case, astrophysics presents an exciting possibility which may add to our understanding of all that is related to this text.

Practical Theology and Ethics

This kind of inquiry brings in the third dimension of the integrative enterprise. In addition to exegesis and theology, what practical real-life issue could be related to Genesis 1? *What can teachers and leaders do to help people connect biblical truth with their daily lives? How can the truth be presented in a way that is not completely foreign to nonbelievers?*

This introduces another section of questions. I have offered questions for biblical studies and for systematic studies. Next, I will explore questions which can help integrate these studies with practical disciplines. Just as

14. cf. von Rad, *Genesis*, 53.

the move from biblical studies to systematic studies widened the scope in multiple directions, so the move to practical disciplines again widens the scope further. Practical disciplines could include apologetics, homiletics, counseling, environmentalism, pro-life and justice issues, evangelism, and more. For the purposes here, questions will be considered in three practical disciplines: liturgical, formational, and missional.

Liturgical

The beliefs of the community of faith are expressed not only in written form, but in liturgical form. What the community believes manifests through worship as well as writing. An examination of what was/is done is required to gauge biblical, historical, and present belief systems. Questions in this category include: *What does this text reveal about God's design for worship? How did the New Testament era and early church function in light of this text? How have liturgies across the centuries been shaped by this text?*

In Genesis 1, this genre of questions is illustrated for example by, *If God is a God of order, how can some claim that a historic liturgical pattern for worship is hindering to the move of the Holy Spirit? If God's exemplary seventh day was a time of resting not from fatigue but in the sense of peaceful celebrative satisfaction, how can the community of faith shape its time together to nurture peace and the celebration of what God has done in its midst during the previous week? How might such a focus for a worship service impact seeker-sensitive models? How do other passages throughout the canon inform this Genesis 1 message regarding worship?*

Formational

Just as with the community of faith corporately, so it is with individuals' formation. At least to some extent, belief is evidenced in behavior and character. Questions in this category of practical formation include: *What does this text reveal about God's design for personal piety (that is, godliness, the manifestation of God's character in an individual believer)? What does this text reveal about ways to nurture personal piety? What does this text reveal about hindrances to personal piety?*

In Genesis 1, this genre of questions could include: *How would I put into words what the nature of God is, in whose image I have been created? And therefore, what is godly character? What are some of the basic purposes for which humanity was made? And therefore, how do I grow closer to God the Creator by better fulfilling these purposes?*

Missional

Given the presupposition that God's nature is one of purpose, especially the purpose of his own self-revelation and expression of love, then Scripture as his self-revelation will include insights regarding God's will concerning the community of faith's involvement in that mission. Questions in this missional category include: *How can this text be used to express God's nature in a winsome way to people inside the community of faith? How can this text be used to express God's nature in a winsome way to people outside the community of faith? What does this text reveal about how God's nature informs mission? How does God's character of sacrificial love, wisdom, patience, constancy, justice, tolerance and the like inform mission?*

In Genesis 1, this genre of questions is illustrated for example by the questions: *What are all the ways God expressed power in a generous way in Genesis 1? Why did God do these things? Can we expect God to act in similar ways as time goes by, and in the lives of people today? What is the first mission God entrusted to humanity? Has God changed or rescinded this first mission? Given God's nature, and humanity's 'imago dei', how then is humanity to go about fulfilling this first mission?*

Continuing Interdisciplinary Conversations

One can see that integrative interpretation is no small task! With so many disciplines and categories of questions, no one person could hope to specialize in them all. Thus, we return to the goal of nurturing the conversation between disciplines. It will take multiple scholars from diverse disciplines to enter into careful dialogue to tackle such a project. Yet, how exciting the results will be!

The sample questions above can in some way already be seen to rely upon insights from questions in other areas. Black and white categorization is not the goal of these lists. Beyond these, it is also necessary to ask questions which intentionally target multiple disciplines, especially with a view toward the ramifications, the 'so what,' of all of the rest of the inquiries. Here are just a few examples of countless possible integrative questions. They will move beyond our focus on Genesis 1 in order to help generate such questions in additional areas.

How are pneumatology and ecclesiology to be related in light of this text? For example, if a pneumatological study has shown the design of God to be to create one new people of God, one priesthood, *how might a text be understood to impact the working of the Holy Spirit in ecclesiastical settings such as seating at the Lord's Supper, membership in the body, and leadership in the body?*[15]

Given the answers to Christological and formational questions, *what personal piety is conducive to pneumatologically informed interpretation?* For example, *if a Christological study has shown the consistency of the second person's ongoing communion with God in the context of community, and a formational study has revealed the principle that piety is improved likewise through community, then what qualifications could be esteemed on an interpreter's resume in addition to degrees and publications, both in terms of lifestyle, and in terms of evidence of spiritual maturity in community?*

Another conversation between theology proper and ecclesiology might ask: *How might the universal church become more mature if theological insights were embraced? Are liturgical ramifications to even the most basic revelations of God's nature, such as his being the only true God, a Trinity, transcendent, and also continually immanently involved?* The church matured when speaking as a majority in the orthodox arena and grew out of Deism, and, from the perspective of this interpreter, it is more mature as it clarifies arguments against Unitarianism and Universalism.

Given the Passover paradigm in Hebrew Scripture and New Testament scholarship supporting the paschal nature of the Last Supper: *What insights can be gained regarding God's design for the ongoing practice of remembrance in the community of faith?* This question integrates both concentrations within biblical studies, as well as theological, and ecclesiastical studies. The ramifications of its conclusions can impact the liturgical life, the personal piety, and the missional strategy of the current community of faith.[16]

Considering theology proper and a biblical study of the Pastoral Epistles: *How can in a particular congregational setting, current sociological studies which show a decrease in meaningful relationships and an increase in a desire for a sense of acceptance and belonging?*

This study would likely take the course of articulating characteristics of the divine community, characteristics of Paul's relationships and interactions with the New Testament era churches, and a practical analysis of how the contemporary congregation is investing time and money and gifts. It would be wise to then ask, *Is the congregation equipped and focused on meeting these actual needs?*

In Genesis 1, this genre of integrative questions can be illustrated by building upon questions posed above. Refer back to the question from the formational category, *How would I put into words what the nature of God is,*

15. cf. Stephenson, *Dismantling the Dualisms.*

16. cf. Bubbers, *Scriptural Theology.*

in whose image I have been created? One can integrate that question with exegetical, canonical, and Christological questions. *What insights can be gained into this question about Genesis 1 through the canonically complementary book of John, especially regarding the character of Christ? What aspect of my own character is the Holy Spirit currently hovering over, working on, to bring it more into alignment with the image of God as revealed in Jesus' character in the gospel of John? And, how might I cooperate or participate in this work of God in me?*[17]

Referring to terms in the biblical studies genre of questions for Genesis 1, an integrated interpretation could investigate such questions as: *What is the meaning of "us" and "our"? There are several suggestions, including a heavenly court,*[18] *divine address (and humanity similar to a vassal king),*[19] *and divine plurality*[20] *(encoded reference to the Trinity).* Consider articulating clearly, *what is the place in history and what are the presuppositions of each of these scholars, von Rad, Sarna, and Mathews? What impact does this have on their conclusions?* Given that the meaning is divine plurality, *What insights can be gained about the interrelationships of the persons in the godhead integrating biblical study, theology proper, Christology, and pneumatology? How do these insights inform the decision-making dynamics of a congregation considering a conversation between biblical study, theology, and ecclesiology?*

Conclusion

While seeking answers to all of these questions, it is important to keep in view the guiding principle of God's nature. All other questions are corollaries to "What is God revealing about himself?" The foundational and overarching question, "Who is God?" leads to the immediately relevant and personal question, "How then are we to live?" All the meanings and effects of an integrative interpretation of Scripture will be consistent with God's own nature.

These sample questions help to provide a way for each discipline to remain distinct yet also enter into dialogue with the others, with an ultimate aim of furthering the community of faith's comprehension and appropriation of God's self-revelation. Asking good questions and listening for and

17. cf. The Center for Anglican Theology, online course www.CenterATLAS.org, *Nurturing Christlike Character through Spiritual Formation.*

18. von Rad, *Genesis*, 57.

19. Sarna, *Genesis*, 14

20. Mathews, *Genesis*, 162.

developing richer answers within a circle of disciplines makes better for better conversations in the family of faith.

Bibliography

Book of Common Prayer. New York: The Church Hymnal Corporation, 1979.

Bubbers, Susan. *A Scriptural Theology of Eucharistic Blessings*. LNTS 495. London: T. & T. Clark, 2013.

Hamilton, Victor P. *The Book of Genesis: Chapters 1–17*. Grand Rapids: Eerdmans, 1990.

Hays, Richard B. *Reading Backwards: Figural Christology and the Fourfold Gospel Witness*. Waco: Baylor University Press, 2014.

Mathews, Kenneth A. *Genesis 1–11:26*. New American Commentary 1A. Nashville: Broadman & Holman, 1996.

Reno, R. R. *Genesis*. Grand Rapids: Brazos, 2010.

Ross, Allen P. *Creation & Blessing: A Guide to the Study and Exposition of Genesis*. Grand Rapids: Baker, 1998.

Sarna, Nahum M. *Genesis*. The JPS Torah Commentary. Philadelphia: Jewish Publication Society, 1989.

Slattery, Charles Lewis. *The Gift of Immortality*. Boston: Houghton Mifflin, 1916.

Stephenson, Lisa P. *Dismantling the Dualisms for American Pentecostal Women in Ministry*. Boston: Brill, 2012.

von Rad, Gerhard. *Genesis: A Commentary*. Philadelphia: Westminster, 1961.

Westermann, Claus. *Genesis 1–11: A Commentary*. Minneapolis: Augsburg, 1974.

10

Biblical Theology in the Service of Ecumenism

Eschatology as a Case Study

Gregory S. MaGee

Introduction

In recent decades advances in eschatological thought from a biblical-theological perspective have helped forge a growing eschatological consensus among biblical scholars and theologians.[1] Groundbreaking biblical theologians such as Geerhardus Vos, Oscar Cullmann, George Eldon Ladd, John Bright, and Herman Ridderbos made significant contributions that have paved the way for much shared eschatological perspective among theologians, even those from previously opposing "camps" such as covenant theology and dispensational theology.[2] In this study the specific features of biblical theology that fostered this consensus in eschatology will be identified and examined, and potential contributions of biblical theology to other long-standing areas of contention in Christian theology will be considered. At times proposed strengths of

1. In this study the spotlight has been placed on advances in biblical theology within the past one hundred years. In a broad sense, biblical theology has a history that stretches back thousands of years. Biblical-theological thinking is apparent in the Old and New Testaments and many places throughout church history.

2. Also crediting biblical theology for growing agreement between dispensationalists and covenant theologians is Helyer, *The Witness of Jesus, Paul and John*, 113–17.

biblical theology will be inspected and clarified by drawing out contrasts with traditional systematic theology.[3] Near the end of the essay, the potential for collaborative efforts towards theological unity in the church from biblical and systematic theologians will be explored.

The Need for Ecumenical Progress

The challenge of ecumenism is to foster understanding and shared worship and mission among believers without diluting the importance of biblical truth or the church's theological heritage in the process. Ecumenical movements from earlier generations have been criticized for losing their biblical and historical moorings, but Christian thinkers in recent years have championed a revamped ecumenism that takes the biblical call to both truth and unity seriously.[4] Biblical writers speak about a common faith (Titus 1:4) and common salvation (Jude 3). Jesus's prayer for believers' unity in John 17 and Paul's exhortations for preserving unity found in passages such as Eph 4:4–6 place unity among believers high on the priority list for Christians.

The church in this generation still needs an ecumenical mindset and commitment.[5] Biblical unity, however, is not easily attained. While the ancient creeds of the church provide a strong starting point for ecumenism, the goal of a theologically robust and shared faith that still has room for diversity on secondary issues can be achieved only with the help of additional resources. In this essay, I contend that the field of biblical theology is particularly well suited for advancing theologically substantive ecumenical efforts.

3. Even though this essay is primarily an endorsement for biblical theology's suitability for identifying theological common ground, systematic theology has historically already contributed greatly to this cause, especially through the early ecumenical creeds.

4. See Thomas Oden's critique of earlier attempts at ecumenical endeavors in *The Rebirth of Orthodoxy: Signs of New Life in Christianity*, 55–65. See also Packer and Oden, *One Faith*.

5. I do not endorse an ecumenism that attempts to unite Christians under one organization but rather an ecumenism in which believers from different Christian traditions, denominations, or fellowships are willing to honor one another as fellow believers, enjoy constructive relationships with one another, and work together for the cause of Christ in various ways. For a similar perspective, see Scobie, *The Ways of Our God*, 78.

Which Biblical Theology?

As recent works have made clear, there are a number of different approaches within the field known as biblical theology.[6] The discipline has been seen to span the territory from a history of religions focus (with its reticence about moving beyond descriptions of observed theology) to approaches that are hybrids of biblical theology and systematic theology (as some would characterize the theological interpretation of Scripture). For the purposes of this essay, I will exclude biblical theology that is purely descriptive (BT1 in Klink and Lockett's spectrum)[7] but include other movements that are frequently associated with biblical theology (BT2, BT3, BT4, and BT5).[8] What these systems (from BT 2 to BT5) share in common is the attempt to understand the diversity of canonical literature as part of a coherent and progressing story from Genesis to Revelation. The parts and whole of the story are organized according to movements and themes that are native to the Bible's own language and thought-world. The theology that emerges out of a study of the Bible in its unity and diversity, Old and New Testaments, is then related and applied to the ongoing life and mission of God's people.[9]

Biblical theology is indeed diverse in its approaches, and the aim of this essay is not to try to eliminate differences of method. One need not insist on uniformity in method to recognize that the ways of understanding the biblical witness that are promoted within the broad field of biblical theology have been instrumental in advancing theological common ground.[10]

6. Treier, *Introducing Theological Interpretation of Scripture: Recovering a Christian Practice* 110–19; Treier, "Biblical theology or theological interpretation of scripture? Defining the relationship," 24–28; Köstenberger, "The Present and Future of Biblical Theology," 446–59; Klink and Lockett, *Understanding Biblical Theology*.

7. BT 1, or "Biblical Theology as Historical Description" (see Klink and Lockett) is not particularly beneficial for advancing ecumenical efforts, precisely because it seeks to distance itself from ecclesial entanglements.

8. BT 2 is the "history of redemption" approach, BT 3 is "worldview-story" (overlapping with narrative theology), BT 4 is "canonical" theology, and BT 5 is "theological construction" (related to theological interpretation of Scripture). See Klink and Lockett, *Understanding Biblical Theology*, for a more comprehensive treatment of the varieties of biblical theology.

9. Admittedly, different aspects of this description are more commonplace among different varieties of biblical theology. Diversity, progressive revelation, and language and concepts native to the Bible are favored more on the BT 2 side of the spectrum, BT 2 and BT 3 speak of "parts' fitting within the "whole," a "story" focus flourishes with BT3, while canonical unity and relevance for the life of the church are preferred emphases within BT 4 and BT 5.

10. Bartholomew contends that "a variety of approaches may be legitimate and even complementary" even as the different methods exhibit "recognition of the Bible as canonical and the ancient sense of its inner unity that comes from Christian faith"

The goal of this essay is not to insist on a common scholarly method within biblical theology. Rather, the purpose is to propose enlisting the help of biblical theology to create a greater awareness of a shared theological vision among believers in Christ.

Consensus in Eschatological Understanding

The potential for ecumenical progress that is fueled by biblical theology has already been observed in our understanding of eschatology.[11] Pioneering biblical theologians such as Vos, Cullmann, Ladd, Bright, and Ridderbos helped attain significant breakthroughs in the area of eschatology in past generations. These theologians introduced new ways of thinking about eschatology, including new terms and categories that are now taken for granted among biblical theologians today. Evidence of this consensus is seen frequently. Some form of Vos's "overlapping ages" diagram surfaces in works by theologians from a variety of backgrounds.[12] Language of "already and not yet" dominates discussions of Christ's past, present, and future work.[13] Scholars regularly pinpoint the kingdom of God as a central biblical theme and speak about the kingdom in terms of "pulling the future into the present" or "the sovereign rule of God . . . breaking into the present world, the earth."[14] And scholars from various theological confessions more readily endorse the biblical association between eschatology and ethics.[15]

In addition, more recent works by scholars (Blaising and Bock, Goldsworthy, Schreiner, Alexander, Hamilton, Beale, and Gentry and Wellum, for instance) reflect the gains achieved by the earlier generation of

("Biblical Theology," 89).

11. Köstenberger also observes a movement towards some commonly shared eschatological ideas ("The Present and Future of Biblical Theology," 459).

12. See Vos, *The Pauline Eschatology*, 38; Fee and Stuart, *How to Read the Bible for All Its Worth*, 147; Gentry and Wellum, *Kingdom through Covenant*, 601.

13. Ladd, *A Theology of the New Testament*, 59, 64–69; Ridderbos, *Paul: An Outline of His Theology*, 52–53; Witherington, *Jesus, Paul and the End of the World*, 33, 52; Scobie, *The Ways of Our God*, 92–93; Helyer, *The Witness of Jesus, Paul and John*, 141–44.

14. The first quote is from Bock, "The Kingdom of God in New Testament Theology," 28; the second is from Wright, *Surprised by Hope*, 201. Witherington also speaks of "God's divine saving activity breaking into human history" (*Jesus, Paul and the End of the World*, 60). These scholars follow in the tradition of Bright, *The Kingdom of God*; Ridderbos, *The Coming of the Kingdom*; Ladd, *Jesus and the Kingdom*; and Ladd, *The Presence of the Future*.

15. See for instance Bright, *The Kingdom of God*, 222; Ladd, *A Theology of the New Testament*, 120–34; Ridderbos, *Paul*, 494–95; Witherington, *Jesus, Paul and the End of the World*, 48, 180; Bock, "The Kingdom of God in New Testament Theology," 49.

theologians.[16] Some of these recent studies may be seen as modifications of existing systematic theologies (whether dispensational or covenantal) or hybrids combining the strengths of the two systems. In all cases, biblical theology has played a pivotal role in reshaping and refining eschatological views in directions of greater agreement with other systems.

Biblical Theology and Ecumenism, with Application to Eschatology

Biblical theology offers certain advantages over systematic theology for creating ecumenical common ground that is still theologically robust.[17] The purpose of this section will be to analyze characteristics of biblical theology that facilitate the church's growth in truth and unity.[18] These different strengths will be observed in operation with the eschatological views that Christian theologians from various backgrounds have subscribed to in recent decades. The ability of biblical theology to promote consensus can be traced back to two general areas: the organizing strategies of biblical theology and the open-endedness of biblical theology.

Organizing Strategies of Biblical Theology

Biblical theology, by design, adopts a number of organizing strategies for understanding Scripture. These organizing principles are effective for

16. See Blaising and Bock, *Progressive Dispensationalism*, 212–83; Goldsworthy, *According to Plan*, 210–34; Goldsworthy, *Christ-Centered Biblical Theology*; Schreiner, *New Testament Theology*; Alexander, *From Eden to the New Jerusalem*; Hamilton, *God's Glory in Salvation through Judgment*; Beale, *A New Testament Biblical Theology*; and Gentry and Wellum, *Kingdom through Covenant*, 39–80; 591–716.

17. The modern differentiation between biblical and systematic theology has roots in Johann P. Gabler's famous address in 1787: "An Oration on the Proper Distinction Between Biblical and Dogmatic Theology and the Specific Objectives of Each." Traditionally and simplistically the distinction between the fields has been stated as an inductive versus confessional approach to theology. Today BT1, which is excluded from this essay, fits most comfortably with many of Gabler's successors in biblical studies. Current systematic theology pursues more nuanced goals and is much less confessionally-driven. Moreover, there is often significant overlap between the two disciplines today (seen especially in the theological interpretation of Scripture, which can be "claimed" by both biblical and systematic theologians).

18. It should be mentioned that the Trinitarian and Christological heritage of systematic theology is impressive, and other unity-building characteristics of systematic theology will be highlighted later in the chapter.

forging theological common ground, as has been demonstrated consistently in the study of eschatology.

Categories Arising Directly from the Bible

First, in keeping with the inductive approach to biblical interpretation that is associated with biblical theology, biblical theologians show preference for categories that are more directly derived from the Bible itself.[19] In fact, many biblical theologians consider this to be a defining feature of biblical theology.[20]

This feature of biblical theology creates a collection of commonly observed and acknowledged categories for discussions of theological viewpoints. Instead of beginning with dogmatic or confessional allegiances when approaching biblical texts (and perhaps even using specific texts as evidence in support of a dogmatic tenet),[21] biblical theologians attempt to let the biblical categories govern theological inquiry, and they can appeal to these commonly identified categories in discussions of finer points of doctrine.[22]

In the specific realm of eschatology, Oscar Cullmann appealed carefully to biblical terminology about time (καιρός, αἰών, the present age, the age to come, once for all) to demonstrate that underlying assumptions about God's intervention in history had changed with the appearance of Christ.[23] Whereas Old Testament believers looked towards the future in anticipation of God's culminating work, Christ's decisive ministry became the new pivot-point for history, so that Christians now looked back in history, as well as forward to consummation.[24] Cullmann's new insights were not accidental

19. This is not to suggest that one can attain a perfectly objective understanding of the Bible through biblical theology. Theological presuppositions are still significant factors to be aware of in biblical theology (see Vanhoozer, "Exegesis and Hermeneutics," 63; Vos, *Biblical Theology: Old and New Testaments*, 25).

20. See definitions in Ladd, *A Theology of the New Testament*, 25; Vanhoozer, "Exegesis and Hermeneutics," 53; Carson, "Systematic Theology and Biblical Theology," 100; Bartholomew, "Biblical Theology," 88.

21. It is true that this rigid approach to systematic theology has fallen into disfavor among many scholars since the time of Barth, but it is still detected regularly at a more popular level.

22. It should be noted that among systematic theologies there is still significant variety regarding the relative preference for dogmatic categories versus biblical ones (see the discussion in Vanhoozer, "Systematic Theology," 773–79), with trends away from extrabiblical organizing structures.

23. See Cullmann, *Christ and Time*, 38–50, 121–25.

24. Ibid., 81–93.

but part of an intentional effort to allow biblical rather than dogmatic categories to set the agenda.[25] Because Cullmann's proposals about time were so closely tied to the language of Scripture, later generations of theologians have been able to adopt them as well as the eschatological implications that follow from them.[26]

Emphasis on the Storyline of the Bible

Second, biblical theology more readily exposes the most important features of the biblical storyline, and these defining events within the larger narrative are used to organize the smaller movements and theological reflection within the story and stories.[27] Advocates of biblical theology often pursue theological understanding within a narrative or redemptive-historical framework.[28] A focus on narrative or redemptive history promotes ecumenism in two main ways. First, a narrative approach highlights a number of easily recognized and broadly agreed upon turning points within the story.[29] By necessity, a complex story such as the story of God's creating and redeeming work presented in the Bible must be summarized more generally, by appealing to the major features of the story.[30] These major features then become rallying points for shared faith and understanding. Second, a narrative orientation invites readers to embrace the story as their own and discover their place

25. As demonstrated by Dorman, "The Future of Biblical Theology," 254–55.

26. See for instance Ridderbos, *Paul: An Outline of His Theology*, 42–43; Ladd, *A Theology of the New Testament*, 46–47.

27. See Vos, *Biblical Theology*, 26.

28. Wright offers an apologetic for reading the Bible as narratives within a larger narrative in "Reading Paul, Thinking Scripture," 60–62. See also Hays, *The Conversion of the Imagination*, xvi; Helyer, *The Witness of Jesus, Paul and John*, 384.

29. Though prominent biblical theologians such as Wright, Dumbrell, Hays, and Goldsworthy leave their unique imprints on their presentation of the biblical story, there are still strong similarities in their conception of God's work throughout history, as they detect common movements from creation, fall, the covenants, covenant failure and exile, incarnation, crucifixion and resurrection, the outpouring of the Spirit, the ministry of the church, the return of Christ, and new creation. Further examples of these common features are given in the arena of eschatology in the paragraph that follows.

30. Green (*Practicing Theological Interpretation*, 29) summarizes the Bible's basic narrative structure as follows: "the Bible narrates the work of God: from Genesis to Revelation, from creation to new creation, with God's mighty acts of redemption, in the exodus from Egypt to the promised land and the new exodus of Jesus's life, death, and resurrection, the center points in God's grand story." Though biblical theologians also speak more specifically than this about the biblical story, they typically recognize a basic structure such as the one Green proposes.

within the story as it continues.[31] As a result, seeing biblical truth within its greater story-shape helps believers move more naturally from doctrine to ethics in their individual and corporate experiences.

For eschatology, scholars have arrived at significant agreement about both key events of the biblical story and the participation believers should aspire to within that story. The key events marking the age to come include the announcement and demonstration of the kingdom of God in Christ's first advent, the ascension and session of Christ, the return of Christ, the resurrection from the dead, and the new heavens and new earth. These events surface as significant eschatological milestones when the Bible is viewed as a developing story.[32] Viewing the shape of the overall story places the spotlight on these major events rather than on relatively minor features such as the intermediate state, the rapture, or specific incidents within a tribulation period. While these latter topics need not be ignored altogether in biblical theology, they are kept in proper proportion within the broader narrative framework, encouraging a better balance between the parts and the whole of the biblical witness. Disagreements about relatively minor eschatological events are not enough to detract from the commonly affirmed features of the biblical storyline, which helps preserve a unified affirmation about the major features of biblical truth.[33]

As a corollary, biblical-theological attentiveness to believers' fitting involvement in the grand story of God's redemptive work has encouraged a growing awareness of the biblical connection between eschatology and ethics. No longer is eschatology seen as something predominantly otherworldly in its interests and concerns. Theologians desiring to link doctrine and ethics have found ample precedent for this combination in the Scriptures, with the pairings of the Day of the Lord and repentance in the Old

31. This emphasis on a believer's participation in the drama of redemption has arguably surfaced most frequently in the BT 3 ("worldview-story") and BT 5 ("theological construction") varieties of biblical theology. Since the latter category (BT 5) overlaps so much with systematic theology, it is not surprising that the idea of participation in God's story has gained momentum within systematic theology circles as well (see Vanhoozer, "Systematic Theology," 778).

32. Ironically, these events are the very ones trumpeted by theologians in the early centuries of the church, in the ecumenical creeds. Biblical theology, in its narrative or redemptive historical orientation, helps the church stay true to vital turning points that have been identified within orthodox theology all along.

33. There will always be some disagreement about which events and truths are "major" and which are "minor." The organizing strategies of biblical theology (language, story, and themes explicitly mentioned and repeated within the canonical witness) aim to clarify what is major and what is minor (in other words, to discern what is or is not stressed overtly and consistently in biblical texts). Taking cues from what is seen as consensus in historical theology is surely helpful here too.

Testament, kingdom and discipleship in the Gospels, and the return of Christ and moral vigilance in the New Testament letters.

Sensitivity to Major Biblical Themes

Third, the thematic sensitivity of biblical theology supports building confessional consensus. This advantage is derived in part from the previous two mentioned. The themes are drawn from what is emphasized in Scripture itself and are located within their proper context as part of the larger story presented in the Bible. Biblical theologians have proposed a number of biblical themes that have gained wide acceptance among biblical scholars as being central to the Bible's storyline and world. Paul House sees this collection of themes as "a lengthy enough list of major themes to do justice to the theological breadth of the Bible, yet short enough to give the discipline some recognizable continuity."[34] Prominent biblical themes are pillars for unity around which more peripheral details can be arranged.[35] Even when different interpretations are offered on specific passages, the common pillars remain as reference points for shared understanding.

Themes that are prominent in biblical theology's treatment of eschatology include kingdom, new covenant, resurrection, judgment, restoration, and new creation/consummation. These themes find their meaning as part of the broader narrative of how God has and will make all things new in Christ. The themes are not understood as part of intricate theological systems as they are in systematic theology. The whole (the narrative) makes sense of the parts (the themes), which is a relationship that reflects how those themes are described within the Bible itself (i.e., as part of a larger story).

As a specific example, N. T. Wright appreciates the potential for thematic centeredness to help correct skewed theological constructs and bring them more in line with an ecumenical perspective. Wright espouses using a primary eschatological theme such as the bodily resurrection as a starting point for understanding both the biblical picture of heaven and how a Christian should live on this earth.[36] Wright contrasts this proposal with the

34. House, "Biblical Theology and the Wholeness of Scripture," 276. See also Scobie's advocacy for a "multithematic approach" in *The Ways of Our God*, 87, 93–94.

35. Historically, the rule of faith and the classic creeds of the church have also served this function. Biblical theology does not remove or replace those traditional anchor points but adds to them and enriches the common understanding of Scripture with contributions such as covenant, temple/presence of God, exodus, exile, servants of God, image of God, and new creation.

36. Wright, *Surprised by Hope*, 148.

medieval project of "developing the picture of purgatory and rearranging present Christian life around it."[37] Wright explains that Joseph Ratzinger has helped changed the orbit of Catholic eschatology by moving the center away from purgatory back to more pivotal biblical themes such as the final judgment.[38] In short, a strategy favored by biblical theology, namely, to give preference to cardinal biblical themes and to organize lesser themes around them, can help eliminate or diminish theological idiosyncrasies and thus contribute to ecumenical common ground.

The above organizing methods for biblical truth provided by biblical theology are insufficient as the exclusive ways to understand the Bible.[39] But biblical theology's organizing strategies (using the Bible's own language and categories, highlighting the overall narrative trajectory of the Bible, and affirming central biblical themes) help establish the basic parameters for sound theological judgments without insisting on hasty conclusions about the more obscure and peripheral theological propositions that tend to spark disagreement and debate.

Open-endedness in Biblical Theology

The second area of strength for the purpose of ecumenism involves the open-endedness of biblical theology that makes room for both diversity and new discoveries.[40] This characteristic of biblical theology helps cultivate an environment for theology that is more "generative" than limiting. Viewing the biblical witness from a biblical theological perspective can lead to significant breakthroughs in theological understanding. Breakthroughs are not as likely when explicit commitments to uphold well-defined, long-standing theological systems take high priority.[41] Freed from its need for allegiance to

37. Ibid., 166.

38. Ibid., 167.

39. Christopher Wright notes that whatever "map" is used for summarizing or explaining Scripture, whether systematic or biblical theology, will inevitably create some "distortion" of the biblical message ("Mission as a Matrix for Hermeneutics and Biblical Theology," 138–39). Mead notes critiques against "thematic and topical approaches for leveling the Bible's theological diversity; and the narrative method for needing to clarify historical and theological referents" (*Biblical Theology*, 138).

40. The strengths of openness throughout this section are most effective within broader common agreement on central biblical emphases. A strong awareness of what is central (from the contributions of the various biblical and theological disciplines) provides accountability for theologians in the pursuit of new insights.

41. Constructive systematic theology contributes to breakthroughs in how theology is understood and applied in current settings. But biblical theology's version of openness is more directed towards identifying the Bible's internal theological message in all

relatively fixed and detailed theological systems biblical theology creates a good environment for innovation. And breakthroughs and innovations are conducive to ecumenical progress because they offer opportunities to overcome impasses that were previously seen as set in stone. Several distinguishing features of biblical theology promote greater openness to new insights.

Comfort with the Unity and Diversity of the Scriptures

First, biblical theology is attuned to both unity and diversity within the canon. The unity provides a basis for ecumenical common ground, while the diversity allows plenty of room for investigation and varying viewpoints. Though the two disciplines may construe unity within the biblical canon somewhat differently, evangelical biblical theology and systematic theology are similar in their recognition of that unity.[42] Balancing unity with diversity is where biblical theology often diverges from systematic theology more substantially.[43] Biblical theologians typically do not value as high a degree of logical consistency on a detailed level in their theologies, since they do not expect that level of consistency in how various corpora in the canon treat specific topics. This typically gives biblical theologians a higher tolerance for unresolved tensions in theological conclusions.[44]

In eschatology, even within the synoptic gospels and within the Pauline corpus, there is diversity in how the kingdom of God is described.[45] The theme of kingdom is flexible enough to depict the reign of God in either this age or in the age to come, in either internal/spiritual or visible/material terms.[46] Similarly, salvation, new creation, and related ideas are described as past, present, or future realities, without any thought of contradiction.[47] Since the biblical witness itself reflects a diversity of perspec-

---

of its complexity and avenues of exploration.

42. See Vanhoozer, "Systematic Theology," 775.

43. See for example Goldsworthy, *Christ-Centered Biblical Theology*, 28–29; Scobie, *The Ways of Our God*, 99–100.

44. Since sound biblical theology builds upon detailed exegesis, conclusions will reflect that careful interaction with specific passages. But biblical theologians tend to resist harmonizing the differing details from various passages, preferring to leave unresolved tensions lingering rather than import an artificial consistency into the texts with their theological conclusions.

45. For similarities and differences between Jesus's and Paul's descriptions of the kingdom of God, see Witherington, *Jesus, Paul and the End of the World*, 67–68, 73–74.

46. See Vos, *Biblical Theology*, 397–411; Ladd, *A Theology of the New Testament*, 63–69.

47. The diversity in how kingdom and salvation are described can be seen from

tives on this topic, biblical theologians can be comfortable with a range of conclusions or even "both/and" proposals that give credit to the breadth of the biblical witness.

As an example, when Jesus proclaims "the kingdom of God is at hand" (Mark 1:15), reasonable interpretations could put more or less relative weight on the immediacy of the kingdom's arrival or the extent to which the kingdom will have a visible or largely internal manifestation. Similarly, when Paul speaks of his salvation from imprisonment and hardship (2 Cor 1:10; Phil 1:19–20), there is an ambiguity of reference that opens possible windows into the past, present, and future aspects of salvation, not to mention the potential outcomes of removal from immediate danger and eschatological vindication. These texts are part of a coherent yet fluid biblical presentation of kingdom and salvation within the eternal plans of God.

Flexibility in Keeping with Progressive Revelation

Second, biblical theology typically allows for progressive revelation within the scriptural accounts of God's redemptive work in the world.[48] According to biblical theologians the promise-fulfillment structure of the OT and NT, the typological correspondences between the testaments, or more specific concepts such as "mystery" confirm the inherent progressive nature of biblical revelation.[49] The assumption that God progressively reveals himself in action and word means that faithful synthesis of biblical material is more complex than simple internal consistencies across passages from different locations in the canon.[50] There is development within the canon, leaving more room for discovery of nuances that could be missed otherwise.

For instance, in biblical theology, the principle of progressive revelation facilitated the breakthrough in how the present age and age to come should be understood in the Bible. It is now widely recognized that from Old to New Testament there was a transition from a two-age schema to an

---

corpus to corpus but also even within a corpus. Some see a higher emphasis on realized eschatology in Colossians and Ephesians than in Paul's earlier letters, for example.

48. See Vos, *Biblical Theology*, 14–16. More debatable and beyond the scope of this essay is the question of whether to infer an extended progression of revelation beyond the canon, as explored in the redemptive-movement hermeneutic put forward in Webb, *Slaves, Women & Homosexuals*. See also the debate over this approach in *Four Views on Moving beyond the Bible to Theology*.

49. The biblical idea of "mystery" denotes God's revelation of previously-hidden truth about his purposes for the world.

50. See Carson, "Systematic Theology and Biblical Theology," 101–2; Goldsworthy, *According to Plan*, 30–32.

era of overlapping ages brought about by Christ's incarnational ministry. Through the revealed mystery of Christ and his work, whether from the teaching in Jesus's parables or in the later apostolic exposition of Jesus's significance, Jesus's early disciples came to understand that the ultimate Day of the Lord was not arriving in full force, even though Jesus was demonstrating the arrival of God's kingdom to the world. This critical insight derived from biblical theology expanded theologians' conception of eschatology beyond just the future to include the manifestation of eschatological blessings in the present age as well.[51]

Creative Intertextuality that Resists Rigid Systematization

Third, the intertextuality that is favored in biblical theology fosters sensitivity to the often subtle but profound ways that the narrative of salvation history unfolds across biblical texts. The works of Richard Hays have been influential in this realm.[52] Intertextuality recognizes creative connections between passages (a more "right brained" approach), which promotes seeing theology from new perspectives.[53] These fresh insights can help overcome interpretive stalemates between belief systems that are governed by more conventional confessional approaches. Similarly, studies on the use of Old Testament within the Old and New Testaments have drawn attention to the diverse ways that later writers have interacted with both specific earlier texts and seminal biblical themes in their later works.[54] Sensitivity to the rich complexities of how biblical authors are inspired by and engage with their theological heritage promotes openness to learning and willingness to refine theology in the light of ongoing discovery. Ecumenism flourishes the more that all parties recognize the provisional nature of theological understanding on the frontiers of biblical studies.

51. For an overview of the scholarly progression from "consistent eschatology" to "realized eschatology" to "inaugurated eschatology, see Helyer, *The Witness of Jesus, Paul and John*, 133–44.

52. Hays, *Echoes of Scripture in the Letters of Paul*; Hays, *Conversion of the Imagination*.

53. Hays promotes sensitivity to "unstated or suppressed points of resonance" between one text and its source material, with an awareness of "whispered or unstated correspondences" between the texts (Hays, *Echoes of Scripture in the Letters of Paul*, 20). But even this poetic approach to intertextual echoes is guided by tests that evaluate the likelihood that these echoes are relevant features of the text (ibid., 29–32).

54. See for instance the introduction in Beale and Carson, *Commentary on the New Testament Use of the Old Testament*, xxiv–xxv.

For studies in eschatology, appreciating the extensive allusions and echoes of the OT in Revelation has helped set a better agenda and surface more appropriate questions for interpreting the book.[55] Keys to interpretation of Revelation now more commonly include a deeper awareness of the images, language, and theology of Old Testament books such as Genesis, Isaiah, Ezekiel, Daniel, and Zechariah. This helps readers get properly oriented to the divine story that was launched throughout the Old Testament, has taken surprising and dramatic turns owing to the person and work of Jesus, and is awaiting completion in the eschaton.

Application to a Specific Passage—Isaiah 65:17–25

The ecumenical benefits of a biblical theological approach can be observed when the tools are applied to the eschatologically rich depiction of a new heavens and earth in Isa 65:17–25. Perhaps more than any other Old Testament text, this passage gives a rich description of God's new creation work for his people and his world.[56] There are many questions in Isa 65:17–25 that could prematurely divert the interpreter's focus away from the primary contributions of the discourse. Does verse 20 imply that there will still be death in the new heavens and new earth? What did the Old Testament saints understand about resurrection and life after death? Does this passage describe the millennial era or the final eternal state of our existence? While these are important questions that should be examined and whose proposed solutions should be articulated according to the needs of the audience, they do sidetrack the interpreter from what is even more central to the passage.[57]

Isaiah 65:17–25 and the Organizing Strategies of Biblical Theology

As encouraged by the organizing strategies of biblical theology, giving preference to the passage's own categories and themes within the broader story of the Scriptures moves the reader from the topics of millennium

55. Beale's commentary on Revelation provides the most extensive exploration of the countless resonances between the OT and Revelation (*The Book of Revelation*). See also Beale, *John's Use of the Old Testament in Revelation*.

56. Related new creation imagery is also found in passages such as Ps 48:1–3; Isa 11:6–9; 25:6–9; 27:13; 66:20–23; Ezek 20:40–42; Joel 3:17–18; Amos 9:13–15; Zech 8:3–8,12.

57. That central message also happens to be one that aligns comfortably with the emphases reflected in centuries of teaching within the church.

and the eternal state to topics more native to the passage: creation, new creation, triumph over suffering and sorrow, life, fruitfulness, blessing, *shalom*, and covenantal fellowship with God. These themes, prevalent throughout the Bible, are located within a canonical story that moves from creation to a frustrated and corrupted creation to a new creation. In this specific passage the covenantal people of God are promised God's restored blessing in the midst of that story, as indicated by the strong contrast in verse 17: "For behold, I create new heavens and a new earth, and the former things shall not be remembered or come into mind" (ESV). The prophet follows with rich descriptions of dramatic reversals. The emotions will change from the "weeping" and "distress" of the people to God's own "rejoicing" in those people (verse 19). Premature death will be replaced with long life (verse 20), and people will flourish in a productive, fruitful, and secure existence (verses 21–23). God's people will enjoy his immediate presence and help (verse 24), and *shalom* will prevail among natural enemies in the animal world.[58]

Both the themes and the story reflected in Isa 65:17–25 enjoy widespread recognition and affirmation among theologians from different perspectives. Instead of running aground on the debated systematic renderings of this passage (life in the millennium versus life in the eternal state), the organizing strategies of biblical theology surface the central theological thrust of the passage and its accompanying themes, which creates common rallying points for believers who approach the text from different theological perspectives.

Isaiah 65:17–25 and the Openness of Biblical Theology

Using the tools of unity in diversity, progressive revelation, and intertextuality, readers discern that Isa 65:17–25 contributes to a coherent yet unfolding story, with links both to its past and its future in salvation history. The intertextual relationships between this passage and others prior and subsequent to it are intricate.[59] The passage alludes to past and ongoing obstructed reception of God's blessings for his people, reaching all the way back to

58. Mark 1:13 may picture the initial fulfillment of this peace when wild animals are mentioned in Jesus's temptation account (Dumbrell, *The Search for Order: Biblical Eschatology in Focus*, 183).

59. Oswalt (*Isaiah 40–66*, 655) describes the results in Isa 65:17–25 from the interplay with various other texts as "an impressionist canvas." He notes that "although precise definition is not always possible, the one bright impression is unmistakable: our God has the power to banish sin and sorrow forever."

the opening chapters of Genesis.[60] The passage depicts God liberating the people from past covenantal curses (Deut 28:30) that were bearing down on the nation. At the same time, Isa 65:17–25 anticipates the future fulfillment of abundant life within a transformed world by means of God's gracious intervention. The passage is even one source of imagery for the new creation description in the closing chapters of Revelation (especially Rev 21:1–5). This movement of progressive revelation across the canon allows the reader to see theological development from passage to passage (instead of getting "stuck" on how the specific details may differ).

Two specific intertextual resonances also punctuate central features of the biblical story in an imaginative way. Verbal and thematic correlations between Isa 65:25 and Isa 11:1:6-9 suggest that the broader passages (Isa 65:17–25 and 11:1–10) portray two perspectives of the same eschatological future. As a result the "shoot from the stump of Jesse," the promised Davidic king to the throne (Isaiah 11), emerges as the catalyst for the realization of the new heavens and new earth (Isaiah 65).[61] Jesus Christ, the Spirit-empowered fulfillment of this figure, moves the story from creation in Genesis to new creation in Revelation. A second probable instance of intertextuality is found in the enigmatic comment of Isa 65:25 that "dust shall be the serpent's food." Though scholars are not unanimous in acknowledging an echo of the curse against the serpent from Gen 3:14, this is the best explanation for the inclusion of the humiliated serpent at the end of the vision of creatures otherwise at peace in Isa 65:25.[62] The prophecy provokes satisfaction that part of the glorious new creation consists of the continued subjection of hostile forces opposed to God's rule.[63] These specific occurrences of intertextual creativity enhance central aspects of God's saving story in evocative ways, without comprehensive specification of the exact details of consummation. This relatively unmarked terrain within the more defined landscape of the passage engenders a mix of theological stability and humility that contributes to theologically-sound ecumenical progress.

60. The new heavens and earth, along with the repeated language of God creating, recalls the original creation account. As is mentioned below, the passage also alludes to Genesis 3:14. It is also possible that the language of full and fruitful life in Isaiah 65:20–23 envisions a return to Eden and a reversal of the curse (Seitz, *Isaiah 40–66*, 544).

61. Childs, *Isaiah*, 538–39; Goldingay, *Isaiah*, 369; Dempster, *Dominion and Dynasty*, 175–76, 181.

62. *BHS* posits, though without support from variant readings, that this mention of a serpent may be a gloss, and some others assume that this is the case (Westermann, *Isaiah 40–66*, 407, 410–11; Whybrew, *Isaiah 40–66*, 278–79; Blenkinsopp, *Isaiah 56–66*, 284, 290).

63. See Goldingay, *Isaiah*, 369.

Biblical and Systematic Theology as Allies

One aim of this book is to explore the interdisciplinary approaches to reading and understanding the Bible. So far this essay has highlighted the benefits of biblical theology for ecumenical cooperation, but progress towards theological accord and growth is a collaborative effort.[64] In particular, systematic theology has a valuable place alongside biblical theology in discussions about eschatology and other areas of theology.[65]

It bears mentioning time and again that much ecumenical common ground over the centuries has been attributable to the rule of faith and early creeds of the church. These doctrinal safeguards arose out of confessionally-sensitive communities of worship and in response to erroneous conceptions of what it meant to believe and speak faithfully about God. The systematic outworkings of generations of brilliant and devout theologians have left a legacy of doctrinal stability in central matters of the Persons and works of Father, Son, and Spirit.

Systematic theologians are also more attuned to the need to tie together the various details of passages into a coherent scheme (for instance, in proposals about how eschatological events are understood to unfold).[66] Biblical theologians would acknowledge the need for additional development of theology on a detailed level, and part of this involves disciplined and comprehensive ordering of material, which systematic theology provides more readily than biblical theology does.[67] In addition, the precision and consistency valued especially by analytic theologians proves advantageous in philosophical and apologetic discussions. A more precise definition of terms and concepts are expected in those settings, along with a higher level of internal coherence within a belief system that is being defended.

64. Susan Bubbers' chapter in this volume highlights this effectively. See also House, "Biblical Theology and the Wholeness of Scripture," 270.

65. Vos insists that the disciplines are distinct but equally valid ways of capturing the breadth of the biblical witness (Vos, *Biblical Theology*, 23–25). A survey of the range of approaches to the discipline of systematic theology would require a separate essay.

66. Vanhoozer notes that systematic theology puts forward a theology that is "more suitable for displaying the overall conceptual consistency of the biblical witness as a finished and complete work" and places "the church's situation in its cultural-historical context in light of the gospel in it canonical context" ("Systematic Theology," 775, 778). Helyer (*The Witness of Jesus, Paul and John*, 24) describes systematic theology's undertaking in this way: "Systematic theology has the enormous task of articulating the truths of Christianity both for the church and over against the competing world-views and non-Christian theologies of the contemporary world."

67. House notes that the overarching themes of biblical theology "require elaboration and schematization" ("Biblical Theology and the Wholeness of Scripture," 276). Biblical theology provides many tools for elaboration, but fewer for schematization.

Biblical theology is also indebted to systematic theology's attention to the life and health of the church. The very concern for ecumenism in the first place is strengthened greatly by a hearty appreciation for the "one, holy, catholic, and apostolic church." Systematic theologians are often more aware of contemporary questions of interest and are more prepared to address those questions in ways that benefit the church.[68] Even the introduction of new terms and concepts that are still faithful to the "judgments" of the Bible can strengthen the church as it moves forward in truth, unity, and maturity.[69]

Equipped with the perspectives and discoveries of both biblical and systematic theology scholars can engage in constructive conversations about differences while still recognizing the common core beliefs that continue to unite them. As these conversations have occurred in the area of eschatology, some theological differences, while not being eliminated altogether, have been diminished, leaving less of a gulf between opposing positions.

Other Applications and Conclusions

Other topics for which biblical theology could act (and has undoubtedly already acted) as a catalyst for theological unity include the nature and authority of Scripture, atonement, election in salvation, cosmology, and ethics. By reinforcing consensus in the center and flexibility on the margins for these various debated topics, biblical theology is well suited to move the discussion forward in the direction of greater agreement and understanding, without extinguishing the passion for further discovery in these areas.

The methods of interpreting Scripture according to the language, story, and themes of the Bible, along with reading with sensitivity to canonical diversity, progression, and intertextual complexity are among the tools that biblical theology brings to the table for ecumenical progress. These tools contribute to a reinforcement of central features of the biblical witness but not at the expense of ongoing discovery and diversity. Biblical theologians have made significant contributions towards eschatological consensus that is firmly rooted in the authority of God's revelation but is

68. See Carson, "Systematic Theology and Biblical Theology," 101. Bartholomew identifies inattention to contemporary and practical concerns as a weakness in the history of the discipline of biblical theology ("Biblical Theology," 89–90). Especially in more historically-oriented streams of biblical theology (particularly BT 1 on Klink and Lockett's scale), contemporary application is surrendered entirely to systematic theologians (Klink and Lockett, *Understanding Biblical Theology*, 38). Proponents of theological interpretation of Scripture (BT 5), on the other hand, would see ecclesial contexts as highly relevant to the biblical scholar's work (ibid., 169–70).

69. See Yeago, "The New Testament and the Nicene Dogma," 87–100.

broad enough to be considered truly ecumenical in scope. Perhaps biblical theology can be mobilized in similar ways to build consensus in other theological areas as well.

Bibliography

Alexander, T. Desmond. *From Eden to the New Jerusalem: An Introduction to Biblical Theology*. Grand Rapids: Kregel, 2008.

Bartholomew, Craig G. "Biblical Theology." In *DTIB* 84–90.

Beale, G. K. *The Book of Revelation*. Grand Rapids: Eerdmans, 1999.

———. *John's Use of the Old Testament in Revelation*. Journal for the Study of the New Testament Supplement Series 166. Sheffield: Sheffield Academic Press, 1999.

———. *A New Testament Biblical Theology: The Unfolding of the Old Testament in the New*. Grand Rapids: Baker, 2011.

Beale, G. K., and D. A. Carson, eds. *Commentary on the New Testament Use of the Old Testament*. Grand Rapids: Baker, 2007.

Blaising, Craig A., and Darrell L. Bock. *Progressive Dispensationalism*. Grand Rapids: Baker, 1993.

Blenkinsopp, Joseph. *Isaiah 56–66: A New Translation with Introduction and Commentary*. Anchor Yale Bible. New Haven: Yale University Press, 2003.

Bock, Darrell. "The Kingdom of God in New Testament Theology." In *Looking into the Future: Evangelical Studies in Eschatology*, edited by David W. Baker, 28–60. Grand Rapids: Baker, 2001.

Bright, John. *The Kingdom of God: The Biblical Concept and Its Meaning for the Church*. New York: Abingdon-Cokesbury, 1955.

Carson, D. A. "Systematic Theology and Biblical Theology." In *NDBT* 89–104.

Childs, Brevard S. *Isaiah*. Louisville: Westminster John Knox, 2001.

Cullmann, Oscar. *Christ and Time: The Primitive Christian Conception of Time and History*. Translated by Floyd V. Filson. Philadelphia: Westminster, 1964.

Dempster, Stephen G. *Dominion and Dynasty: A Study in Old Testament Theology*. Downers Grove, IL: InterVarsity, 2004.

Dorman, Ted M. "The Future of Biblical Theology." In *Biblical Theology: Retrospect and Prospect*, edited by Scott J. Hafemann, 250–63. Downers Grove, IL: InterVarsity, 2002.

Dumbrell, William J. *The Search for Order: Biblical Eschatology in Focus*. Grand Rapids: Baker, 1994.

Fee, Gordon D., and Douglas Stuart. *How to Read the Bible for All Its Worth*. 3rd ed. Grand Rapids: Zondervan, 2003.

Gentry, Peter J., and Stephen J. Wellum. *Kingdom through Covenant: A Biblical-Theological Understanding of the Covenants*. Wheaton: Crossway, 2012.

Goldingay, John. *Isaiah*. Peabody, MA: Hendrickson, 2001.

Goldsworthy, Graeme. *According to Plan: The Unfolding Revelation of God in the Bible*. Downers Grove, IL: InterVarsity, 1991.

———. *Christ-Centered Biblical Theology: Hermeneutical Foundations and Principles*. Downers Grove, IL: InterVarsity, 2012.

Green, Joel B. *Practicing Theological Interpretation: Engaging Biblical Texts for Faith and Formation*. Grand Rapids: Baker, 2011.

Gundry, Stanley N., and Gary T. Meadors, eds. *Four Views on Moving beyond the Bible to Theology.* Grand Rapids: Zondervan, 2009.

Hafemann, Scott J., and Paul R. House, eds. *Central Themes in Biblical Theology: Mapping Unity in Diversity.* Grand Rapids: Baker, 2007.

Hamilton, James M. *God's Glory in Salvation through Judgment: A Biblical Theology.* Wheaton, IL: Crossway, 2010.

Hays, Richard B. *The Conversion of the Imagination: Paul as Interpreter of Israel's Scripture.* Grand Rapids: Eerdmans, 2005.

———. *Echoes of Scripture in the Letters of Paul.* New Haven: Yale, 1989.

Helyer, Larry R. *The Witness of Jesus, Paul, and John: An Exploration in Biblical Theology.* Downers Grove, IL: InterVarsity, 2008.

House, Paul R. "Biblical Theology and the Wholeness of Scripture: Steps Toward a Program for the Future." In *Biblical Theology: Retrospect and Prospect,* edited by Scott J. Hafemann, 267–79. Downers Grove, IL: InterVarsity, 2002.

Klink, Edward W. III, and Darian Lockett. *Understanding Biblical Theology: A Comparison of Theory and Practice.* Grand Rapids: Zondervan, 2012.

Köstenberger, Andreas J. "The Present and Future of Biblical Theology." *Themelios* 37.3 (2012) 445–64.

Ladd, George Eldon. *Jesus and the Kingdom: The Eschatology of Biblical Realism.* New York: Harper & Row, 1964.

———. *The Presence of the Future: The Eschatology of Biblical Realism.* Grand Rapids: Eerdmans, 1974.

———. *A Theology of the New Testament.* Grand Rapids: Eerdmans, 1974.

Mead, James K. *Biblical Theology: Issues, Methods, and Themes.* Louisville: Westminster John Knox, 2007.

Oden, Thomas C. *The Rebirth of Orthodoxy: Signs of New Life in Christianity.* New York: HarperCollins, 2003.

Oswalt, John N. *The Book of Isaiah: Chapters 40–66.* New International Commentary on the Old Testament. Grand Rapids: Eerdmans, 1998.

Packer, J. I., and Thomas C. Oden, *One Faith: The Evangelical Consensus.* Downers Grove: InterVarsity, 2004.

Ridderbos, Herman N. *The Coming of the Kingdom.* Philadelphia: Presbyterian and Reformed, 1962.

———. *Paul: An Outline of His Theology.* Translated by John Richard de Witt. Grand Rapids: Eerdmans, 1975.

Schreiner, Thomas R. *New Testament Theology Magnifying God in Christ.* Grand Rapids: Baker, 2008.

Scobie, Charles H. H. *The Ways of Our God: An Approach to Biblical Theology.* Grand Rapids: Eerdmans, 2003.

Seitz, Christopher. *Isaiah 40–66.* Nashville: Abingdon, 2001.

Treier, Daniel J. "Biblical Theology and/or Theological Interpretation of Scripture? Defining the Relationship." *Scottish Journal of Theology* 61 (2008) 16–31.

———. *Introducing Theological Interpretation of Scripture: Recovering a Christian Practice.* Grand Rapids: Baker Academic, 2008.

Vanhoozer, Kevin J. "Exegesis and Hermeneutics." In *NDBT* 52–64.

———. "Systematic Theology." In *DTIB* 773–9.

Vos, Geerhardus. *Biblical Theology: Old and New Testaments.* Grand Rapids: Eerdmans, 1948.

———. *The Pauline Eschatology*. Grand Rapids: Eerdmans, 1930.

Webb, William J. *Slaves, Women & Homosexuals: Exploring the Hermeneutics of Cultural Analysis*. Downers Grove, IL: InterVarsity, 2001.

Westermann, Claus. *Isaiah 40–66: A Commentary*. Translated by David M. G. Stalker. Old Testament Library. Philadelphia: Westminster, 1969.

Whybray, R. N. *Isaiah 40–66*. New Century Bible Commentary. Grand Rapids: Eerdmans, 1975.

Witherington, Ben, III. *Jesus, Paul and the End of the World: A Comparative Study in New Testament Eschatology*. Downers Grove, IL: InterVarsity, 1992.

Wright, Christopher J. H. "Mission as a Matrix for Hermeneutics and Biblical Theology." In *Out of Egypt: Biblical Theology and Biblical Interpretation*, edited by Craig Bartholomew, et al., 102–43. Grand Rapids: Zondervan, 2004.

Wright, N. T. "Reading Paul, Thinking Scripture." In *Scripture's Doctrine and Theology's Bible: How the New Testament Shapes Christian Dogmatics*, edited by Markus Bockmuehl and Alan J. Torrance, 59–71. Grand Rapids: Baker, 2008.

———. *Surprised By Hope: Rethinking Heaven, the Resurrection, and the Mission of the Church*. New York: HarperOne, 2008.

Yeago, David S. "The New Testament and the Nicene Dogma: A Contribution to the Recovery of Theological Exegesis." In *The Theological Interpretation of Scripture: Classical and Contemporary Readings*, edited by Stephen E. Fowl, 152–64. Cambridge, MA: Blackwell, 1997.

www.ingramcontent.com/pod-product-compliance
Lightning Source LLC
LaVergne TN
LVHW050628100826
845148LV00011B/1777
9781498229661